THE WINGS OF DAWN

To W. Chiles Plummer, who is a big help to the world, with assurance of my high esteem. Jay N. Darling, alias Ding

Jay N. "Ding" Darling was haunted by what he considered to be the inadequacies of the first duck stamp design. For more than 2 decades following the issue of his "Mallards Alighting" stamp, Darling sketched variations with "improved" positions for the birds' wings and feet and gave the sketches to influential friends. Chiles "Cap" Plummer from Cheyenne, Wyoming, was, along with Darling, one of the founding fathers of the National Wildlife Federation. *(Courtesy National Wildlife Federation)*

THE WINGS OF DAWN

The Complete Book of North American Waterfowling

GEORGE REIGER

STEIN AND DAY/*Publishers*/New York

First published in 1980
Copyright © 1980 by George Reiger
All rights reserved
Designed by David Miller
Line drawings and endpapers by Roy Grinnell
Printed in the United States of America
Stein and Day/*Publishers*/Scarborough House
Briarcliff Manor, N.Y. 10510

Library of Congress Cataloging in Publication Data

Reiger, George, 1939-
The wings of dawn.

Bibliography: p. 299
Includes index.
1. Waterfowl shooting—North America.   I. Title.
SK331.R44   799.2′44′097   78-788
ISBN 0-8128-2498-9

For my many hunting companions
With whom I've shared
Soggy sandwiches and cold coffee,
Jammed ejectors and flooded blinds,
Leaky waders and frozen fingers,
And outboard-severed decoy lines.

But especially for John S. Gottschalk
Who bears the vicissitudes and triumphs of waterfowling
With humor and dignity;
And for my son, Christopher,
With the prayer he will know
The Wings of Dawn for decades to come.

CONTENTS

INTRODUCTION

ALTHOUGH SNOW still lies in patches on the north sides of the hedgerows and ice forms on quiet fresh waters at night, the lengthening days draw paired mallards and whistling flocks of pintail from the Carolinas to our seaside farm in Virginia.

The themes of nature—like those of history—are continuity and change. Winter does not descend all at once like a gloomy curtain across the land with the first fall of snow. Laughing gulls are gradually replaced by ring-billed gulls from the Midwest, and bald eagles tarry until the first peregrine falcons come from the tundra.

In April, spring does not burst forth in a paroxysm of greenery, driving Jack Frost north in sudden retreat. Red-winged blackbirds sometimes serenade a frosted pond; sleet silvers the sulfur boughs of forsythia.

Long after the widgeon and bufflehead have left for Canada, when the ospreys are already nest-building and catching bass and bream in the warming shallows of irrigation ponds, the blue-winged teal arrive at last, careening up creeks and pitching into the sloughs like exuberant revelers late for a party. "Hail! Hail! The gang's all here!" their chatter proclaims—but finding the fiesta gone on without them, they leave as abruptly as they came to follow the early birds to the prairies.

Summer passes slowly. It is a time of waiting—a time for watching corn and soybeans grow. Wasps fill their burrows with paralyzed spiders, and mosquitoes and greenhead flies guard the emerald marsh. We console ourselves with flounder and bluefish, sometimes tuna and king mackerel, but mostly we are waiting for the time when we hear again the muttering of black ducks in the creek bottoms at dawn.

In September, we shoot dove and rail. Unlike waterfowling, we make no special plans to take these birds. For the first week after the corn or soybeans are out of the fields, any likely-looking cedar or clump of honeysuckle in a hedgerow will suffice for a blind for the powdery-gray birds that pour in to feed on the agricultural tailings.

Rail are more a gift of the gods. If a northeast wind pushes a high tide well over the marsh so that most havens for the reclusive birds are submerged, you get shooting. If not, you may go an entire season without push-poling a punt or paddling a canoe up to a tiny island of nearly drowned spartina grasses and having clapper rail, and maybe a stray sora or two, flutter up and away downwind while you fire and fumble for more shells as birds continue to emerge from the tiny tump—like clowns emerging from little cars at the circus.

As the days grow short, and sun-burnt leaves begin to fall, your anticipation of waterfowling becomes a preoccupation. You try to concentrate on chores, but you are quickly out of the house when you hear geese pass overhead, and the first pied-billed grebe in the pond is a herald for the game birds which follow.

Blinds are rebuilt, or fresh cedars are staked around the periphery of old structures. While you paint decoys or patch waders, your secondary senses make familiar resolutions capped by the perennial hope: "This season will be perfect."

All shots will be clean kills, and all downed birds will be found. This year you'll have more than one chance at a Canada goose—and this year you won't miss. The adult red-breasted merganser drake you'd like for a mount will fall to a splendid pass shot. The gray-faced dog, your alter ego, will survive another winter, and next spring his memories will chase themselves in whimpering dreams near your feet and in your heart.

These promises and a sense of life's purpose are concentrated in the precious few moments when the unseen sun has blued the firmament and wood-sculptured ducks lure their living kind from the dark skies above. Tucked in a layout boat, the dog between your knees, trembling with the cold and anticipation, you watch a pair of black ducks move like wraiths over a shadowy waterscape.

One hundred yards away, the birds start to settle, then rise and turn, eager for food, but eager, too, for the presence of other birds to indicate "all's well." You cannot call, for the slightest movement will be seen, and you fear to breathe lest your frosty exhalations flare the ducks.

They pass out of sight beyond your right shoulder. You lie numb, convinced they have gone and won't return. Then there is the whisper of wings overhead and you rise up. The ducks are just starting to slide toward the decoys, and your sudden movement causes them to strain away. With your eyes locked onto the form of the farthest bird, there is no awareness of sound as the duck shudders, rolls to one side, and begins to tumble to the water. There is no precise memory of the second shot as the other bird folds and lands with a "plop" in the soft mud of the marsh. When you look for your dog, he is halfway back to the layout boat with your first bird.

Another season has begun, and life is strangely renewed by the taking of life. You are part of nature's harvest, and in the killing, you learn to crave the perpetuation of waterfowl as only a waterfowler can. Duck hunting is essential to your well-being. It is re-creation in the original sense of that word. The wings of dawn have become extensions of your very soul.

I apologize to any of my western readers who may feel I have slighted their region by featuring waterfowling anecdotes and examples from Back East. A writer—even an outdoor writer—must describe what he knows best, and as a hunter and bird observer, I am largely a product of the Atlantic Flyway. Yet in defense I will suggest that lessons learned in a local marsh can usually be applied anywhere on the continent. Canada geese are as suspicious of mid-season additions to a blind in Oregon as they are in Maryland; drake mallards are as receptive to good calling in Utah as in South Carolina; and scaup are as reluctant to come to decoys next to a high embankment in New Mexico as they are in New York. My understanding of waterfowl has been strengthened by owning a farm where I can raise ducks, photograph and study them, and, in the fall, hunt their wild kith and kin. Furthermore, the knowledge and skills I have developed in Virginia have stood me in good stead on waterfowling trips to Arkansas, California, South Dakota and Texas—just to name four of the ten states west of the Mississippi where I have been privileged to hunt.

I owe so many debts to so many people for stimulating or sharing my enthusiasm for this project, it would be a hopeless task to try to name them all. I will thank Larry Jahn, vice-president of the Wildlife Management Institute, for having read the original manuscript and suggesting several ways to improve it. Bob Hines, chief of the audio-visual division of the U.S. Fish and Wildlife Service, was a great help (as he always is) in tracking down certain necessary illustrations—as were Bob Elman, editor-in-chief of Winchester Press; Peter Gedeon, director of exhibits for the Chesapeake Bay Maritime Museum; and several patient people at the Library of Congress.

A list of my literary sources is provided in the bibliography. However, this list says nothing of my gratitude to half a hundred guides from California's Central Valley to Maryland's Eastern Shore; to the perception and sympathy of Richard and Brownie Borden; to visits with Dale Whitesell and the Ducks Unlimited gang in Chicago; to my years of laboring and learning at the National Wildlife Federation; to the moral support (and companionship in the marsh) of Jack Samson, editor-in-chief of *Field & Stream;* and to early-morning outings with my brothers with whom I have hunted or birded from Alaska to Florida. To these and many, many more, my thanks.

GEORGE REIGER
Heron Hill
Locustville, Virginia

ONE: THE FIRST WATERFOWLERS

"And I brought you into a plentiful country, to eat the fruit thereof and the goodness thereof; but when ye entered, ye defiled my land, and made mine heritage an abomination."

The Book of the Prophet Jeremiah, 2:7

RECORDED HISTORY in what today constitutes the United States spans a little over four hundred and fifty years. It begins with the shipwreck and subsequent imprisonment of Cabeza de Vaca by Gulf Coast Indians in 1528. Compared to the spectrum of events that make up the chronologies of ancient Crete and Egypt, Ebla, Sumer and Mesopotamia, American history is but a minute to their quarter hour.

If Americans are remembered in millennia to come, it will be because for a few brief centuries, we were the inheritors of all history. While we were not the first to use fire, the wheel, the plow, or the ax, we inherited these tools and refined them to meet the new conditions of a new continent.

So it is with waterfowling. Americans were not the first people to hunt ducks for sport with firearms and dogs. And American Indians were not the only people who from ancient times hunted from blinds and with decoys. Any person who depends on a knowledge of nature for his daily bread must learn the ways of wildlife or perish. To suggest, as some American folk-art historians have done, that the concept of live or facsimile birds used to lure other birds to a blind where hunters were hidden occurred first to people living in North America is to deny common sense to every other prehistoric family of man.

In the tomb of Tutankhamen, ruler of Egypt more than three thousand three hundred years ago, a small golden shrine was found which honored Nekhabet, the vulture goddess of Elkab. On the left side of the shrine, in the upper panel, the king is standing in a boat made of papyrus stems and throwing a boomerang at wildfowl out of sight to the viewer's right.

In his left hand Tutankhamen is clutching several live decoys by the legs. How do we know the birds are decoys and not part of the king's bag? Because ancient Egyptian artists depicted dead game in limp, head-down positions. The ducks held by the king are fluttering with alert heads.

In the panel below, Tutankhamen is sitting on a stool at the edge of a papyrus marsh shooting wildfowl with a bow. A tame lion stands on one side while the queen sits in front of the king, passing him an arrow with

More than a thousand years before this golden shrine honored Nekhabet, the vulture goddess of Elkab, was fashioned for the tomb of Tutankhamen, an Egyptian hieroglyphic was carved into the concept: "You throw your bomerang against them. It is a million which fall to the whistle of its wind: Green-throated geese, laughing geese, pintails." Eventually an Egyptian office was established which supervised the activities of waterfowlers. Hunting in the marshes became so popular that a permit system was established to regulate the kill of ducks and geese, as well as to bring in additional revenues to the government. Sebek-hotep, governor of Fayum Province, was given the title "Overseer of the Swamps of Enjoyment," and the position "Chief Fowler of the Kingdom" carried with it the influential and lucrative title of "Chief Treasurer." *(Photograph courtesy the Metropolitan Museum of Art)*

one hand and pointing to the birds with the other. A duck is falling, pierced by an arrow, and the king is drawing on still another. Except that live decoys are no longer legal in the United States and few modern duck hunters use boomerangs or bows, the shrine of Nekhabet shows that the forms of waterfowling have changed little in at least thirty-three centuries.

What does make the American experience unique is that the discovery of the New World gave humankind a chance to develop a culture based on the primary lesson of history—namely, that all wealth and social stability arise from the thoughtful management of natural resources. Tragically, only an educated minority have ever understood that principle, and the discovery of America with its apparently unlimited resources only served to postpone our day of reckoning by five centuries. People from an overcrowded Europe, where natural resources were either depleted or controlled by the aristocracy, suddenly found a continent of opportunity two months away across the sea. The earliest immigrants came to exploit the fishes, furs, and forests, but even they subsisted on waterfowl.

Never before, and never again, will man see such clouds of ducks, geese, swans, and cranes as once passed across the face of North America. Not in all the history of creation had climate, earth, and evolution joined in such perfect harmony to fill the skies and thousands of millions of wetland acres with seasonal clouds of wildfowl. Although several great waterfowl concentration areas still exist in eastern Europe, Africa, and Asia, all such places combined do not equal the variety and magnitude of the autumn flight that once tumultuously swept down North America's Atlantic and Mississippi Flyways. Not the richness of the Nile, the Ganges, nor the Yangtse Delta could compare with the tens of thousands of square miles of rivers, marshes, and brackish water flats in and around the Chesapeake Bay, where abundant food and generally ice-free water provided a good living for over half the canvasbacks and whistling swans on earth—to name just two of the more than 30 species of waterfowl that still frequent this largest estuary in the contiguous United States.

In the north and to the west, tens of millions of bogs, potholes, and ponds had been left by the retreat of the Laurentide Glacier barely 10,000 years ago, and birds reproduced in staggering numbers and funneled down the Delaware and Susquehanna, the Missouri and Mississippi, the Colorado and Columbia, just as other fowl in lesser numbers still moved down Europe's Danube, Dnieper, and Volga. Wherever great rivers of the Northern Hemisphere flow to permanently open water and submerged foods, ducks, geese, and swans flow with them. Yet, perhaps, never in their 25 million years of evolution had waterfowl found such optimum circumstances as prevailed in the New World following the most recent retreat of ice toward the northern pole. Then Europeans arrived with gunpowder, no-deposit commerce, and nonreturnable industry, and the dismantling of Eden began.

Instead of learning from past mistakes, the immigrants and their descendants who have been born here have used new technologies to deplete all resources more completely and at a faster rate than ever imagined possible by our pre-Christian era or even medieval ancestors. Waterfowling today has many themes, and one of the most compelling is that, inevitably, we are hunters in and of the past.

In 401 B.C., Xenophon led the withdrawal of a mercenary Greek army from Persia. It is curious that this retreat should be better known and honored than many military victories, but then we only know ancient history from the people who recorded it, and Xenophon himself set forth the details of this "exemplary campaign."

He also wrote about his former commander-in-chief, Cyrus the Younger, and suggested that his military prowess resulted from his love of hunting. (Unfortunately for Cyrus, his hunting and military skills did not allow him to overthrow his brother, King Artaxerxes II, who killed Cyrus at the battle of Cunaxa which then triggered Xenophon's retreat.) Addressing Cyrus's ghost, Xenophon recalls that:

You often used to get up in the dark in the hardest winter weather and set your nets or traps before the birds were stirring, so that the place should seem entirely undisturbed. And your trained birds worked with you against their mates while you lay in ambush, seeing without being seen, and practiced catching the birds before they could take wing.

In the first "Cynegeticus," Xenophon wrote that:

To the gods themselves is due the discovery, to Apollo and Artemis, patrons of the chase and protectors of the hunt. At [their] feet sat many a disciple, to whom they taught the mystery of hunting. The first efforts of a youth emerging from boyhood should be directed to the institution of the chase, after which he should come to the rest of his education. . . . Of the many pleasures to which youth is prone, this one alone is productive of the greatest blessings.

Xenophon was a pupil of the great intellectual martyr, Socrates. So was Plato, but Plato was far less the man of action than Xenophon. The undrained marshes of northern Greece and Macedonia once served as important way stations to waterfowl on their annual migrations between Europe and Africa. The Greeks hunted such birds in the late summer and fall, and Plato was disgusted by the fascination wildfowling had for so many of his countrymen. He probably thought this hunting unworthy entertainment for enlightened minds, but he claimed his dislike was based on the sport's capacity to "bewitch" its participants. In *The Republic,* he complained that hunting is "one of those pleasures of which we cannot be rid." Plato felt such enthusiasm was degrading, but then Plato was a snob.

Bows and boomerangs, nets and snares, were all used by ancient waterfowlers of the Mediterranean world. However, the sling was probably the most effective and popular weapon for the ordinary hunter who could not afford more elaborate paraphernalia and merely jumped his ducks from streams and ponds. Smooth pebbles from the shore or streambed were his expendable ammunition, and even minimal practice made most any son of a sheepherder proficient with this simple weapon.

A painting on a sixth-century B.C. Etruscan tomb depicts a lad slinging a rock into a flock of rising fowl. Another tomb painting, also done about 2,500 years ago, at Tarquinia in Italy shows three hunters in two boats using slingshots to kill three ducks flying overhead.

The essentials in life rarely change, although essential skills—in this case, the ability to hit flying fowl with a sling or bow—may deteriorate. During the First World War, journalist Richard Harding Davis visited the border between Greece and Serbia and, among other impressions, saw that "between the road and the margin of the lake [Doiran?] were bamboo reeds as tall as lances, and at the edge of these were gathered myriads of ducks. Fishermen were engaged in bombarding the ducks with rocks. They went about this in a methodical fashion. All around the lake, concealed in the reeds and lifted a few feet above the water they had raised huts on piles. In front of these huts was a ledge or balcony. They looked like overgrown bird-houses on stilts.

"One fisherman waited in a boat to pick up the dead ducks, and the other hurled stones from a sling. It was the same kind of sling as the one with which David slew Goliath. . . . The one the fisherman used was about eight feet long. To get the momentum he whirled it swiftly above his head as a cowboy swings a lariat, and then let one end fly loose, and the stone, escaping, smashed into the mass of ducks. If it stunned or killed a duck, the human water-spaniel in the boat would row out and retrieve it."

During Europe's so-called Dark Ages, falconry established itself above the bow, sling, and net as the aristocratic way to hunt waterfowl. Guns had not yet been developed, and by the first century A.D., the advantages of using birds to extend a hunter's reach were obvious to the tribes of people filtering into Europe from central Asia, where falconry had long been practiced on the steppes of Turkestan.

Aristotle reminds us that hawks were used to hunt marsh birds in ancient Greece. And Pliny the Elder (23-79 A.D.) reports in his *Historia Naturalis* that: "In the district of Thrace inland from Amphipolis men and hawks have a sort of partnership for fowling: the men put up the birds from woods and reed-beds and the hawks flying overhead drive them down again."

However, this was not falconry in the purest meaning of that word, first, because the hunting birds were not, in fact, falcons, but hawks—an important distinction when it comes to pursuing swift prey like teal and mallards—and second, because the hawks were often used in conjunction with dogs to harass or distract quarry so that the human hunter could get into position to use his net, bow, or sling.

Falconry is the use of trained raptors to strike down airborne game birds over open spaces. Marshes and moorlands where waterfowl and shorebirds abound provide ideal settings for the stoop and kill of a well-trained falcon. Since Europe was once rich in such landscapes, it is not surprising that as early as the sixth century A.D., a Burgundian law should stipulate that anyone stealing a falcon was to have six ounces of flesh plucked from his behind by the kidnapped and presumably recovered bird.

Since falconry is a *sport* with all the original nonprofit connotations of that word—that is, there is no way a falconer can capture enough meat with his bird to support even himself, much less a family—falconry quickly became a pastime of Europe's leisured classes: the nobility and the clergy. While a hierarchy of birds was drawn up to distinguish the various falcon species according to the political power of their respective users, in reality, such distinctions were difficult to enforce. For example, although priests were supposed to confine themselves to the flying of kestrels (commonly called sparrow hawks in America), many priests preferred peregrines (duck

Sic fluuialis anas capitur cane, fulminis iƈfu   *Dum percuƈus obit, pennafque in flumine ƒpargit .*

This party of Dutch gunners from Hans Bol's *Venationis, Piscationis et Avicupii Typii* (1580–1588) is using waterfowling techniques much like those described by Benvenuto Cellini half a century earlier in his *Autobiography*. Note the use of retrievers and the fact the hunters "pot" their birds on the water. The size of their weapons makes such sport more in the tradition of punt-gunning than wing-shooting from the shoulder. *(Reproduction courtesy Elman Pictorial Collection)*

hawks), and the lower clergy sometimes owned such birds even though peregrines were officially ranked as the prerogative of dukes and earls. On the other hand, only kings and princes were supposed to hunt gyrfalcons. However, these birds were uncommon even in earlier centuries, and a crowned head might have to settle for a peregrine or even the lowly goshawk.

All falcons, except the small merlin (pigeon hawk) and smaller kestrel, were used to take ducks and herons, and the aristocracy hunted waterfowl with falcons until less conspicuously consumptive lifestyles for aristocrats became the order of the day toward the end of the eighteenth century. Besides political upheaval that helped sweep falconry into a temporary eclipse, the advent of improved firearms obviated the time-consuming capture and training of falcons as a first step to successful waterfowling. Such convenience has appealed to the busy middle classes of the sixteenth through twentieth centuries. Ironically, today's revival of falconry is being led, not by wealthy Arab sheiks, but by middle-class Americans who find fulfillment in dedicating themselves to falcons and dawns in the marsh.

Although the first portable firearm was constructed in the middle of the fourteenth century, its usefulness in shooting waterfowl was not generally perceived for two more centuries, during which time the original gun model was greatly refined in accuracy, weight, and reliability. About the same time, the breeding of dogs for flushing and retrieving game birds became important activities for kennel masters under Italian and Spanish noblemen.

In his *Autobiography,* Benvenuto Cellini describes how he would take one or another of his several hunting dogs into the marshes near Rome to hunt wildfowl. One of his favorite animals was a "shaggy dog, very big and handsome" given to him by the Duke of Florence, Allessandro de Medici. This "beast was capital as a retriever," writes Cellini, "since he brought me every sort of birds and game I shot." This beast also served as a watchdog in Cellini's goldsmith shop and once saved it from being robbed. Several days later the dog attacked the would-be thief in a crowded Roman square, and after the man confessed to his crime, he was taken away and hanged.

Let us turn back the clock four and one-half centuries to the late afternoon of January 5, 1537 to share Cellini's discovery of the heat-retaining merits of goose-down clothing:

It was close upon nightfall, and during the day I had shot a good number of ducks and geese; then, as I had almost made my mind up to shoot no more that time, we were returning briskly toward Rome. Calling to my dog by his name, Barucco, and not seeing him in front of me, I turned round and noticed that the well-trained animal was pointing at some geese which had settled in a ditch. I therefore dismounted at once, got my fowling piece ready, and at a very long range brought two of them down with a single ball. I never used to shoot with more than one ball, and was usually able to hit my mark at two hundred cubits [about 100 yards], which cannot be done by other ways of loading [that is, by using smaller bird shot]. Of the two geese, one was almost dead, and the other, though badly wounded, was flying lamely. My dog retrieved the one and brought it to me; but noticing that the other was diving down into the ditch, I sprang forward to catch it. Trusting to my boots, which came high up the leg, I put one foot forward; it sank in the oozy ground; and so, although I got the goose, the boot of my right leg was full of water. I lifted my foot and let the water run out; then, when I had mounted, we made haste for Rome. The cold, however, was very great, and I felt my leg freeze, so that I said to Felice [Cellini's companion]: 'We must do something to help this leg, for I don't know to bear it longer.' The good Felice, without a word, leapt from his horse, and gathering some thistles and bits of stick, began to build a fire. I meanwhile was waiting, and put my hands among the breast-feathers of the geese, and felt them very warm. So I told him not to make the fire, but filled my boot with the feathers of the goose, and was immediately so much comforted that I regained vitality.

This illustration from Sir Ralph Payne-Gallwey's *Book of Duck Decoys* provides a nineteenth-century view of what a decoy looks like, but no explanation of how it was used. To learn that, notice in the photograph, *top right,* how the "piper dog" works away from the ducks, never looking at them or giving them cause for alarm. The dog's pacing—directed by her master, Jim Worgan, chief warden for the Boarstall Decoy in Buckinghamshire, England—lures the birds deeper and deeper into the enmeshed tunnel until the sudden appearance of a man at the tunnel entrance causes the birds to flush and fly around the bend where they are trapped. The first decoy in Britain was constructed in 1665 by Hydrach Hilens, a Dutchman, for King Charles II. *(Illustrations courtesy WAGBI magazine) Bottom right* is the Delta Waterfowl Research Station in Manitoba about 1954, not long after construction of the only working decoy (bent, greenhouse-looking affair in left lower center of the picture) in the New World. Built by Dr. Robert McCabe and Sir Peter Scott, the decoy is used to trap and band wild ducks. However, banding represents only one of the many research facets of this important non-governmental institution. *(Photograph courtesy Robert McCabe)*

In Northern Europe, waterfowlers had learned how to use dogs and/or tame ducks to lure inquisitive wildfowl into tunnel-shaped duck cages or *ende-kooi,* as the Dutch called them. From this word evolved the English term "decoy," which originally referred to the elaborate duck trap, then to the tame ducks used to lure wild birds, and finally to the wooden facsimiles used for the same purpose.

All European watermen knew how to design a simple duck trap into which wild birds were lured under a low doorway by a trail of wheat or other grain. When the grain was consumed, the ducks stood upright and could not find the low opening again. (This system is still used by outlaw duck trappers in the United States.) The Dutch method involved a net tunnel with a large mouth into which wild birds followed tame birds and then panicked toward the back of the tunnel when a man wading or in a boat suddenly appeared at the mouth of the trap.

The British refined this technique by introducing "tolling dogs" to lure the inquisitive wildfowl into the tunnel and then closing off their retreat while the birds were absorbed in watching the pacing antics of the dog. Charles II constructed the first improved duck decoy in what today is St. James's Park in the heart of London. The king's kennel master trained spaniels to serve as tollers, and the king's aviary keeper, Edward Storey, clipped the wings and banded (the English say "ringed") the more unusual waterfowl to induce them to stay and breed in the park. In the decade between September 1660 and June 1670, Storey spent £246 18s. on "oat-meal, tares, hemp-seed, and other corn for the birds and fowls." The modern equivalent of this amount is something over $7,500 a year for duck food.[1]

In the eighteenth and nineteenth centuries, tolling dogs (but not decoy structures) were used in North America, especially in Maryland and Virginia. And until the middle of this century, tolling dogs were used in Canada, chiefly Nova Scotia, by hunters hiding behind driftwood along the shores of lakes which are waterfowl staging areas for the fall migration. Vincent Potier of Yarmouth developed a strain of tolling dog which in size, coat, and color closely resembled the red fox. This animal would run

---

[1] This amount was undoubtedly supplemented by donations from courtiers who wanted to impress the king with their love of waterfowl. Later in the seventeenth century, William III built a blind on Duck Island in which he spent long hours observing ducks and geese in the park. William, also, issued stern edicts for the protection of these birds.

Although dogs have been used in waterfowling for hundreds of years, they have served mostly as flushers and retrievers. This nineteenth-century hunter is probably unaware that the spaniel-like dog alongside him is superbly suited by size and temperament to be trained as a tolling dog. So employed, the spaniel could lure large flocks of ducks within range of the hunter instead of merely retrieving those few birds the hunter will manage to pass-shoot from his poor place of concealment. *(Courtesy Elman Pictorial Collection)*

up and down the shore, occasionally emitting a sharp bark, and ducks and geese would swim in to see what was causing all the commotion. So long as the birds stayed several yards off the beach, they knew they were safe from the "fox"—but not, as it turned out, from the hunter's gun. Unfortunately, this tradition is dying, if not already dead, and you would be hard put to find even a single tolling dog in the Maritime Provinces, where once there were many.

There are two aspects of waterfowling sometimes assumed to be peculiarly American: the use of blinds and the use of artificial birds to lure ducks close to the blinds. In Europe, however, both swans and sea ducks were shot from concealment and over decoys (in the modern sense of that word). In Scandinavia swan decoys were put out near patches of water on frozen lakes, and hunters would either conceal themselves among the ice floes, hide under white sheets, or stalk the birds from behind white screens mounted on runners after wild swans had flown in to join their fake brethren.

Until the development of superior firearms in the sixteenth century, such elaborate preparations were not often made for ducks or even geese, because these birds offered too small a target for the then unwieldy and unreliable guns and even crossbows. The European archer, who prided himself on the distance he could project an arrow, was insufficiently skilled at the specialized craft of rapid-fire, close-range shots at flying prey with which his North American contemporaries, the Indians, had been familiar for many centuries. When Scandinavians hunted scoters and oldsquaw, they would catch the birds with nets set on the diving ducks' feeding grounds or slung in a flyway across an inlet or channel. These methods were preferred to gun or bow until even the close of the nineteenth century.

In the New World, Central and South American Indians had developed still another device for waterfowling: the blowgun. While the Aztecs also used nets much the way the Scandinavians did to trap ducks trading through a particular flyway,[2] the Aztecs often jumped waterfowl while wading or paddling in canoes and brought the birds down with darts fired from blowpipes. The Conquistadors were given several such jewel-encrusted devices by Montezuma, along with "twenty golden ducks, beautifully worked and very natural looking," according to Bernal Diáz's diary of 1521. Cortés later ordered these birds to be melted into ingots.

Tragically, soldiers have often taken art and beauty for granted, and frequently they are indifferent observers of the passing scene. Thus, we have no records from the sixteenth century of French and Spanish waterfowling expeditions in North America, although they doubtless occurred, if for no other reason than to supply camps with food. Army officers have sought recreation in hunting for centuries before the lieutenants of Alexander the Great took time out from their march to India to stalk ducks along the Euphrates.

The first record of an American duck hunt is dated as late as May 28, 1687, and describes an outing the previous fall. Baron Lahontan, Lord Lieutenant of the French Colony in Newfoundland, found himself that September at the north end of Lake Champlain in the Missisquoi Delta:

[2] One frame in the Codex Florentino comprising Aztec paintings on display at the Laurentian Library in Florence, Italy, depicts an Aztec removing ducks from a net stretched between two poles.

Decoys fashioned from feathers, skins, rush, or wood have been used for many thousands of years. This drake canvasback from Lovelock Cave, Nevada, just happens to be our oldest example—approximately 800 A.D. *(Photograph courtesy of Museum of the American Indian, Heye Foundation)*

. . . accompany'd with thirty or forty of the Savages that are very expert in shooting and hunting and perfectly well equipped with the proper places for finding waterfowl, deer, and other fallow beasts. The first post we took up was upon the side of a marsh or fen four or five leagues in circumference; and after we had fitted up our huts, the savages made huts upon the water in several places. These water-huts are made of branches and leaves of trees, and contain three or four men.

For a decoy, they have the skins of geese, bustards [probably herons], and ducks, dry'd and stuff'd with hay. The two feet being made fast with two nails to a small piece of a light plank, which floats around the hut. This place being frequented by wonderful numbers of geese, ducks, bustards, teals, and an infinity of other fowl unknown to Europeans; when these fowls see the stuff'd skins swimming with the heads erect, as if they were alive, they repair to the same place, and so give the savages an opportunity of shooting 'em, either flying or upon the water; after which the savages get into their canoes and gather 'em up.

This French correspondence was first translated in 1703. The English were always interested in knowing what their French adversaries were up to in the New World. However, the English needn't have been concerned the French were getting more of the wildfowl resources than they were, for sixty-six years before Baron Lahontan wrote his letter, Edward Winslow of the Massachusetts Colony sent another letter to prospective Pilgrim immigrants advising them to bring hefty smoothbore muskets for the marvelous waterfowling to be had near Plymouth: "Let your piece be long in the barrel and fear not the weight of it, for most of our shooting is done from stands."

The use of dead or artificial birds for decoys (as contrasted with the tame, live birds used for so many centuries by Europeans and Asiatics), the craft of duck calling, and the use of "stands," "huts," or as we call them today, "blinds," have long been essential ingredients of American waterfowling. Such refinements, especially the use of duck and goose calls, still distinguish our sport from Europe's, where waterfowl are mostly pass shot from behind sea walls or rush panels as the birds trade between resting and feeding areas.

There is another, more subtle, contrast between European and American hunting traditions to be read between the lines of Winslow's quote. In England, "stand shooting" was a privilege reserved for the gentry. In America, it was a necessity, reserved for every man.

Captain John Smith, of Pocahontas fame, and the man who coined the term "New England," was the New World's first real estate promoter, and he composed hyperbolic phrases about nearly every aspect of American life, conveniently overlooking hostile natives, biting flies, and strange new diseases. Such little problems didn't seem to exist in Smith's Chesapeake, which he described as "a country that may have the prerogative over the most pleasant navigable rivers; heaven and earth never agreed better to frame a place for man's habitations."

As far as rations went, "In winter there are great plenty of swans, cranes gray and white with black wings, herons, geese, brants, ducks, widgeon, dotterel [shorebirds], oxeyes, parrots [the now-extinct Carolina parakeet], and pigeons.[3] [There is] of these sorts great abundance, and some other strange kinds, to us unknown by name."

Elsewhere Smith speaks of the New World as a place where "nature and liberty affords us that freely which in England we want, or it costeth us dearly . . . [In America, there are no] hard landlords to rack us with high rents, or extorting fines . . . [no] tedious pleas in law to consume us with their many years' disputation for justice . . . here every man may be master of his own labor and land . . . and if he have nothing but his hands, he may set up his trade; and by industry quickly grow rich."

According to Sir William Dugdale's *Origines Juridiciales,* swans and cranes in England cost an exorbitant ten shillings apiece as far back as

---

[3] Mourning doves are field birds; Smith is probably referring to the forest-loving and now-extinct passenger pigeons.

Before the advent of the camera, nineteenth-century artists designed flying ducks so they rather more resembled jet-propelled aircraft with swept-back wings than the furiously flapping fowl which photography has taught us to see. This woodcut was made for Charles E. Whitehead's description of waterfowling in *Wild Sports in the South; or, The Camp-Fires of the Everglades,* published in 1860. Note that decoys, even in primitive Florida, were considered a necessary part of a duck hunter's equipment. *(Reproduction courtesy Elman Pictorial Collection)*

1555—when the Crown, to whom these birds belonged, permitted such royal fare to be sold at all. Seventy-five years later in America, such birds cost no more than the price of shot, powder, and a little effort to collect them.

Thus, it is not a farfetched notion that the abundance and availability of wildlife in the New World were important ingredients in the rise of democracy, a political system in which game belongs to everyone [4] until

[4] The unfortunate corollary to the concept of game belonging to everyone is that it belongs to no one. Wildlife protection and law enforcement is a more difficult proposition in the New World than in the Old, where the poacher's ultimate victim is a landowner who defrays his taxes or pays for game management through the sale of game. With a vested interest in wildlife, a landowner is clearly an injured party when poachers rob his property. British courts recognize this vested interest, and confirmed poachers are given stiff penalties. In the New World, the poacher, as a member of the society which owns the wildlife, is only injuring himself in stealing wildlife without a license, out of season, or in excess of the legal limit. Therefore, American courts have traditionally treated poachers lightly.

In 1937, Joseph P. Knapp, the founder of More Game Birds in America, Inc., and Ducks Unlimited, and three of his colleagues were arrested in North Carolina for shooting five ducks over their legal limits. When the federal prosecutor asked which one of the hunters had violated the law, Knapp's attorney replied: "The respondent has taken up the torch [of conservation] from failing hands and passed it on, and the wave of interest for the preservation of wildlife now evident in America and the Dominion [of Canada] is largely due to him. If the officials of this generation cannot properly appraise him and appreciate him, those of the future will, for when the ducks, geese and other wildfowl again swarm over Currituck Sound and nearly blot out the sun, the credit will be his, and his prosecution will then appear in its true and ridiculous light."

The judge must have been impressed by such flowery rhetoric, for he only fined Knapp $5—a dollar for each of the illegal ducks.

taken into possession. While the hunting traditions of Europe were usually based on property, those of America were based on need and effort. While only aristocrats and their associates could shoot waterfowl in overcrowded England, every farmer's son in spacious America was expected to go to the nearest river to harvest migrating mallards.

This was the bright side of our system. The dark side is presaged in Captain Smith's words that anyone "may set up his trade; and by industry quickly grow rich." While surplus game had long been sold in Europe, its taking had never involved professional shooters paid so many ounces of gold for a barrel of ducks. In the New World, John Jacob Astor had made a fortune (enough to buy major portions of Manhattan Island) by managing a small army of trappers. Why could not similar fortunes be made, some people asked, by managing teams of professional waterfowlers? Thus was born the concept of the market hunter who, like Astor's trappers, would devastate significant wildlife resources that took decades to recover, or, in some cases, never did.

TWO: COMMERCIAL HUNTING

"There are those whose only claim to a place among duck hunters is based upon the fact that they shoot ducks for the market. No duck is safe from their pursuit in any place, either by day or night. Not a particle of sportsmanlike spirit enters into this pursuit, and the idea never enters their minds that a duck has any rights that a hunter is bound to respect. The killing they do amounts to bald assassination—to murder for the sake of money. All fair-minded men must agree that duck hunters of this sort should be segregated from all others and placed in a section by themselves. They are the market shooters."

Grover Cleveland, in 1906

OVERSHOOTING can and has devastated many wildlife resources. Recreational—that is to say, properly regulated—hunting has never depleted a single form of wildlife. This is an important distinction which wildlife protectionists rarely bother to make in their condemnation of sport hunters.

A corollary rule of wildlife management is that artificial propagation and stocking do not always succeed in restoring a depleted species. In fact, we know next to nothing about the breeding requirements of literally dozens of endangered species and could not artificially propagate them even if the U.S. Congress budgeted the funds to do so. Sir Peter Scott in *The Swans,* implies that North Americans have been fortunate the trumpeter became our endangered swan species, rather than the whistling swan, because the trumpeter responds well to captive breeding, while the whistling swan does not.

So-called subsistence hunting raises still another issue. Wildlife protectionists are generally inclined to support the "right" of native Americans to take fish and wildlife when and where they desire with no restrictions on the numbers involved. This, despite the fact protectionists are disposed to eliminate all forms of recreational hunting.

The theory is that native Americans, relatively few in number and limited in mobility, can never have the impact on a resource that highly mobile and superbly armed European-Americans can have. However, such thinking is both naive and illogical. What does it matter how superbly equipped a sport hunter is if he is prohibited from killing more than seven eiders a day? And what does it matter how little mobility an Eskimo woman has if with a snare-pole she can eradicate an entire nesting colony of eiders in a day for their eiderdown skins?

Subsistence hunting, without any limitation on season and daily bag limit, is precisely as effective as unrestricted market hunting in devastating a wildlife resource. Indeed, in the case of northern-nesting waterfowl, it is often more effective. Nesting birds are more susceptible to harassment than wintering birds. Merely the physical strains involved in producing eggs, incubating them, protecting and finding food for the young, is enough to exhaust adults. In order to provide the birds with an opportunity to recover, nature has designed a quiet recuperation period after nesting known as the summer moult.

However, when native Americans compound the tensions of reproduction with human egg-collecting and hen-snaring and interrupt the recuperation period with flightless-bird roundups, they are doing more than reducing bird populations by those numbers actually killed and consumed. They are eroding the stamina and possibly the will of a species just before the rigors of fall migration.

Thus, whistling swans have abandoned the Perry River region of Arctic Canada, and eiders have been displaced from several once important breeding ranges between Alaska and Labrador. By contrast, the native peoples of Iceland, Scandinavia, and Siberia have developed a tradition of eider "farming" in which eiderdown and eggs are collected under regulated conditions. Female eiders are so strictly protected, they become tame to the point of domestication. In some areas, eiders have developed dense colonies under the auspices of man, and concentrations of several hundred nests per acre are found on Novaya Zemlya, the huge island separating the Barents and Kara Seas. Meanwhile at Hooper Bay, which lies north of Nunivak Island on the Alaskan coast, native persecution has so reduced breeding populations of eiders that one species, the Steller eider, no longer nests there at all. So much for the righteous tradition of subsistence hunting.[1]

As a rule of thumb, while unregulated shooting was the principal cause of North American waterfowl declines in the last century, the deterioration of prime nesting and wintering habitats has had the greatest adverse impacts in this century. However, there are areas of overlap. For example, overshooting (not to mention trapping and other illegal forms of killing) of black ducks is probably the major factor in the continuing decline of this species, just as the cutting of swamp and bottomland timber had much to do with the decline of the wood duck in the last century.

Following the Civil War, the food demands of burgeoning urban populations and an improvement in firearms worked together to wreak

---

[1] A still more dramatic example of subsistence overkill comes from New Zealand. Polynesians arrived there about the tenth century A.D., and within 600 years, these stone-age hunters had killed and eaten the last indigenous swan, *Cygnus summerensis*. By the seventeenth century, they had also killed the last moa.

In 1854, when this woodcut was made by C. Minton for *Gleason's Pictorial,* the Canada goose was a trophy more because of its size, wariness, and scarcity than because of its flavor. In fact, there was no great market for what epicureans termed its "coarse flesh," and in the Atlantic Flyway, snow geese were sold as "white brant" so as not to have the tainted word "goose" stand in the way of profit. *(Reproduction courtesy Library of Congress)*

incredible devastation on many forms of wildlife. The advent of the semi-automatic shotgun has even been cited as a principal reason for the decline of waterfowl. Many sportsmen still refuse to hunt with this weapon, perhaps feeling that the blood of troubled species or the vanished Labrador duck is on its bolt. Yet the thoughtful historian recognizes that the laws of supply and demand dictated by a geometrically-progressing human population toward the end of the last century inspired both the need for more game and the means, including the rather late development of semiautomatic shotguns.

Ironically, the turn-of-the-century decline of the canvasback and redhead duck had as much to do with America's growing demand for more wheat, corn, and other grains as with overshooting. Agricultural priorities led to massive drainage projects throughout the Midwest so that, for example, by 1910, less than five percent of Iowa's original wetlands remained intact. Thus, more wheat meant fewer ducks, and this robbing of Peter to pay Paul has had more to do in the long run with the decline of waterfowl than the invention of any firearm or even the shooting of thousands of birds daily on such prime grounds as the Chesapeake's Susquehanna Flats.

Unlike most other forms of hunting in North America, where pioneering/subsistence and aristocratic/sporting traditions merge, so that a fortunate grouse or turkey hunter derives as much pleasure from his woodcraft and shooting skills as he does from presenting the hunt's harvest to his family and guests, waterfowling is still haunted by the pioneering and market hunting past. The magnitude of the slaughter that took place between the 1850s and 1910, and which can be verified by old freight slips and bills of lading for barrels of birds, reinforces the legends about sky-darkening flocks of ducks and geese. Modern waterfowlers collect the artifacts of that murky era, not as talismans to future slaughter, but because ancient decoys, shotguns, and brass shells are reminders of a day when our nation's values and lifestyle were simpler, more confident, and still touched by a reverence for the unknown, and our continent's resources were nearly as abundant as they had been when our forefathers first arrived.

Cobb Island

Nathan Cobb, his wife, and their three sons sailed from Cape Cod in 1833 to the Eastern Shore of Virginia, where Cobb bought a barrier island with several hundred bags of salt boiled from a seep he found on his chosen land. Although the Cobb boys all went to the mainland to find wives, they returned to their father's island to raise their children on surf-caught fish and beach-shot shorebirds. Even before the Civil War, Nathan Cobb and his three sons shot ducks by the barrel for northern markets—exceptional weeks, averaging up to 150 birds per day per man—then stayed up most of the night plucking and dressing the black duck, pintail, canvasback, redhead and brant that brought 50 cents apiece—approximately ten dollars per bird in today's inflated currency. Canada geese were seldom shot for the market since, before the advent of their upland feeding habits, goose flesh was considered too coarse for urban epicureans. For this reason, when the wary and flavorful greater snow geese were shot, they were marketed as "white brant" so as not to turn away potential buyers adverse to the idea of eating a "wild goose." When the Cobbs had a shipment ready, they would load the birds aboard one of their Cobb-built sloops and put out to sea in search of a northbound schooner with whose captain they would negotiate a fair freight price. Once the bargain was made, the barrels were lifted aboard and sent on their way to A. & M. Robbins, wholesalers of New York City.

The Cobbs purchased powder by the 25-pound keg, and when breech-loading shotguns were introduced, the boys loaded their own brass 8- and 10-gauge shells. Some of the double-barreled weapons they shot weighed several pounds more than the heaviest modern 10- and 12-gauge magnum shotguns, and the barrels measured up to 38 inches in length. Somehow the Cobbs learned to handle these unwieldy pieces with precision and to make shots on bunched or crossing birds in order to keep their daily totals under one shot per duck.

When northern manufacturers and financiers who had been enriched by the Civil War looked for more southerly playgrounds, they gravitated to Cobb's island, possibly because he was a Yankee like themselves or simply because by the late 1860s, the fame of the place was nearly nationwide. Soon the Cobbs were receiving two or three requests a week from sportsmen for guide services. The Cobbs invested every dollar they could from their gunning profits into a hotel and clubhouse, ballroom, chapel, improved wharf, a coal-burning steamer (the *NWA Cobb,* named for the brothers Nathan, Jr., Warren, and Albert), and other amenities to serve the gentlemen and their ladies who had sometimes tasted Cobb Island ducks long before they had an opportunity to come south to shoot their own. The island resort became so popular, visitors soon asked to buy lots near the clubhouse, and the Cobbs sold mere patches of shifting sands for as much as $5,000 apiece. Most of the wealthy buyers, like the elder Cobb himself, came from coastal Massachusetts.

Even before the patriarch died in 1890, the island was changing physically, shifting west and north, but also shrinking as the Atlantic imperceptibly rose year by year. The number of ducks, brant, and shorebirds had greatly diminished, and the Cobbs were reduced to shooting "strikers," the local name for terns. The most valuable of these to the millinery trade in

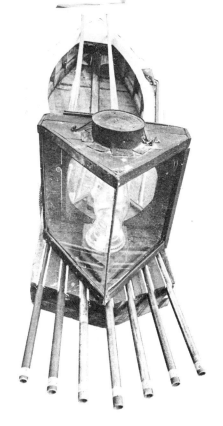

Left: A battery mounted in the bow of a flat-bottomed skiff built by Ira Hudson of Chincoteague, Virginia.

Right: A gunning light rigged atop a 7-barrel 12-gauge battery for deadly night work. *(Photographs courtesy Chesapeake Bay Maritime Museum)*

Boston and New York was the tiny least tern *(Sterna albifrons),* for which the Cobbs received 15 to 25 cents apiece. Even as the sea rose, and the numbers of birds dwindled, the center of commercial duck shooting in the mid-Atlantic, and of the sport hunting clubs that grew up in conjunction with such activity, shifted south to Currituck, Albemarle, and Pamlico Sounds where you can still hear stories about suppliers who sailed catboats and small sloops among the sometimes smoke-shrouded shooting rigs, paying golden half-eagles ($5) for braces of canvasbacks—then taking the money in again when they sold the gunners shot and powder or shells at scalper's prices. Fortunes were made in market hunting, but as in the case of Astor's trappers or Cabot's whalers, the men at the top of the pyramid got rich. The men at the bottom, the men who risked early death to trap beaver in Indian country or to hunt whales or waterfowl in unholy weather, made enough to get by from year to year, or perished in the process. Today much of Nathan Cobb's Sportsman's Paradise is under the sea, and brown sharks pursue croaker and spot across the site of the ballroom floor and into the slough where the chapel once stood. Cobb Island brant decoys and canvasback sink-box weights from Currituck Sound are poignant reminders of the men who loved waterfowl and independence in equal shares, but who destroyed the former to prolong the latter.

Punt Gunning

Even the nonhunting public is fascinated by this era of abundance turned to scarcity. Perhaps, people are really more intrigued by tales of riches to rags than the other way around. The mere sight of a gigantic punt gun or a row of barrels welded together to form a battery [2] evokes fantasies of mayhem and slaughter. Lem Ward of Crisfield, Maryland used to enjoy titillating the gunning groupies found at most any decoy show by saying, "Once you go big gunning, you'll never hunt another way."

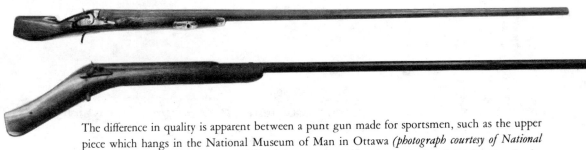

The difference in quality is apparent between a punt gun made for sportsmen, such as the upper piece which hangs in the National Museum of Man in Ottawa *(photograph courtesy of National Museums of Canada, Ottawa)*, and the bare-bones, stove-pipe affair made for night shooting in the Chesapeake, such as the lower piece which used to hang in the Abercrombie & Fitch gun room.

However, the preferred method of "big gunning" the Chesapeake was less pleasant than memory allows. First of all, the guns themselves were often jury-rigged, stovepipe affairs as liable to blow up in the gunner's face as at the ducks. In the mid-Atlantic, winter weather is highly erratic, and in a shallow bay a sudden breeze can bunch up waves with a mysterious cross-chop guaranteed to sink a small skiff unless it is beached in a hurry. The roll

---

2 The word *battery* is also used in the mid-Atlantic as a synonym for sink-box. Actually a "sink-box" was originally a very low, decked-over, skifflike affair which was made to float at water level by flooding one or more compartments under the gunwales and floorboards. The so-called battery was larger, often designed for two shooters, and surrounded by canvas or thin wooden panels or "wings." The sink-box was towed or sometimes even rowed into position; the battery normally had to be carried out to the gunning grounds aboard a tender. Since the sink-box had a very local and rather short-lived existence, and because most people think of the word *battery*, as Webster's dictionary does, in the context of "a grouping of artillery pieces" or "a number of similar articles, items, or devices arranged, connected, or used together," I will continue to use *battery* when referring to guns with three or more barrels and *sink-box* as a floating device for shooting from a reclining position below the waterline.

Former Director of the U.S. Fish and Wildlife Service, Albert M. Day, inspects a number of punt guns obtained on the Eastern Shores of Maryland and Virginia. On either side of the long guns, note the less romanticized but far more lethal multi-barreled batteries. *(Photograph courtesy U.S. Fish and Wildlife Service)*

call of punt gunners who never made it home is a long one, and, perversely, that only adds to the glamor of their names.

The preferred method was to hunt on still, moonlit nights, or on dark nights with a large bow light, and seek ducks silhouetted by the moon's glow or illuminated and fascinated by the bow light. If your skiff was painted white, and if you kept a low profile behind a cannon loaded with a pound and more of shot and aimed over the bow, you could get within 80 yards (optimum range for the big guns) of resting birds before the flare of a match touched to the powder train or a paddle slapped on the hull caused the birds to jerk their heads up and to start into the air where a confusion of stretched necks, extended wings, and exposed flanks resulted in a consequent confusion of dead and dying fowl after the cannon's roar and the smoke had drifted away.

In the darkness, the loss of crippled ducks was shameful, and the inheritor of such inhumane waste is the modern waterfowler who makes no particular effort to recover his crippled birds. Given the circumstances of waterfowling—that is, hunting hard-to-kill birds over or near a watery environment in which the birds can swim faster and dive better than any dog, and in which they can hide so no human eye or canine nose can detect them—lost birds are a regrettable, but inevitable, facet of the sport. However, to be careless about the pursuit of cripples, to hunt without a dog or at dusk when the odds are increased that a wing-tipped duck will know a lingering death, that is criminal behavior. Market gunners rationalized that "time is money" and unsuccessful shots fired at skulking cripples were precious pennies taken from their modest profits. The modern hunter has no such cruel excuse.

The kills per discharge of a punt gun were rarely the popularly imagined 100-plus birds. Sixty-seven ducks is the biggest single-shot bag that Paul Martial of Smith Island, Maryland, can recall,[3] and a team of fast shooters working from a sink-box could be far more lethal with the expenditure of only a little more shot and powder. In a single day in 1878, Charles S. Hawkins, shooting on Long Island's Great South Bay from a sink-box tended by Wilbur R. Corwin, killed 640 ducks, mostly greater scaup, which were shipped to New York City from Bellport at 25 cents a pair. On another occasion in the same area, Judge H. A. Bergen, tended by Richard B. Hamel, killed 98 black duck, 64 broadbill, and one gadwall between 9 A.M. and 1 P.M.

Sink-Boxes

The sink-box shooter had two advantages over his punt-gunning colleague in that a sink-box's shooting was done in the daytime and all targets were airborne. Although it is easier to hit a swimming duck, it is easier to kill a flying one, even if both are centered with the shot pattern. As any hunter knows who has fired half a dozen shells at a swimming cripple, there

---

[3] Connecticut decoy carver Charles E. "Shang" Wheeler owned a double-barreled 4-gauge shotgun that was fired from a punt into a flock of greater scaup—the first barrel at birds on the water; the second as the ducks got airborne. The two shots killed 81 broadbill outright and when a 12-gauge shotgun was used to collect the cripples, the total came to 127 ducks. This is the greatest single-effort kill from a punt that I have been able to locate which has some documentable credibility.

WILD DUCK SHOOTING ON THE POTOMAC.

By 1850 (the year of this woodcut), waterfowling had fallen into two, not always easily distinguished, categories: sport hunting and market hunting. Although this chap on the Potomac River in a sink-box (sometimes called a battery) seems to be enjoying himself, the large number of fowl he is killing makes it more than likely that the surplus will be sold by his guides standing by in the sloop as a bonus for their services. *(Reproduction courtesy Library of Congress)*

are many holes in a pattern once the shot flies 60 or more yards. A duck's head and neck will fit any number of these holes, and a distant duck's back sheds lead or steel about as well as it does water. However, by waiting for birds to get close before shooting and then swiftly reshooting any downed birds with their heads still up, many sink-box shooters were able to average one dead duck for every shot fired by making up the "deficit" caused by follow-up shots with periodic kills on crossing and overlapping birds.

Sink-boxes were awkward, heavy, and frequently hazardous contraptions. They required sturdy blocks and tackles to launch from a tender, and an hour or more was required to set out the 300 to 500 decoys that sometimes surrounded these "floating coffins." [4] Panels or wings resting on or just under the water provided stability, and a lip of lead around the coffin center kept out the water which always threatened to flood and sink the box.

Weight was a delicate matter, not only regarding the size of the gunner—big men generally became tender men and did relatively little shooting except when chasing cripples downwind of the stool—but regarding the distribution of ballast as well. Remarkably, while sink-box shooters were always wet and occasionally had to swim for their lives, relatively few were lost due to the proximity of the tender picking up dead waterfowl and keeping the gunners supplied with shot and powder. Careless handling and occasional swampings caused the loss of iron decoys used to weight the stabilizing wings or panels, and in recent years divers have made a small industry of searching for these relics on Long Island Sound, the Susquehanna Flats, in North Carolina waters, or any waterfowl wintering areas where sink-boxes were used. The iron decoys are then sold for prices nearly as heavy as the birds themselves.

In sink-box shooting, unlike punt gunning, teamwork was essential to a successful outing. Normally, if one bird was killed for every three shots fired, the families of four men (two in the box or boxes, and two in the tender) would break even and survive another winter. If a shooter did worse than that, he was soon out of the box. If he did better, well, the skipper might be able to afford a new mainsail for the tender instead of continually patching the old.

Commercial Traditions and the Law

One modern habit of American waterfowlers which is looked on with dismay by European sportsmen, but which may be an inheritance of the teamwork of market gunning days, is the tendency of a dominant shot in a

---

[4] Eugene V. Connett attests that Long Island gunners Wil Corwin and Henry Gould could set a sink-box and about 150 decoys in precisely 20 minutes. Furthermore, they could pick up the entire rig to be launched elsewhere in 19 minutes. Needless to say, this Corwin-Gould team was exceptional. In some instances, where a sink-box included several hundred decoys, it was set in the fall and pulled in the late spring. Periodically the sink-box was pumped out and decoys were added to the stool to replace those that storms and tides had carried away.

However much modern sportsmen would like to forget that our forebearers often shot more waterfowl than they could use, it happened. These two college boys have obviously had a busy day of gunning at Buffalo Lake, Alberta, and we can only hope they were able to give away or sell their fifty geese so the birds didn't go to waste. *(Photograph courtesy Library of Congress)*

party of three or four hunters to shoot the other hunters' limits as well as his own. Such waterfowlers either do not know or care that they are not entitled to shoot more than one limit of birds, even when the other hunters involved are perfectly happy for him to do so. This law is essentially unenforceable, for how can a warden prove against the testimony of two or three witnesses that one man did all the shooting?

In the United States we have dozens of public laws governing circumstances which sportsmen in other nations handle through club codes. Although we have substituted law for personal ethics (which are the foundation of sportsmanship), we have not at the same time explained to the custodians of the law why such laws exist or provided wardens with adequate muscle to enforce the laws. In all the United States, there are approximately 200 federal conservation enforcement agents to supervise not only migratory wildlife laws, but laws affecting endangered species and, along the coasts, marine mammals.

Ironic and even tragic situations are reported every year in which harried wardens treat honest hunters like the worst kind of poachers, and soured sportsmen frequently allow their hunting ethics to slide with the justification that such standards only handicap them vis-à-vis the many unapprehended lawbreakers in the field. Furthermore, such ethics do not earn the esteem and public respect formerly associated with the word *sports-man*. Hunters once policed their own ranks, and there was as much pride in this facet of the sport as in well-made shots. Today bureaucrats make laws for other bureaucrats to enforce, and many of these laws have more to do with hunting morality and the convenience of the enforcers than the needs of waterfowl resources. Whether a law "means well" is irrelevant. What matters is whether the law can be enforced, and there is simply no way the federal government will ever hire enough wardens to replace the concerned sportsmen who once represented the chief protection for wintering ducks and geese throughout America.

As Richard L. Parks noted more than thirty years ago, "Waterfowling laws too often play into the hands of the unscrupulous. 'To a shorter hunting season!' 'To less shooting!' 'To fewer hunters on the marshes!' These are toasts of the duck trappers as they pluck our ducks and guzzle their rotgut beside the roaring woodstove by night. For one duck trapper can bag more black ducks in a season than a thousand license-paying sportsmen."

With the passing of the waterfowling clubs—which began in 1935 with a 30-days' hunting season and a prohibition against the use of live decoys and made official in 1978 by Congressional approval of a tax law that no longer permits individuals or industries to treat clients to a day of hunting or fishing and write off the expense as entertainment—and with the decay of personal hunting standards, it is no more a matter of ten percent of all hunters being slobs, but more like most of us being slobs ten percent of the time. As Benjamin Franklin once observed, "So convenient a thing it is to be a *reasonable* creature, since it enables one to find or make a *reason* for everything one has a mind to do." The list of rationales for criminal behavior in duck hunting include: for baiting, "I feed more than I kill"; for shooting over the limit, "I only get out once or twice a season, so I'm only taking what I'd get if I went more often"; and for shooting before or after legal hours, "My watch is probably slow (or fast)."

Such codes and their violations are an old affair and are rooted in the nineteenth-century struggle between the sportsmen and commercial gunners for possession of waterfowl resources. The future doesn't look any brighter or less hypocritical. Young men are awed at waterfowl festivals, decoy shows, and Ducks Unlimited dinners, when retired outlaw gunners tell the youngsters what it was like to shoot dozens of ducks a day and then

Although nearly blinded and crippled by duck poachers in 1947, John Buckalew recovered and is still active in waterfowl research. Here he is on a recent banding expedition on the Delmarva peninsula. *(Photo by George Reiger)*

demonstrate how to hide the overkill in hollow goose decoys; or "outlaw historians" demonstrate with aerial transparencies the contrast between poorly concealed bait in a pond and the same pond "so you'd hardly know there was anything there."

Conservation officials, even migratory wildlife refuge administrators, seem to be as entertained by such presentations as the young hunters in the audience. However, by glamorizing the outlaw tradition, the sponsors of such show-and-tells may be contributing to the perpetuation of many of our resource problems by encouraging young men, who might not have thought of shooting a dozen ducks a day, or of baiting a pond, to sample the experience—"just to see what it was like." At least, that's what they tell the wardens when they are caught.

A letter from John H. Buckalew, former manager of the Chincoteague National Wildlife Refuge, to his boss in Washington, D.C., briefly and heroically describes the true face of outlaw gunning better than any number of sermonettes on the subject. The letter is dated February 25, 1947:

Before daylight on the morning of February 22, I made an attempt to apprehend two or three persons who, according to information I had received, had been going on the refuge and killing waterfowl. At approximately 1:30 P.M., I was walking north along the road leading through the woods bordering the side of the refuge. I had stopped and looked back along this road for possibly a minute or so. When I looked up the road I saw two men starting to run across it toward Assateague Channel, on the west side of the island. Both men had shotguns, and one carried a bag containing a number of ducks. When these men found that I had seen them, they started running back into the thick brush, dropping the bag of ducks. At the time I saw them, they were approximately 75 yards from me. I told them to stop and started in pursuit.

Within a very short distance I had gained on them until only about 30 to 35 yards separated the hunters and myself. At this time one of the men jumped behind a tree and fired, the charge striking me in the left side and chest. As I ducked toward the shelter of another tree, he fired again, the charge this time striking me in the face and arms. Before I could recover from the shock of the shots and clear my eyes of blood, both men had disappeared in the thick brush. . . .

P.S. You may find a number of errors in this and other correspondence for today, as I have not yet regained the use of my right hand.

The Federal Bureau of Investigation was called into the case, and, although the identities of the poachers were well known, just one man was brought to trial, convicted, and received a shockingly mild two-year sentence. There is nothing romantic or Robin Hoodish about attempted manslaughter.

First Waterfowling Laws

The attempt to protect waterfowl with legislation goes back nearly two hundred and seventy years to the Massachusetts Colony's prohibition against the use of camouflaged canoes and sailboats in the hunting of ducks and geese. We don't precisely understand how this law was meant to protect waterfowl when the more obvious solutions of a closed season and a daily bag limited were not explored. Possibly the restriction was created by those who felt, as many English gunners still feel, that it is unsportsmanlike to disturb resting birds. For example, certain chapters of the Waterfowlers Association of Great Britain and Ireland (WAGBI) prohibit their members from jump shooting which, after hunting over decoys, is the American waterfowler's most popular way to take ducks.

Another possibility is that the statute was created to give local birds some respite during the summer moult, when waterfowl are unable to fly. Unfortunately, this law also bound the winter hunter and would have prevented him from retrieving many crippled birds—had he honored the law. Since there were no wardens to enforce this legislation, colonial ad-

Although this 1890 photograph taken in the Dakotas looks like the results of a hard day's shooting for the market, the quality of the men's firearms (note the bison skull against which the guns are stacked), the presence of dogs, and the fact the hunters are dressed à la mode indicate these nineteenth-century gentlemen have been recreating, not commercial gunning. *(Photograph courtesy Library of Congress)*

This was pure market gunning— one hundred and seventy-five scaup and redheads. Photographer C. L. Wasson entitled this 1902 pose: "It wasn't good weather for ducks." *(Photograph courtesy Library of Congress)*

ministrators may have helped set the precedent for ignoring wildlife protection laws that unfortunately, for many people, continues to the present day.

Whatever the reason, this early law was at least indicative of the fact that by 1710 the people of Massachusetts recognized that waterfowl had already decreased in numbers from their amazing abundance in the 1600s.

By the beginning of the nineteenth century, the situation had deteriorated to such an extent that there was real tension and even bloodshed between men who hunted ducks for recreation and those who did it for a living. Industrialization and the draining of wetlands had begun in a big way, and sportsmen and commercial gunners were competing for the best, but shrinking, waterfowl wintering grounds. Sportsmen had the inside track in political and economic pull, but the commercial men had the advantage of living year around along the bays and marshes where the birds were found.

There was ambiguity in the fact that not all sportsmen were pure in heart, for many of them sold the ducks they killed, both to defray the expenses of a hunt and to rationalize their overkill—that is: "the birds won't be wasted." In many ways, the situation was analogous to the current struggle between recreational anglers and commercial fishermen for dwindling marine resources, such as striped bass and bluefin tuna. Even the way to distinguish the impure sportsman from commercial man runs about the same: Namely, the sportsman doesn't have to sell his catch for a living while the market man does.

In 1831, an event occurred which is a kind of milestone in the struggle between the two groups. A young English aristocrat arrived in America as an exile from his own land. Henry William Herbert, who would one day be known to the sporting world by the pseudonym "Frank Forester," was the son of the Honorable William Herbert, Doctor of Laws, member of Parliament, and the grandson of Henry Herbert, Lord Portchester, first Earl of Carnarvon. We don't know the reason Henry William Herbert was expelled from his family, but it was doubtless some matter of honor which may have, in reaction, made the young man a shining example of sporting honor in his adopted country.

Although Herbert was an outsider who offended many Americans with his English manners and accent, as well as his outspoken condemnation of our reckless use and waste of all natural resources, he found several close and influential friends and with them enjoyed the excellent hunting still

Henry William Herbert's (1807–1858) English aristocratic background enabled him to perceive the abuses perpetrated on wildfowl in the name of American democracy. This perception did not make him popular with politicians, but his journalistic attacks on battery gunners and spring shooting helped spearhead the first efforts to eliminate such practices at the state level. *(Reproduction courtesy New York Public Library)*

then to be found on the fringes of New York City. His experiences helped make him in time a particular enemy of William Henry Seward's plan to industrialize southern New York State. William Seward is best remembered today as the U.S. secretary of state who negotiated the purchase of Alaska from czarist Russia. However, prior to the Civil War, he was governor of New York and a great proponent of railroads and other industrial improvements. Frank Forester attacked Seward's encouragement of unplanned development and laced the word "improvement" with the same touches of irony that modern conservation writers have applied to "progress."

Without formal training in wildlife management (there was no such discipline in the 1830s), Henry William Herbert understood that the two greatest evils confronting wildlife and the future of sport hunting were overshooting and habitat destruction. (Unfortunately this perception did not prevent Herbert himself from racking up some staggering daily kills, but then our cultural heroes are rarely perfect.)

Herbert urged the banning of sink-boxes because their effect was to destroy great numbers of ducks "on their very feeding grounds, where most they desire to be quiet and unmolested, as in the end, if long persisted in, to

Low profile sink-boxes and boats were used by sportsmen as well as commercial hunters. This 1890 photograph by George Barker illustrates a blend of both designs. We call them "duck punts" or "layout boats" today, and they are still the most efficient way to hunt diving ducks—so long as the wind doesn't pick up and roll a few gallons of water down your neck.*(Reproduction courtesy Library of Congress)

make them entirely abandon the flats on which it is practiced." English sporting tradition has always preferred pass shooting to decoy or jump shooting, and Herbert recognized the several advantages occurring to a gunner who was able to shoot offshore from a concealed position surrounded by a few hundred decoys. Herbert also recognized that most of these rigs were worked by market men. Even when the sink-box operators took out a pair of "sports" for a day of shooting, the majority of birds were kept by the operators for sale as part of their guide fee. This racket was also used by the Cobbs in Virginia when they persuaded their summer guests to shoot terns for sport. The clients paid for guiding services, paid for all the shells they used—the shells loaded by the Cobbs and marked up above the cost of labor and materials—and the Cobbs got to sell all the birds shot by their guests. There were no accountants nor income taxes to pay.

In 1838, the New York legislature banned sink-boxes (or as it called them, "batteries") on Long Island, the area of the state where these rigs were most used. However, as previously noted, writing a law does not guarantee that it will be respected. Herbert's real effort began when he publicly condemned Long Island "sportsmen" who continued to use sink-boxes for fun and profit. Herbert contrasted them with the commercial gunners of the Jersey Shore who are "bold, hardy, lawless, and some say, half-piratical race, half-fowlers, half-fishermen, and more than half-wreckers, who are apt to enforce the laws of their own enactment by the strong hand and with the aid of their Queen Anne's muskets and a handful of heavy shot."

Herbert knew that even though there were no legislated covenants against such acts, outsiders who attempted to hunt from a sink-box or sail a boat equipped with a swivel cannon on Barnegat Bay sometimes disappeared—permanently. The rough treatment accorded strangers was not because the Jersey gunners knew or cared much about the reasons for the dwindling supply of ducks. The coastal fowlers were concerned with protecting their income from the birds today and were little interested in arguments favoring bag limits and seasons that would save the birds for tomorrow. The Jerseyites regarded the local, but seasonal, duck supply in a possessive manner, and they didn't allow anyone, who wouldn't at least hire a local guide, to shoot "their ducks."

Herbert's ideal hunter resided along the shores of the Chesapeake. This is curious and even amusing today, considering the Chesapeake is one of the nation's last strongholds of the outlaw tradition. Still, in Frank Forester's day, waterfowling on the Chesapeake was controlled largely by the members of private clubs who paid full-time caretakers to maintain the club's equipment, decoys, and buildings, and to patrol the grounds. Maryland, according to Forester, was where "the strong hand of the lawful and sportsmanlike gunners . . . alone carries out and vindicates the operation of the law; and is not without desperate, and at times even bloody affrays, that the poachers are prevented from carrying on their ruinous trade."

Brought up in the English aristocratic tradition, Herbert carried with him the notion that setting aside wild places exclusively for the recreation of man was both sensible and proper. He was horrified by the American attitude that wildlife was free and anyone's for the taking. It is, therefore, ironic that sink-boxes were finally outlawed in the present century as much to democratize waterfowling as to protect the resource. While sink-boxes frequently helped the boatless hunter when the shooting offshore kept diving ducks moving about on a calm day rather than permitting them to raft up safely out of range, several influential wildlife authorities felt that, following official demise of the market hunter, only the very rich could afford to own and operate a sink-box, and such exclusivity was opposed to American recreational ideals. One wonders what English-bred elitists, like Henry William Herbert, would have thought of that argument!

Throughout the century-long debate on the sink-box, anyone suggesting that the deadly and disruptive nature of the contraptions could be governed with bag limits and seasons was apparently shouted down by both sides. The presumption has long riddled waterfowling laws that "while I'm an honest guy, the next fellow isn't." Many of those who opposed sink-boxes insisted that no man would go to the trouble of maintaining such a contrivance unless he could shoot several dozen ducks a day; or that even if he had honorable intentions, once the ducks started pouring in, he would lose control and keep firing until he was out of shells.

Canadians have a more mature (or naive, depending on your point of view) outlook. If you are not upset about the possibility of disturbing birds on their nesting or feeding grounds, you will still find the sink-box a legal blind in a few areas across the border and an exciting way to greet migrant ducks and geese as they move through the Maritimes. Since American waterfowling seasons in states from the 40th parallel south don't get going until November, a trip to Canada in September or October will provide

Market hunting is still not dead. These feedbags filled with over 100 redheads were seized on the Eastern Shore of Maryland not many years ago. So long as exclusive restaurants and foreign embassies in Washington, D.C. continue to offer top dollar for illicit *wild*fowl, market hunting will go on. *(Photograph courtesy U.S. Fish and Wildlife Service)*

you with an early start. Lying below the waterline on a bed of sweet-smelling straw and watching from under your cap as a flock of scaup side-slip and spill wind from their wings while piling into the decoys is one of the highlights of American waterfowling and still available at Tabusintac, New Brunswick.

Henry William Herbert opposed the practice of spring hunting, sensibly arguing that every bird shot during the nesting season was equivalent to shooting next year's crop as well.

"The American snipe lays four eggs," Frank Forester wrote. "The death, therefore, of every snipe during spring shooting is equivalent to the death of five of these beautiful and sporting little birds."

In 1846, Rhode Island became the first state to prohibit the spring shooting of black ducks, wood ducks, woodcock, and snipe. However, political pressure from the business-as-usual boys eventually forced the Rhode Island legislature to rescind this law. The same thing eventually happened in New York State with the law against sink-boxes. By the time

Henry William Herbert died, it was clear to many thoughtful and concerned hunters that if any success was to be had with waterfowl protection, the initiative must come from the federal government. The states simply lacked the integrity or intestinal fortitude to take the necessary steps on their own, or to make their conclusions stick.

However, the federal government and states' rightists opponents would be busy with the issue of human slavery throughout the middle of the nineteenth century, and it wasn't until the 1870s that the federal government got involved, even then indirectly, in wildlife protection. It is a shame Henry William Herbert could not have lived to see national acceptance of some of the principles he introduced or championed. However, he would have had to live until this century before that happened. Instead a disillusioned "Frank Forester" committed suicide on May 17, 1858.

THREE: THE CONSERVATIONISTS TAKE OVER

"To bring back the ducks in their old-time abundance, the gunners must agree to
Stop spring shooting;
Limit the size of bags for a day and a season;
Stop the sale of game."

George Bird Grinnell, in 1901

"One of the things I've learned as I've gone along is that you never dream big enough."

Ira Noel Gabrielson, in 1969

THE PROFESSIONAL careers of George Bird Grinnell (1849–1938) and Ira Gabrielson (1889–1977) spanned more than a century of American history, and their activities mirror the development of conservation from a largely untested theory to proven principle supported by law. As a young man, Grinnell shot passenger pigeons with the grandsons of John James Audubon in rural Manhattan; as an old man, Gabrielson was active in the fight to preserve wetlands from urban development all across the country. Several different careers were known to these two men, who also knew each other.

Most conservationists realize that our ever-burgeoning population makes it impossible to recover this continent as it once was. However, prophets of conservation like Grinnell and Gabrielson inspire us in our attempts to create a more coherent world based on nature and science. Conservation has evolved from a fragile truth to a dynamic faith with millions of adherents and a large and growing clergy of trained biologists, ecologists, and economists. Every creed is based on the deeds and sacrifices of early practitioners and martyrs, and conservation today would not occupy such a lofty place among men's philosophy and goals except for the pioneering work of Grinnell and Gabrielson.

Although Grinnell's father was a prominent New York businessman, the rural upbringing of his son inclined the boy toward the study of nature. So grateful was young Grinnell for the influence of the Audubon family, he later created in 1886 the first national bird protective society in the United States and named it for John James Audubon.

Grinnell was, in some respects, an American edition of European aristocratic traditions. Certainly he was imbued with the same refined sense of honor and noblesse oblige that had motivated Henry William Herbert. Grinnell's father had had many business dealings with southern planters who were later ruined by the Civil War. The elder Grinnell was ruined as well. He incurred debts from which lesser men would have run. However, in 1873, Grinnell's father not only paid his many creditors the money he owed, but he supplied interest on the debts as well. George Bird Grinnell looked back on this deed as the finest achievement of his father's life.

Although George Bird Grinnell was more attached to Audubon's widow and her grandchildren (his contemporaries), Grinnell named America's first bird protective society for John James, the hunter and artist. This portrait of Audubon was painted by John Syme in 1826. *(Courtesy Elman Pictorial Collection)*

Such admiration of integrity was the foundation of Grinnell's concept of the sportsman-naturalist. However, unlike his cultural hero, Henry William Herbert, Grinnell reinforced his ideals and love of nature with the intellectual discipline of scientific training. Indeed, Grinnell would deserve a footnote in conservation history if for no other reason then, that he was the first (and one of the few) outdoor writers ever to earn a scientific doctoral degree, in Grinnell's case, in ornithology.

However, the catalog of George Bird Grinnell's accomplishments is far more significant than that, and not even *The New York Times,* which first called him "the father of conservation," could begin to assemble all the facts of his long and productive life. Just a few highlights will indicate the magnitude:

· In 1870, Grinnell went west with Othniel C. Marsh and helped discover fossil proofs to reinforce Darwin's theory of evolution.

· In 1874, he was in the Black Hills with George Armstrong Custer when gold was discovered and only missed being slaughtered two years later at the Little Big Horn because he was detained at Yale University cataloging material from the earlier expedition.

• Grinnell explored the region of the Continental Divide running north into Canada, and so impressed was he by this magnificent country, he became the principal mover in the successful effort to create Glacier National Park.

• Grinnell was a great friend of the Pawnee, Blackfeet, Gros Ventre, and Cheyenne, and as a respected ethnologist, he helped secure several rights and reservations for the red man.

• In 1887, he and Theodore Roosevelt founded one of hunting's most prestigious fraternities: the Boone and Crockett Club.

• From 1876 to 1911, Grinnell was editor of *Forest and Stream,* the foremost sportsman's publication of its time, and he wrote wisely and prolifically on a broad range of outdoor and natural-history subjects.

• In 1901, he published *American Duck Shooting,* the first book ever devoted to North American waterfowling and conservation. Although much of its information is dated, the very age of the anecdotes adds to their historical value and does not at all detract from their charm.

Like all compelling personalities, Grinnell had disciples, and, perhaps, the most worshipful was John P. Holman, for many years the managing editor of *Forest and Stream.* For younger men, Holman was our best, if not our only, link to Grinnell and his nineteenth-century world of wildfowling. Although John was a treasure trove of memories in this own right, he always subordinated his past to the "grand master," Grinnell.

Seated in Holman's home in Fairfield, Connecticut—a home John had built in an area which was once thought to be off the beaten track—the roar of traffic on Interstate 95 beyond the trees on the lower lawn occasionally shook the house with the speed and violence of monstrous trucks. Yet John's descriptions of yesteryear were so absorbing, they transformed the noise into a background murmur.

"Despite broad experience," said John, "George Bird Grinnell was not an excellent wing shot. However, he was not afraid to have other people know it, which was unlike most other well-known sportsmen of his time. George once observed after a particularly horrendous miss, 'It is astonishing how much room there is in the air around a duck!' and then he'd chuckle about the miss as though the red gods had played a joke on him. He didn't use the excuses the rest of us concoct when a bird flies by unscathed.

The year is 1915, and John Holman has just snapped a photo of his guide towing the boats and decoys across Barnegat Bay, New Jersey. "That was a miserable season," recalled John. "Duck populations were so far down I was lucky to get one drake canvasback in three days of hunting. That's not disdain, but incredulity, in my expression. Cans were never abundant in New Jersey, but this was the only duck that came near the decoys all weekend. Notice my full shell vest. Maybe the bird was deranged. There was nothing wonderful about those particular 'good old days.' I hope American hunters never again see waterfowl populations as low as we knew them in the 1910s and again in the thirties." *(Photographs by John P. Holman)*

"Because of George's modesty, when he talked about hunting, you put yourself into his stories. He would laugh while describing some perfectly awful flubs, but he'd say little about his fabulous shots. When he told you he made a perfect double on a pair of widgeon after his hunting partner had already missed the birds, the story was unquestionably true because he had spent rather more time telling you about how he had missed three easy black duck shots in a row."

George Bird Grinnell used similar storytelling techniques in his writing, and his anecdotes are enriched with detail. He knew and tried to teach that the least part of many of our most successful trips is the killing of game. In a paradox, never to be understood by nonhunters, killing becomes essential to hunting, but it is rarely essential to our best memories of the sport.

Let us go back nearly ninety years and sit with George Bird Grinnell in a duck blind on the shores of Currituck Sound:

It surprises one—though, of course, it is only natural—to see how many birds there are, which are not waterfowl, that come close to the blind entirely unsuspicious of its occupant. Hawks and sometimes, during gray days, owls hunt over the marsh, eager to prey on the blackbirds and sparrows whose haunt is here. Gulls often pass near the decoys, and occasionally one sees flying through the air a loon or cormorant. Sometimes one of the latter may be seen perched over the water on a stake of some deserted bush blind. Eagles [1] and buzzards, of course, and the ever-present crow, are constantly searching over the marsh and over the water, looking for dead and wounded ducks. . . .

Besides these, in and among the reeds live blackbirds, sparrows, marsh wrens and rails, any of which will venture close to the blind. Sometimes a little Carolina rail [2] in its peregrinations along the water's edge will even walk into the blind and gaze at its occupant with bright, dark eye, uncertain what he may be. It is amusing sometimes to see two or three men and a dog go crashing through the cane in hot pursuit of one of these little birds, who must laugh to himself at the clumsy efforts made by his pursuers to capture him.

Often a wisp of snipe or two or three individuals pass within gunshot of the blind, or a single bird, like a bullet from the sky, may drop on some nearby point of the marsh,

[1] Bald eagles are a rare sight for modern Atlantic Flyway wildfowlers. However, in December 1975, conservation administrator John Gottschalk, wildlife artist Ned Smith, and I turned back the clock as we watched a pair of eagles from a duck blind search for crippled game in the coastal marshes of Virginia.
[2] Sora rail, called "Carolina rail" in the Carolinas to distinguish this species from the larger Virginia rail.

Following the War Between the States, there was a veritable boom in field sport activity and art. However offensive or silly "Black Duck Shooting" might be by modern standards, it should be viewed as an example of an era (1879) when Currier and Ives could be sure of a national market for humorous prints based on waterfowling. *(Reproduction courtesy Library of Congress)*

and run briskly about over the mud to the water's edge, probing with busy bill for food which is hidden beneath. In like manner now and then a killdeer plover or a pair of yellowlegs may fly in from beyond the marsh, and hurry along over the mud as if greatly pressed for time.

Herons, of course, are abundant in the marsh, and are of three sorts. The night heron—in New England called quawk—and the bittern are seen less often here than the great blue heron, which in these parts is known by an apparently unmeaning name—"forty gallons of soup." This bird is common here, and often comes close over the blind, or alights in the water near it.

It is interesting to watch one when it is fishing. Its huge wings and long straddling legs make a great commotion over the water when it alights, though there is no splash when it puts its feet down. The moment that it has folded its wings, however, it straightens its legs, neck and body, and for a long time stands bolt upright, absolutely motionless, looking for all the world like a straight, weathered stick standing out of the water. In this position it resembles anything rather than a bird, and its attitude is extremely ungraceful. The position and the entire absence of motion are due, I suppose, first to its desire to see whether any enemy is in the neighborhood; and second to give its prey, which may have been frightened by the shadow of its passing body, time to recover from this alarm.

After a period of stillness which may last five or six minutes, but seems to the watcher much longer, the heron, still holding its neck straight and stiff and its bill pointed somewhat upward, takes a cautious step and then stands still for a moment. Then seemingly reassured, it moves on with slow, careful steps, its head turned a little on one side, evidently searching the water for its food. It does not take the conventional heron attitude until it sees some little fish that is within reach. Then very slowly it draws

The even earlier (1870) "Wild Duck Shooting" illustrates the idealized image of the sportsman we still nurture today. He has taken a young man, possibly his son, and his retriever with him, and, besides limiting his kill to a few birds, he is well groomed and dressed like a gentleman. *(Reproduction courtesy Library of Congress)*

in its neck and darts out its strong, keen bill, and usually captures its prey; not always, however, for I have several times seen one miss his stroke.

These are big birds, and birds, too, that one seldom has an opportunity to kill, yet it always seems to me a pity to shoot at them. They can be eaten, to be sure; yet no one who has ducks and geese to eat would be likely to prefer heron. Unless the gunner has some use for it, it does not, to me, seem worthwhile to kill any bird. Life is something so mysterious that it should not be lightly destroyed, and I have no sympathy with the wantonness which leads many shooters to try their guns on every robin, swallow, nighthawk or bat that may fly near to them. This is commonly done "for fun," or to see "whether I can hit it"; but it is all wrong.

Such sentiments were not as prevalent in the nineteenth century as they are today. That they are can be attributed more to the writings of George Bird Grinnell than the laws which many of his writings helped create. In a recent sociological study conducted under the auspices of the U. S. Fish and Wildlife Service and Yale University's School of Medicine, psychologist Stephen R. Kellert concluded there are three categories of hunter, rather than the more commonly perceived two: meat hunter and sportsman. While Kellert still perceives a meat-hunter type, he prefers to call him the "utilitarian."

Kellert then divides the sportsman into "dominionists" and "naturalists." The former is absorbed by displays of skill, competition, achievement, and companionship; the latter has a strong interest and affection for wildlife and the outdoors, and he is perfectly content to hunt alone, for his sense of being an integral part of nature is heightened by solitude.[3]

Although such distinctions are intriguing and useful for debate, they are ultimately invalidated by the complexity of the human spirit. Most sportsmen have overlapping veins of "dominionist" and "naturalist" sensibilities, and all of us (I hope) hunt for food. Certainly we know that a seed-fed mallard or teal is a supreme treat for the palate, and we pity less fortunate souls unable to obtain anything closer in taste than Long Island Duckling à l'Orange.

Doubtless, there were days when Grinnell enjoyed companionship afield, and there were hours when he preferred solitude. Certainly, he enjoyed his roast canvasback as much as the next nineteenth-century gentle-

---

[3] In his *Fishing and Shooting Sketches* (1906), Grover Cleveland made similar distinctions between "market shooters," "dead shots," and "serene duck hunters."

Although Theodore Roosevelt is the U.S. President most often associated with the birth of conservation, such men as Benjamin Harrison (who created the first combination national wildlife refuge and wilderness area in 1892) and Grover Cleveland (who supported restrictions governing the activities of market hunters) did much to improve the national climate for waterfowl. President Cleveland is shown testing his new 14-foot, 30-pound aluminum duck-hunting boat, designed by W. H. Mullins of Salem, Oregon. Aluminum boats were very rare and expensive in the 1890s; now they are very common and relatively inexpensive. *(Photographs courtesy Library of Congress)*

MR. CLEVELAND'S NEW TOY--A BOAT 14 FT. LONG MADE OF ALUMINUM AND WEIGHING 30 POUNDS.

MR. CLEVELAND'S DUCK BOAT.

It Is Made of Aluminum, Weighs Thirty Pounds, and Is the Lightest Duck Boat in the World.

President Cleveland has the lightest duck boat in the world. It is made of aluminum. It is fourteen feet long and weighs exactly thirty pounds.

This boat was presented to the President by W. H. Mullins, of Salem, O., who is the first boat manufacturer to use aluminum for this purpose. One was exhibited at the recent sportsman's exposition, and it set people who are fond of duck shooting to thinking.

A boat that will carry two persons and may be lifted easily with one hand is a useful contrivance, particularly in such waters as the Adirondack lakes, where frequent portages are necessary. The softest stroke of the paddle will set it in motion. Its draught is so small that it can run among the thick reeds where the ducks love to hide in the daytime. Painted green, it can hardly be distinguished from the rushes.

The President will doubtless take much comfort in his new and remarkable craft. Air-tanks at bow and stern make it unsinkable, so that it is as safe as a wooden duck-boat.

man. Yet his words "life is something so mysterious that it should not be lightly destroyed" characterize him as a "naturalist" above all, and he becomes America's first great sportsman in that tradition after Henry William Herbert.

Kellert's labels are useful in describing trends in waterfowling, if not distinct hunting personalities. The conservation movement was initially based on an alliance between "naturalist" and "dominionist" sportsmen against the "utilitarian" market hunter. In more recent times, according to Kellert's definitions, a struggle for the ordinary hunter's soul is underway between "naturalist" and "dominionist" tendencies in the sporting fraternity. This contest is not merely a moral or philosophical abstraction, for its outcome will affect the future of hunting in North America.

Curiously, the "naturalist," with his sometimes misguided support of unregulated subsistence hunting, has formed alliances with his erstwhile enemy, the "utilitarian." And in some respects the "meat hunter" and the "romantic-esthete" (to use novelist Vance Bourjaily's descriptive phrase for the waterfowler) have more in common than either have with the "dominionist." After all, both are motivated by either a desire or concern for waterfowl resources. The "dominionist," on the other hand, is primarily motivated by the spirit of competition or camaraderie, and he may find as much recreation on a skeet range as in a duck blind.

The "naturalist" hunts ducks because he is fascinated by the mysteries of their existence. The more he hunts, the more he finds himself committed to the perpetuation of waterfowl and their unique and threatened environment. Grinnell, Roosevelt, and many others who made early conservation history were naturalist-hunters, and because they were naturalists first, and hunters second, they naturally (pun intended) became involved with wildlife conservation.

Thus, conservation grows out of a knowledge of nature, and not the other way around as many young "earth watchers" imagine. No man automatically becomes a conservationist just because he makes tax-deductible donations to wildlife-oriented charities. If he isn't obsessed by wildlife, if he doesn't read and talk about wildlife during many of his waking hours, and if he doesn't occasionally see wildlife in his dreams, he may be a hunter, but he is not a conservationist.

A prime example of a conservationist's obsessiveness is found in Teddy Roosevelt's demand that his cabinet officials pay attention to the birdlife

Many of the rituals of waterfowling depend on equipment: decoys, duck calls, or firearms. Here a pair of "serene duck hunters" from Grover Cleveland's *Fishing and Shooting Sketches* (1906) inspect the barrels of their guns while their amused or bemused guide (perhaps both) looks on. *(Reproduction courtesy Elman Pictorial Collection)*

they saw on their way to work so that in cultivating an interest in nature, they would refine their minds for the more mundane chores associated with running a nation. The ethic of conservation is summed up by George Bird Grinnell when he described the activities of the "dominionist" who pops at everything which flies by his blind: "It is all wrong."

In 1872, Maryland became the first state to provide "rest days" for waterfowl. This law was created by sportsmen to provide some relief for canvasbacks and redheads during the nearly six months of the year the birds wintered on or near the Chesapeake. After the turn of the century, although rest-day regulations remained in effect on the Susquehanna Flats, across the rest of the state, this protection was reduced to Sundays only,[4] which pleased clergymen and their sportsmen-parishioners who could pick

[4] Some Maryland clubs and private preserves still maintain rest days. For example, Remington Farms near Chestertown disallows goose and duck shooting on Wednesdays and Thursdays as well as the state-mandated rest day of Sunday.

Probably no one individual had more impact in rallying public opinion against "Game Hogs, Spring Violators, and Game Bootleggers" than Jay N. "Ding" Darling whose cartoons were syndicated in newspapers all across the nation. *(Reproduction courtesy J. N. Ding Darling Foundation, Inc.)*

any other day of the week to hunt, and even market gunners were little affected because as God-fearing men, most did not hunt on Sundays anyway.

The prohibition against Sunday hunting continues to the present in eight states of the Atlantic Flyway. Georgia's prohibition is on a county basis, encouraging some waterfowlers to jump around the state on weekends, depending on where ringbills, wood ducks, and legal shooting coincide. This restriction surprises westerners who cannot understand why many easterners are allowed to trap and fish on Sunday, but not allowed to hunt. Most working men have only their Saturdays and Sundays off to recreate. Therefore, half of a duck hunter's opportunities are eliminated in some eastern states. Although many biologists have expressed their contempt for such arbitrary wildlife management by blue law, the Atlantic Flyway Council voted on the issue a few years ago and decided to leave the matter in the states' hands. Thus, a law with honorable intentions has introduced a sizable chunk of bias against hunters in states with a Sunday hunting prohibition. Since the federal government regards Sunday hunting as legal everywhere, it offers the different states waterfowling options without regard to Sunday exceptions. Automatically, hunters in New York and Florida have a full week more of duck shooting than hunters in Massachusetts and Virginia.

In 1875, sportsmen won their first great victory in their war on "utilitarianism" when the commercial hunting of ducks and geese was outlawed in Arkansas. Still, this law, like many other hunting prohibitions, worked better on paper than in reality. The principal factor that kept market hunting from getting out of hand in Arkansas, which was and is at the heart of North America's mallard wintering range, was poor refrigeration and slow transportation for the slaughtered birds to such then-limited markets as Memphis and New Orleans. The big markets, big money, and hence big gunning occurred along the Atlantic seaboard, where generally cooler weather and faster shipping meant that more birds got to the display stalls in better condition. Those that didn't were sold at half price to the hungry masses of immigrants that formed sizeable populations in Baltimore, Philadelphia, New York, and Boston.

In 1892, President Benjamin Harrison created by executive order what was essentially the first national wildlife refuge. Called the "Afognak Forest and Fish-Culture Reserve" and located north of Alaska's Kodiak Island, this refuge was for migratory fishes (various Pacific salmon species) as well as migratory waterfowl, big-game animals, and forest protection. The Afognak preserve was the inspiration of three people: sportsman and fish culturist, Livingston Stone; secretary of the interior, John W. Noble; and sportsman-naturalist, George Bird Grinnell.

The concept was refined and renewed more than a decade later when Grinnell urged President Theodore Roosevelt to declare Pelican Island, Florida, to be another national wildlife refuge. Since chronologists generally look on four-year presidential terms as the milestones of American history, and since Teddy Roosevelt's service as president was packed with events affecting the rise of conservation, he is generally given credit for creating the first national wildlife refuge. However, Grinnell deserves as much credit for the concept as Roosevelt, and Roosevelt would have been the first to acknowledge his—and the nation's—debt to Grinnell.

By the turn of the century, many states had adopted a licensing program for resident and nonresident hunters, and the Supreme Court had ruled, contrary to English custom and law, that game is the property of the various counties, states, and territories, and not of the individual landowners on whose property the game is found. Serving as a spur to these frail attempts at wildlife management by judicial edict was the extinction of the Labrador duck and the dramatic decline of the wood duck.[5] Apparently, the Labrador duck was never abundant, and in the last decade of its existence, its "market value" was almost exclusively for scientific collections. Grinnell writes that "in the years 1871, '72, and '73, specimens were occasionally exposed for sale in the New York markets, but even at that time the bird had become so rare that ornithologists were on the watch for it, and as soon as a specimen was exposed for sale, it was bought up."

Unlike its near relative, the harlequin duck, which is uncommon along the shores of the northwestern Atlantic, the Labrador duck did not have a Pacific population of its kind to ensure survival for the species once some unknown pressure—perhaps, egging and down collecting on its nesting grounds, shooting for food and scientific collections, alteration of its food

---

[5] In 1901, the same year Grinnell published *American Duck Shooting*, all the New England states (except Rhode Island), New York, New Jersey, and West Virginia made it illegal to hunt or harass wood ducks. Many conservationists thought the ban was too late. However, today over three hundred thousand wood ducks are killed annually in the Atlantic Flyway, and the woodie is the most numerous waterfowl species after the mallard breeding in the eastern United States.

In the drive to end market and plume hunting, ornithologists often winked at such saccharine displays as A. Pope, Jr.'s version of a "widowed" green-winged teal leaving her stricken mate. Unfortunately, gross sentimentality has not faded along with other Victorian attitudes, and it now forms the core of the anti-hunting movement. Recently, James Michener in *Chesapeake* described the emotional and unscientific saga of a Canada goose named Onk-or, his "wife," and his ill-starred "children." *(Reproduction courtesy Library of Congress)*

and habitat requirements, or combinations of all three—caused its downfall in the northwestern Atlantic. John C. Phillips believed "the Labrador duck had very specialized food habits and that changes in the molluscan fauna, brought about by increased population along our coast, may have proved disastrous." Phillips favored this theory because he was able to document significant changes in the numbers and kinds of shellfish found along the New England coast and because he lived through and studied the disastrous decline of Atlantic brant due to the virtual disappearance of eel grass over most of that species's wintering range.

Contributing to the near extinction of other water birds was their slaughter by plume hunters supplying the millinery trade. In 1897, Congressman John F. Lacey had introduced a bill to make the interstate shipment of wildlife products taken in violation of state laws a federal offense. Lacey's bill made the possession of wildlife and wildlife products subject to the laws of states or territories into which they were transported. Lacey's concept was intended to eliminate plume hunting and eventually all commercial hunting of song and game birds by having the federal government uphold, for example, Florida's right to protect nesting egrets and ibises from milliners in Boston or West Virginia's right to protect wood ducks from poultry dealers in Manhattan. (In more recent times, certain endangered species have received similar protection when the federal government upheld the states' right to restrict the transportation or sale of these species's hides, shells, or bone products.) Although Lacey's act failed to make it through Congress immediately upon its debut, President William McKinley signed it into law on May 25, 1900.

The beginning of the century gave promise and optimism to conservationists. However, for a ten-year-old boy from Iowa, the fight to save waterfowl was a remote crusade. In the spring, his prairie skies were still clouded with returning ducks and geese. Without knowing that the sight and sounds of waterfowl were imprinting their beauty and needs on his youthful mind, Ira Gabrielson was already taking steps toward a career that would one day see him picking up the baton of nineteenth-century conservation, refining its meaning and purpose, before in turn passing it on to still another generation of youthful conservationists.

Ira Gabrielson was of John Holman's generation, and like Holman, Gabrielson was an heir to the philosophy of George Bird Grinnell. Grinnell had seen with his own eyes vast herds of bison—their heads like giant fists and bodies like shaggy locomotives—but Gabrielson had seen for himself canvasback drakes playing crack-the-whip with flirtatious hens above the undrained Iowa prairies. Gabe had watched widgeon and teal dart and weave through the evening sky, and the smell of the rich earth had come strongly to his nostrils as he crouched in sloughs and watched ducks turn his way. In the dusk, he had heaved birds over one shoulder, rested his oversize shotgun on the other, and trudged across the newly plowed land to a farmhouse where an oil lamp on the porch gathered darkness and moths.

Gabe had two favorite waterfowling anecdotes from his youth. One involved his first duck; the other, the time his father "killed" a high-flying goose without even pulling the trigger:

Father did not like to hunt. I can recall only once after we moved to the farm [at the turn of the century] that he started to go hunting with me. We started with our guns toward the duck pass, and on the way a flock of geese flew over us at extremely high range. Father raised his old 10-gauge to aim at the birds, and just about that time one of them came tumbling down before he fired a shot. Instead of going on hunting, he picked up the goose and turned back to the house. When I asked, "Why, Dad, aren't you going hunting?" his reply was "No, son, it wouldn't be fair. If I scare them to death just by pointing a gun at them, I hate to think what I'd do if I actually shot at one." Needless to say, the bird had been wounded somewhere down the line and just happened to collapse in the air as the flock went over us.

Father did like to eat ducks, however, and whenever they were in the country, he would say, "Son, if you will go get some ducks to eat, I'll milk the cows for you." My instructions always were to take just enough birds for our needs, not, I am afraid, for conservation reasons, as much as respect for the cost of ammunition. Since milking cows was not the sport I most enjoyed, I was always glad to accommodate and gradually learned to be a pretty fair shot. I can still vividly remember, however, the first duck I actually killed long before we moved to the farm. I was hiking in the early spring along the Little Sioux River looking for the mallards that wintered in the open spots in the river when a string of pintails came by flying single-file. They were close enough for a good shot, and I fired the single barrel 20-gauge I was carrying at the lead bird of the five, and to my amazement, one of the birds back of him came down. This was too deep for me, and I took the problem to Grandpa Whitcomb [the Civil War veteran who lived next door] who was the best authority I knew on any outdoor subject. He explained to me the necessity for leading the birds, for "shooting ahead of them," he called it, and told me the further they were away, the further I had to shoot ahead in order to hit them. This was a novel idea to me, but on trying it out, I began to develop some proficiency as a hunter and became good enough so that I would get ducks nearly every time I went hunting.

While Europe was preparing and then fighting World War I, the U.S. Congress was preparing and then passing some remarkable wildlife legislation. In 1913, the year after Ira Gabrielson finished college and started the first of three years as a high school biology teacher in Marshalltown, Iowa, the Weeks-McLean bill became law, awarding responsibility for the management of migratory game birds to the U.S. Bureau of Biological Survey.

However, as soon as it was evident that Survey employees viewed themselves as scientists, and not wardens, and that there would be little time or money spent on law enforcement, the several sponsors of Weeks-McLean (including George Bird Grinnell) began working for a migratory bird treaty with Canada that would lend the weight of the White House, the State Department, and as it turned out, the Supreme Court to their efforts to establish some kind of federal authority to protect dwindling populations of waterfowl and shorebirds. Interestingly, non-game birds were more substantially protected than game birds in 1913 when the Federal Tariff Act was passed, barring the importation of wild bird plumage and, thereby, effectively eliminating the last major source of feathers for the unregenerate millinery trade.

In 1916, the U.S. Senate ratified a convention between the United States and Great Britain (on behalf of Canada) for the protection of all migratory game birds that pass between our two nations. Although the treaty is generally regarded as featuring waterfowl, it also pertains to the protection and harvest of shorebirds, cranes, band-tailed pigeons, and, as recently amended, crows and ravens. (The Mexican government pushed for international management of the Corvidae in order to strengthen its federal authority in other areas of wildlife law enforcement. The U.S. and Canada went along with the idea, hoping that at the same time, Mexico City would provide greater protection for certain troubled species that concentrate south of the border, such as the redhead duck.)

In 1918, administration of the original treaty was turned over to the Biological Survey with additional funds to hire law enforcement agents. That same year, the Federal Migratory Bird Treaty Act prohibited spring shooting and made the federal government responsible for prescribing the bag limits for all migratory birds. This latter law outraged many states' rightists and dominionist-type sportsmen, and it was soon apparent the act would have to be tested in the courts. The following spring, a federal conservation officer by the name of Ray Holland (who in 1924 would be selected editor of *Field & Stream* magazine) arrested Missouri's attorney general for shooting ducks out of season. When the U.S. Supreme Court upheld the district court's guilty verdict, waterfowl management undisputably became a federal responsibility.

Ira Gabrielson gave up teaching in 1915 to join the Bureau of Biological Survey as an "assistant in economic ornithology." For the next 20 years,

BUT Not A Darned Cent For SEED!

Ding Darling was a master of satire. Even while serving as chief of the U.S. Bureau of Biological Survey, Darling kept up his cartoon attacks on the short-sighted and totally selfish hunters who thought nothing of spending hundreds of dollars a year on such non-essentials as poker games and fancy equipment, yet who squawked about spending two dollars for a state hunting license and one of the new federal duck stamps. *(Reproduction courtesy J. N. Ding Darling Foundation, Inc.)*

Gabe served in the ranks of a growing army of trained conservation workers. By the time he became assistant chief of the Biological Survey in 1935, he was well known and highly respected as a professional wildlife biologist. He had worked his way up from rodent control duties in the Dakotas in 1918 to predator control in Oregon in 1930 to director of game management for the entire Pacific region in 1934, finally to assistant chief of the bureau's division of wildlife research under Iowa compatriot, Jay Norwood ("Ding") Darling.

Gabrielson vividly recalled his first meeting with Ding Darling:

The regional staff and division chiefs met Darling on March 19, 1934, and I thought I had gotten in wrong with him right off the bat. Obviously he was trying to generate enthusiasm and started to tell us that he was going to take all the money appropriated for all lines of work and spend it on waterfowl lands. I sat there expecting some of the division chiefs, or the assistant chief, to tell him that he couldn't do this, but none of them had the nerve. So finally I blurted out something to the effect of "Who has been filling you up?" Ding became very snappy and asked, "What do you mean by that?" "Well," I replied, "I'm all in sympathy with your program of buying waterfowl lands and would like to see more of it done. In my district there is a lot of land that should be in public ownership, but you cannot take the money that is appropriated for specific line items and use it to buy land without going to jail." We exchanged a few words, but the next morning he called me and told me I was dead-right and that he was glad someone had the courage to correct him.

Gabrielson was not a blue blood like Grinnell nor a celebrity like Darling. Gabe was a bureaucrat, in the best, literal sense of that word. However, his methods were not bureaucratic in the modern meaning of a government official who follows a narrow, rigid, or formal routine. Gabe saw what was needed for wildlife conservation, and he proceeded to get it—from the inside out. What Grinnell accomplished with luncheons and weekend outings and Darling did with cartoon propaganda and personal contacts with the press, Gabrielson achieved with government memos and a network of fellow conservation administrators.

Although the Norbeck-Andresen Migratory Bird Conservation Act of 1929 provided for further acquisition of waterfowl refuge lands, the Depression killed any real hope of funding through general revenue. Warden-turned-editor Ray Holland proposed as early as 1920 that what waterfowl needed were revenue stamps purchased by the people who most directly benefited from the resource: waterfowlers. Such tax monies would not be subject to the whims of Congress and could not be expropriated by any other federal agency. They would be used exclusively for the acquisition of wetlands by agents of the Biological Survey.

In 1934, Ding Darling finally pushed through Congress the duck-stamp concept with himself drawing the first design. However, this achievement, linked to his successful lobbying for a larger Biological Survey budget, exhausted his remaining goodwill with Franklin Delano Roosevelt, who had asked him to come to Washington in the first place. Any shock trooper in the corridors of Congress relies on a nonpolitical reputation or surprise tactics to accomplish political goals. Darling used both, but because he was contemptuous of governmental forms and procedures, once his initial attack was made, Darling lacked the temperament for a sustained siege. Perhaps, most important, Darling had created some very influential political enemies. After less than two years in Washington, he resigned and went back to Iowa, but not before making one last major contribution as a conservation administrator. Darling disliked bureaucracy, but he recognized its inevitability. He urged his replacement to be able to deal with paperwork but not be overwhelmed by it. Darling recommended Ira Gabrielson.

The Depression offered lean times; the Depression offered opportunities. Gabrielson seized the opportunities. He almost simgle-handedly put together the 180,850 acres of the Malheur National Wildlife Refuge in Oregon, and he managed to obtain 3,000 acres and $1 million to establish a wildlife research center in Laurel, Maryland, now headquarters for the continent's endangered species rehabilitation efforts and the principal repository of bird-banding information. However, back in the mid-1930s, Gabrielson almost didn't get the facility started when his Civilian Conservation Corps workers ran out of camp because of "lions!"—which turned out to be a solitary bobcat.

When President Roosevelt called for (after much prodding by conservationists) the first North American Wildlife Conference in February 1936, Gabrielson used his participation to introduce more effective federal programs to aid wildlife resources in general, and waterfowl resources in particular. Gabe pointed out that forest, soil, and water resources all had strong federal agencies looking after their interests. States welcomed assistance from the Soil Conservation and Forest Services, but balked at similar help from the Bureau of Biological Survey. Why was this so—especially when the U.S. treaty with Canada gave the states no choice but to accept federal assistance and guidance in matters affecting migratory waterfowl?

Gabrielson noted that many associated federal agencies had contempt for wildlife and stunning ignorance of wildlife's value to mankind. He used the then-recent example of a decision made by officials in the War Department to dig an open sewage canal through the middle of a migratory waterfowl refuge. The officials never bothered to notify the Bureau of Biological Survey before commencing the work and then laughed in the Agriculture Department's face when they were told to stop.

Gabrielson summarized the national needs of wildlife by calling for the following:

1) More land acquisition for the restoration and use of wildlife;

2) Closer cooperation between state and federal administrative agencies regarding wildlife education, development of the national wildlife refuge system, and mitigation of the adverse impacts on wildlife by major state or federal projects;

3) More research to enhance our understanding of wildlife needs;

4) More attention to the problems of pollution and unplanned development; and

5) Better protective regulations based on the needs of wildlife, *and only on the needs of wildlife.*

In 1937, Gabrielson worked for passage of two significant pieces of conservation legislation. The first, known as the Pittman-Robertson Federal Aid in Wildlife Restoration Act, established an excise tax on sporting arms and ammunition to be used on conservation projects throughout the United States and our territories. The funds are distributed to the states according to their hunting-license sales and/or wildlife needs, and over the past forty years, each state has been provided with significant contributions to the maintenance of wetlands and waterfowl protection.

The original act involved a 10 percent excise tax. This was later raised to 11 percent and expanded to include archery equipment with a 10 percent tax on handguns. The proceeds of the tax now exceed $55 million annually and are expected to increase to $135 million per year by 1985. Although habitat acquisition and management consume the lion's share of the revenues, about $10 million a year is spent on hunter education and law enforcement. (In 1978, two wildlife-protectionist organizations challenged the Pittman-Robertson Act in federal court, contending that the management of several dozen game species on 36 million acres of wildlife habitat was detrimental to the well-being of the many nongame species that share these environments. Although the suit was unsuccessful, it cost tens of thousands of taxpayer dollars that could have been better spent on wetlands acquisition and wildlife management.)

The second legislative event of 1937 was confirmation by the U.S. Senate of a treaty with Mexico for the protection of migratory birds and mammals. Of particular concern to both nations were the enormous numbers of waterfowl which winter in Mexico. Nearly one million pintail are found there, along with half a million lesser scaup, ring-necked ducks, and redheads. The treaty with Mexico provided the last essential link in the conservationists' goal of providing this continent's waterfowl resources with comprehensive protection from above the Arctic Circle to within 15 degrees of the equator. Only the far-ranging blue-winged teal, lesser scaup, shoveler, and California-wintering snow geese which nest on Wrangel Island in the Soviet Union, with rare individuals of other species, wander outside the jurisdiction of the Canadian Wildlife Service, the U.S. Fish and Wildlife Service, and Mexico's Sub-Secretariat for Environmental Improvement.

In 1940, Ira Gabrielson oversaw the consolidation of the Agriculture Department's Bureau of Biological Survey with the Commerce Department's Bureau of Fisheries into a new agency with far greater clout in the Congress and with the states than its administrative parents had had separately. When the U.S. Fish and Wildlife Service was born in July of that year, the only logical choice for first director was Gabe. Among his many new professional credentials, he had worked hard in his spare time to finished the graduate work he had begun at Iowa State University nearly one-quarter century earlier, and in 1936, he received his doctoral degree in ornithology from Oregon State University.

Gabe's first love was waterfowl, and although his eclectic mind and far-ranging responsibilities gave him the opportunity to see and count other bird species (at one time, he headed the list of the nation's top ten birders with over 700 species on his life list) and to learn about and gather plants (he transplanted more than 180 species of wild flowers to his 12-acre residence in Virginia), he felt strongly that since the costs of conservation were borne largely by sportsmen, the many fish and wildlife agencies at the state and federal levels had a responsibility to insure that the best interests of the sportsmen were being served. Since waterfowling was and is one of the most popular forms of hunting, every effort should be made to see that the "duck hotels" (Gabe's nickname for the majority of National Wildlife Refuges) are all they should be to guarantee the perpetuation of this invaluable resource.

Even after retiring from governmental service, Ira Gabrielson maintained momentum in conservation work by presiding over the Wildlife Management Institute for the next twenty-four years and by helping to found both the International Union for the Conservation of Nature and Natural Resources in 1948 and the World Wildlife Fund in 1961.

"He never forgot the basic lessons of life he learned on the Iowa farm where he was born," says Wildlife Management Institute president Daniel A. Poole. "He had the common touch, in the best sense of that phrase, and he never forgot the debt he owed—we all owe—to the land and its renewable resources."

If the achievements of George Bird Grinnell's career are associated with the new grounds he broke for conservation, Ira Gabrielson's contribution lies in the lessons he taught through personal example that there is no "peace in our time" when dealing with the forces of social atrophy, economic entropy, and unplanned development. When I told him the year before he died about an attempt being made in Accomack County, Virginia, to convert several hundred acres of prime black duck habitat into a cheap second-home and trailer-park development, Gabe astounded me by saying, "Oh, yes, I know about that. We fought that project back in the thirties when the developer's father attempted to pull off the same deal."

Gabe did not use the words "saved" or "victory" to describe the stalemates involved in preventing marshes from being dredged and streams from being channelized. He knew that many of conservation's triumphs amount to little more than holding actions against armies of environmental Orcs and Balrogs who want to destroy for short-term profits the nation's wetlands. Even toward the end of his life, when he saw the environmental movement gaining hundreds of new adherents daily, he was not less skeptical that we would be able to resist new generations of Dark Riders devoted to despoiling our best remaining wildlife habitat. He had seen fads of enthusiasm for the outdoors and conservation in previous decades, and he had his memories of Iowa before the turn of the century—before 95 percent of its wetlands disappeared beneath the plow.

Ira Gabrielson was not a pessimist; he was a supreme realist. While he trained his disciples well and hard for their daily warfare with mercenary armies shouting such slogans as "The Business of America is Business" and "Progress is Our Most Important Product," he warned there would frequently be casualties and that the ground won decades ago might have to be won all over again today and tomorrow.

However, Gabe believed that since Right as well as Reason were on the side of conservation, eventually we might win the war. "The world we are fighting to save," he suggested, "will bear little resemblance to the world tomorrow. Yet whatever that world may be, it will be a better place in which our grandchildren will live because we have tried to make the world of today a better place for us to live."

FOUR: WHISTLING DUCKS, SWANS, AND GEESE

"It is commonly supposed that goose shooting is very simple, and that they are an easy bird to hit. This is both true and false—true, when they come slowly over one's head, perhaps thirty yards high, facing a moderately strong wind; false, in almost every other way."

William Bruce Leffingwell, in 1888

Whistling Ducks

IT MAY seem odd to think of the two species of whistling ducks found in North America as subtropical equivalents of the swan, but that's what they are. Whistling ducks are smaller, of course, but tropically evolved life forms are generally smaller than their subarctic counterparts, which need larger sizes to maintain body heat.

Whistling ducks share many physical and behaviorial features with swans and geese, such as no difference in plumage between sexes of the same species, no difference in the calls of males and females, relatively permanent pair bonds, and no complex pair-forming behavior or rituals. In addition, there is the curious fact that neither whistling ducks nor swans—unlike other ducks and geese—use much, if any, down to line their nests (which is undoubtedly the reason Eddie Bauer features goose, rather than whistling duck, down in his clothing and sleeping bags!)

The fulvous whistling duck *(Dendrocygna bicolor)* is fulvous-hued, which means its plumage is a dull brownish-yellow. We are fortunate to have a word in English, derived from Latin, which means "dull brownish-yellow," for this interesting bird deserves a better fate than to be called "the dull brownish-yellow whistling duck."

Another common name is fulvous tree duck, which is a misnomer since this species, unlike the black-bellied whistling duck *(Dendrocygna autumnalis),* rarely nests in trees or is even found perched on branches. Of course, this fact also makes the fulvous whistling duck's scientific name incorrect. *Dendrocygna* means "tree swan," and *bicolor* means "of two colors," and we already know the bird is only one color: *fulvous.*

Whistling ducks can be distinguished from all other North American waterfowl by the fact that their long legs extend beyond their short tails. This can be noted either in the hand or when the birds fly by with their broad, rounded wings flapping more like a hurried gull's than a duck's. In addition, like the perching muscovy and wood duck, whistling ducks do not quack. Instead, they make musical whistling sounds which once heard in nature are not easily forgotten. If you live in Florida or along the Gulf Coast, you can hear their lovely calls, which are distinguished from the call of the drake wood duck by their carrying and melodious qualities. (The wood duck's call is comparatively brief and ends on a rising inflection.)

In addition to its dull brownish-yellow color, the fulvous whistling duck can be distinguished from the black-bellied whistling duck by the fact that the former has buffy yellow flank stripes and a grayish-blue bill and feet, while the black-bellied whistling duck has a white lateral stripe separating its brown back from its black belly, and red bill and pink feet. In flight, the black-bellied whistling duck also shows white upper-wing surfaces.

These details are important because both species are showing up increasingly outside these birds' formerly recognized ranges within the United States. The fulvous whistling duck regularly moves up the Atlantic coast to Delaware Bay and its persistence in such northerly latitudes throughout all four seasons of the year has raised the question of whether the species is breeding in the area. Although such northerly appearances may be made by unpaired yearlings which, like most other young ducks, wander widely during their first winter, the fulvous whistling duck is unique among birds in this genus in that it commonly breeds during its first year. In addition, fulvous whistling ducks are not known to be great migrants, and a trek of even a few hundred miles is considered an odyssey.

Fulvous whistling ducks are found in fair numbers in the water management districts south and west of Lake Okeechobee, Florida, and around the Salton Sea in California. They are common in the Louisiana and east-Texas rice belt. In contrast, the U.S. range of the black-bellied whistling duck is almost exclusively limited to southern Texas with a few nesting reports from southern Arizona. However, in Mexico, the black-bellied whistling duck is much more common than its fulvous counterpart.

There may be such things, but a bonafide (that is, a working model) whistling duck decoy must be extremely rare. Gulf Coast gunners say the birds stool so well to other decoys—in fact, when they have a mind to come in, you cannot keep them away—it is not worth the bother to carve a

The Cuban whistling duck *(D. arborea)* is found in the Bahamas, Cuba, Jamaica, Grand Cayman, Puerto Rico, and the Virgin Islands, but for some mysterious reason has never visited the continental U.S.—not even the Florida Keys. Although typical of the genus in overall appearance and behavior, it is distinguished from the fulvous and black bellied whistling ducks by its black bill. Any mainland sightings should be reported immediately to the nearest chapter of the National Audubon Society and the Office of Migratory Bird Management, U.S. Fish and Wildlife Service, Laurel, Maryland 20811. *(Photograph by Glen Smart)*

differently shaped decoy that cannot easily be modified with paint for service as facsimiles of other waterfowl species.

Once whistling ducks are over the decoys, they, like brant, are strangely fragile birds, and relatively little impact is needed to bring one down. A Texas informant insists the sound of the shot kills them, which is typical Texas information. He also says they are delicious, and since the whistling duck diet is composed almost of entirely of seeds and plants, this is certainly to be believed.

However, before any shooter pulls the trigger on a whistling duck, he better be sure such birds are legal game in his state. The Gulf Coast states regard them as fair game, but a fulvous whistling duck in Missouri or the Carolinas should be left alive. If this species is extending its range, which appears to be the case, the protection of pioneering birds *now* may mean regular seasons for this interesting swanlike duck in the years ahead.

If you see a whistling duck far inland from the Gulf Coast—and fulvous whistling ducks have turned up in Oregon, Ohio, and Maine; there is even a breeding record from Kansas—report the circumstances of your sighting to the nearest chapter of the National Audubon Society. Unless you have a photograph of the bird, you may not be believed, for it is characteristic of birders to doubt anything they have not seen themselves. However, do not get defensive or depressed about such reflexive lack of faith. Try to understand that a fulvous whistling duck in British Columbia or Quebec—provinces in which they have, in fact, been seen—are as extraordinary as Loch Ness monsters in the Chesapeake Bay. Chessies, that is.

If you inadvertently shoot a whistling duck in an area outside the bird's normal range, report the circumstances (with a photograph and/or wing) to the Office of Migratory Bird Management, U.S. Fish and Wildlife Service, Laurel, Maryland 20811, or the Canadian Wildlife Service in Ottawa. Professional ornithologists are generally more tolerant of inadvertent shots than amateur birders.

Swans

There are three swan species in North America: the mute *(Cygnus olor)*, the trumpeter *(C. cygnus)*, and the whistling *(C. columbianus)*. The mute is the semidomestic fellow most commonly seen on suburban lakes or city ponds. It is an exotic which may have been first imported from Europe in the eighteenth century. Its spread from Long Island, New York has been poorly documented because the American Ornithological Union (A.O.U.) took little interest in exotics and their spread until this past decade. (Birders have traditionally looked down their noses at introduced species such as the starling or pheasant.) The bird is now found in a wild or feral state mostly along the southern New England and upper mid-Atlantic coasts.

Mute swans appear to be largely nonmigratory once a mated pair has staked out a territory. They can be extremely aggressive during the breeding season and have been known to kill ducks and geese attempting to nest in their vicinity. C. H. Willey, who has studied the species extensively in Rhode Island, feels mute swans may offer a "substantial threat" to humans, particularly children.

Unfortunately, there are many people more taken with the beauty of mute swans than their potential social and environmental impacts. Even today, the bird continues to be introduced to many formerly unaffected parts of the country. The upper Lake Michigan area has a sizable and growing population of mute swans, and feral flocks are now developing in Illinois, Ohio, the Chesapeake Bay, and several southwestern states. Some of these areas are in or close to territories visited by migrating flocks of native swans, and belatedly the A.O.U. and the federal government have decided they have a potential nuisance on their hands. Just what will be done remains to be seen.

About the only way to tell trumpeter and whistling swans apart—unless

Whistling swans are similar to geese in their liking for soggy grainfields on rainy days. While this flock will benefit the farmer by exchanging fertilizer for waste grain, in some areas whistling swans are unpopular despoilers of winter wheat and rye. One whistling swan, which bred 40 miles from the Prudhoe Bay oil fields on the North Slope of Alaska, wintered on the Chesapeake and, for nearly a decade, she and her distinctive neck collar were spotted regularly on her annual cross-continent odyssey. *(Photograph by George Reiger)*

the two species are swimming together and you can compare how much larger the male trumpeter is, with an average weight of 28 pounds versus 16 pounds for the male whistling swan—is by hearing their calls. The trumpeter makes a stentorian, hornlike pronouncement, while the whistling swan has a soft, but high-pitched, bark. A flock of whistling swans sounds like a distant pack of dogs; a flock of trumpeters sounds like the assault on Jericho.

Beginning with Utah in 1962, several western states now offer limited hunting seasons for whistling swans. Curiously, every year there are applicants who seek swan permits, in addition to their regular resident hunting license, with the intention of *not* hunting swans should they receive a number in the lottery drawing. These hunters feel it is morally reprehensible to kill swans, but not other kinds of waterfowl. Some say the whistling swan is too lordly a target, and, perhaps, they associate this species with the tame mute swans seen in parks. Not having hunted the wild and more wary whistling swan—and not planning to—these hunters cannot conceive of it as being a game bird.

On the other hand, such a worldly-wise waterfowler as Van Campen Heilner was "sickened" by his experience of shooting a whooper swan along the German shores of the Baltic. He contrasted the enormous thrill of watching the swan fall and crash like a geyser into the sea with the pathetic sight of its blood-stained body "dying in circles." Heilner reflected, "I always wanted to shoot a swan and now I think I shall never want to shoot another."

Guilt may play a role in a handful of hunters' decisions not to shoot swans. A young Maryland gunner told me about his single (illegal) swan-shooting experience in these words: "There ain't nothing bigger, whiter, and deader in the world than a swan lying neck-out in the decoys. They ain't fit to eat, and when you try to stomp 'im in the marsh, no muskrat house is big enough to hide the thing. Once is enough. You never want to shoot two of 'em."

Custom has it that only cygnets (originally a French word having as much to do with the juvenile's tenderness as its youth) are worth eating. Since young birds are more trusting than their parents, and because young swans can often be distinguished, even on the wing, by their grayish (as contrasted with the adult white) plumage, a swan hunter may decide in advance of his shot whether he wants a juvenile for flavor or an adult for looks.

Given a choice, most waterfowlers would opt for flavor. After all, where do you put a mounted swan? One would look big hanging even from the ceiling of the Grand Ballroom of the Waldorf-Astoria. History supports this choice, for in Europe centuries before the turkey was discovered, along with the New World, cygnets, not adult swans, were kept and fattened for holiday feasts following the summer roundups when the moulting, flightless birds could be caught. The older birds were code marked on their bills and released with the expectation they would produce more cygnets the next spring.

What constitutes a game bird? Or, more specifically, what is a trophy bird in waterfowling?

Unlike the hunting of mammals in which the number of tines or length of an animal's rack or hide are significant measures of its worth, edibility is a more important criterion than size in calculating the value of a duck, goose, or swan. Size, in combination with flavor, often makes for the best trophy. That is why the corn-fed Canada goose rates so high, and why in the days when redhead ducks and canvasbacks fed primarily on *Vallisneria,* the canvasback was ranked above the equally delicious redhead, primarily because the canvasback is a larger bird.

On the other hand, now that the heyday of the market gunner is behind us, certain sporting criteria can and do apply to waterfowling. Scarcity, wariness, and the degree of difficulty experienced by the hunter in obtaining a shot are essential ingredients of the trophy standard. Thus, a black duck's wariness and especially its rarity in the west make it valued far more highly than the lesser or greater scaup, which is everywhere abundant and trusting. Yet, for all that, if the bird in hand has brought with it a sense of achievement, a feeling that the game has been fairly played and won, a bluebill, a coot, even a naive cygnet, may qualify for trophy status.

Hunter-philosopher José Ortega y Gasset suggests that every shot is imbued with a special risk and opportunity. For only an instant, the bird is at the proper range, and if the prey is missed, or if the shot is not taken, another opportunity may not come that day, that season, or ever again. The rarer or more wary the game, the more important the shot becomes as the essential link in the sport's fulfillment. This is why killing is necessary and the culminating moment of the hunting process.

Devoted hunters feel only the slightest affinity for competition target shooters. This is because hunters are involved with the sometimes profound and always solemn business of execution. This is also because hunters know that talent, effort, and opportunity are all essential to a trophy experience. Target shooters employ only talent and effort (which means practice), since they have opportunity without end to earn silver cups and statuettes.

Two of our rarer goose species: Above is the Hawaiian nene that a captive breeding program pioneered by Sir Peter Scott has brought back from the brink of extinction. *(Photograph by Rex Gary Schmidt);* below is Alaska's emperor goose which Van Campen Heilner described as the greatest trophy in all waterfowling. *(Photograph by Sigurd T. Olson)*

Geese

With some waterfowl, the hunter combines shooting skill (perhaps, acquired on the target range) with sharp reflexes, fortunate positioning and good timing to gamble a rarely repeated opportunity on a bird he sees within range on relatively few occasions in his lifetime. The larger, more wary, or more scarce such birds are, the higher the place they occupy in the hierarchy of game. That is why most any species of goose becomes water-fowling's highest achievement.[1]

To simplify our understanding of North American geese, divide all species into four basic color patterns: the Canada goose with its several greater and lesser forms; the snow goose with a blue phase, and the greater and a tiny Ross subspecies; the white-fronted goose with its larger tule subspecies; and the brant divided into Atlantic and Pacific races. Two rare visitors are the emperor goose, which breeds in Alaska and has strayed as far south as California and even Hawaii, and the barnacle goose, which breeds in Greenland and Spitsbergen, but wanders occasionally to New England instead of wintering in northern Europe. (If either of these birds are seen or shot in any of the contiguous 48 states, the fact should be reported to the Office of Migratory Bird Management in Laurel, Maryland 20811.)

THE CANADA GOOSE AND HIS COUSIN

The most commonly hunted goose in North America is the Canada and his seven closely related cousins. When Vaughn Monroe sang of his heart going where the wild goose goes, everyone knew that *Branta canadensis* was the goose he was singing about. The primary reason the Canada is found over most of the continent can be summed up by the word "adaptability." Geese generally mate for life, and the gander shares nesting and fledging responsibilities with the goose. If one of the pair dies, the survivor soon takes another mate. It is nonsense to believe the survivor remains celibate, mourning his or her loss until that bird is either shot or dies of old age. The phenomenal growth of most Canada goose populations over the past half century suggests, if not proves, that the disruption of pair bonds through regulated hunting does not disrupt the species' ability to perpetuate itself. Indeed, if Konrad Lorenz's studies of tame greylag geese can be applied to their wild kin, individual celibacy within flocks of geese is more often a matter of aberrant sexual behavior than the hunter's gun.

Although the Canada goose generally nests on the ground near water, the bird may also nest on cliff ledges or in trees, using abandoned hawk or osprey nests as the foundation for its own reproductive efforts. The Canada goose, like the wood duck, has responded well to human efforts to supple-

---

[1] Remoteness and shyness were the two criteria Van Campen Heilner stressed when he crowned the emperor goose the greatest prize in all waterfowling.

One reason Canada geese have become so abundant is their willingness to nest just about anywhere. Although muskrat and beaver houses have always been popular nesting platforms, biologists have found that putting similarly thatched platforms up a tree or on poles prevents most predators from reaching the eggs and goslings. This "tree goose" was photographed on the Charles M. Russell National Wildlife Range near Lewistown, Montana. *(Photograph by Frank Martin)*

ment nesting options by artificial means. A washtub on a pole, a mound of straw on an anchored raft, or an island of spoil in a golf course pond—all are used by wild pairs of Canada geese which suspend their winter wariness of man for the actual inadvertent protection such locations afford the birds.

The Canada goose learned, even before the mallard, the benefits of man's more efficient, which sometimes means more wasteful, agricultural practices. Huge combines rumble across the nation's farm fields each autumn harvesting in a day what it took dozens of hands to harvest in a week a generation ago. Several corn rows are picked simultaneously, the ears shucked and stripped, and the stalks shredded and spewed back onto the fields for mulch in one clattering, five-miles-an-hour operation. Such marvelous machinery is not perfect, however, and whole ears and many spare kernels are missed by the sheller and disgorged onto the ground. In addition, further waste occurs when the shelled corn is transferred from the combines to 80,000-pound capacity trucks at the edge of fields. In the evening, when the farmers return home, their deserted fields are left to doves and crows, and, in October, to the great migrant flocks of waterfowl.

In recent years, considerable debate—some would call it acrimony—has fired up over the issue of "short stopping." This phrase describes the modern tendency of migratory waterfowl, particularly Canada geese in all four flyways, to winter far north of more ancient wintering grounds. Critics charge that the National Wildlife Refuge System and the previous government policy of growing crops on refuges to feed the birds (so they would not fan out over the countryside and ravage farm crops) are the principal reasons geese do not move as far south as they once did.

Critics correctly point out that concentrating geese at places like Wisconsin's Horicon March or Delaware's Bombay Hook creates situations conducive to avian cholera and other diseases spread by overcrowding. Congressional opponents of short stopping have, therefore, twisted arms within the Department of the Interior to forbid the planting of crops on certain refuge lands and, more recently, to initiate a campaign costing hundreds of thousands of dollars to disperse and discourage geese from building up sizeable populations on National Wildlife Refuges.

Especially stiff political pressure has been brought to bear on the management of Horicon Marsh in southern Wisconsin, where a majority of the geese of the Mississippi Valley population linger throughout the fall. A first attempt to disperse the birds backfired when a drawdown of the marsh's water not only failed to move the geese, but caused an outbreak of botulism. More moderate and long-term steps are now in progress, including the conversion of refuge farm fields to prairie, marsh meadows, and woodlands.

"Our goal is to create new habitat in the marsh for other forms of wildlife," says Jack Toll, Horicon Marsh refuge manager. "The overemphasis on goose protection and accommodation has upset the marsh habitat for songbirds, ducks, and mammals."

A new management plan calls for greatly increased goose hunting activity in fields surrounding the refuge. Large concentrations of geese are to be hazed with air boats and aircraft, and sections of the refuge are to be made uninviting to geese by the random firing of propane-powered noisemakers. The Fish and Wildlife Service hopes to reduce the refuge's Canada goose population to one-tenth its former peak, causing displaced birds to spread south through other states of the Mississippi Flyway.

To date, all these efforts have resulted in only partial success. While the number of Canada geese in the Horicon refuge is down to less than 100,000 birds, the population seems to be stabilizing near that level. Furthermore, the more than 200,000 other geese that used to tarry within the refuge are in no hurry to leave southern Wisconsin.

Francis H. Kortright noted back in 1942 that Canada geese will winter as far north as Nova Scotia and British Columbia along the coasts and "inland as far north as they can find suitable food and large bodies of open water." Open water today is provided by warm-water discharges from power plant cooling systems and the locks and turbines of dams on the tamed Mississippi River. In addition, the quantity of grain formerly provided on Horicon refuge is an infinitesimal fraction of the quantity available on farm fields throughout the upper Midwest. Unless we blow up our dams and power plants and alter the agricultural practices of an entire nation, it is naive and a waste of federal funds to attempt to move Canada geese further south of where moderate winters permit them to stay.

A more dramatic example of short stopping occurs in the Atlantic Flyway, where the former center of goose hunting activity was Mattamuskeet Lake, North Carolina, less than 250 miles—as the goose flies—from the currently favored axis running from Easton to Chestertown, Maryland, and across to Smyrna, Delaware. Since a healthy Canada is capable of flying 250 miles in less than eight hours, even without a tail wind, you would suppose a couple hundred thousand of the more than one million geese found on the Delmarva peninsula every fall would make it down to North Carolina. However, unless the days turn frigid and the creeks and rivers of the Eastern Shore lock up in ice, and waste grain can't be chipped fom the ground with a bayonet, Mattamuskeet does not see many Canada geese.

Of the hundreds of people who have worked over the past half century to create and maintain the Delmarva peninsula Canada goose phenomenon, one of the most interesting was an aviator, engineer, and sportsman who spent a good part of his fortune and the last years of his life proving the thesis that from little flocks of Canadas mighty squadrons will grow. The man died before seeing the fruition of his dream, but his name is remembered in the Glenn L. Martin National Wildlife Refuge on Smith Island in the Chesapeake Bay.

Martin was born in Macksburg, Iowa in 1886 and, like Ira Gabrielson, early experiences on the once well-watered prairies of the Midwest were

A significant casualty of the short-stopping phenomenon was the Mattamuskeet area in North Carolina, once the premier goose hunting grounds in the Atlantic Flyway. *Above:* a quarter-century ago, a hunter swings on some distant birds. *(Photograph by W. F. Kubichek)* Also 25 years ago, Wildlife illustrator Bob Hines holds his daily limit. Today the limit is four birds—in Delaware and parts of Virginia. *(Photograph by Rex Gary Schmidt)*

remembered all his life, generating a special concern for waterfowl conservation. Martin started building gliders in 1907—perhaps inspired to take up aviation by his love of ducks and geese—and from 1909 to 1916, he held all the speed, altitude, and endurance records known to flying. He began his own aircraft construction company in 1911, founded a college of engineering and aeronautical sciences at the University of Maryland in 1945, and received numerous decorations and honorary doctoral degrees. Yet Martin boasted of his early association with The Izaak Walton League of America as though it were his proudest achievement, and he often told audiences that the sight of Canada geese whiffling down onto an autumn field was a far more breathtaking spectacle than an aircraft squadron of even his own design doing barrel rolls close overhead.

In 1940, he bought an eighteenth-century farmhouse on the Eastern Shore of Maryland near Chestertown and improved its vicinity with ponds and a flock of Canada geese. During the next two decades, new generations of Canadas appeared at Broadnox and left each spring for the Canadian subarctic where they reproduced and led their offspring back to Martin's farm in the fall.

When Glenn L. Martin died, his property was purchased and enlarged by the E. I. du Pont de Nemours & Company and renamed Remington Farms. Today this working farm (and profitable as such) sprawls over 3,150 acres, including 26 freshwater ponds varying in size from one to fifty acres. The heart of the wildlife management design for the area is two inviolate sanctuaries with the most important one located near the visitor entrance and comprising a 17-acre pond surrounded by 85 acres of field and shrubs onto which only deer and other wildlife may stray.

Every summer when the geese are in Canada, this pond is drained and plowed to destroy the spore-forming bacterium that causes botulism. In the fall, the pond is reflooded just before the geese return, and a constant water level is maintained by periodic pumping throughout the winter. The entire farm may host 25,000 Canada geese, but this single 100-acre sanctuary is frequently packed with over 10,000 geese.

Remington Farms employs two full-time professional wildlife biologists who run a complex wildlife-management program including the carefully controlled hunting of geese four days a week. The program's emphasis is on the ambience and value of hunting, not the killing. Thus, the quality of the experience is light years away from the Slam-Bam-Thank-You-Ma'am goose-shooting operations found increasingly elsewhere.

No two game species have profited more from modern farming practices than the Canada goose and the whitetail deer. Indeed, the habits of Canada geese have been so altered by the present availability of spilled grains and winter cover crops, the species has become as much of an upland game bird as waterfowl! Whereas Canadas were an uncommon and welcome sight over much of their range, today they are considered a pest by many farmers—but not those at Remington Farms near Chestertown, Md., where this picture was made. *(Photograph by Clark G. Webster)*

I recall a situation in South Dakota where geese were shot from behind palisades cut in the bluffs overlooking the Missouri River. As soon as the members of a fire team collected their one goose apiece—and who knew which was whose goose under such circumstances?—they were hurried out of the trenches and replaced by another squad of shooters. As we bumped along the road heading back to the parking area, a companion looked down at the pile of birds on the floor of the truck and remarked, "This was like being in a Honolulu whorehouse during World War II."

The Canada goose deserves better than this. So do the people who hunt this lordly bird. Had ornithologist Arthur Cleveland Bent ever shot geese from behind a Missouri River palisade, he would not have felt as he wrote in 1925 that the Canada "is so wary, so sagacious, and so difficult to outwit that its pursuit has always fascinated the keen sportsman and taxed his skill and his ingenuity more than any other game bird."

Still, like all birds, the Canada goose is vulnerable on the point that it rarely thinks beyond present need. This is best illustrated by the sanctuary provided at Remington Farms or at any national wildlife refuge which has a visiting population of geese. Comparatively few birds are shot going into such an area. This is because the birds come in high and usually well out of reasonable range, whiffling, barrel-rolling, and spilling wind from their wings to descend on an angle that has them drop a yard for every two yards of forward motion. This is also because hunters in the vicinity recognize that an ingoing bird—hit, but not killed—has the momentum of its descent and the sight of its objective to enhance its will to make a supreme effort to reach the sanctuary. Hence, only first-timers and fools will waste shot and reveal their positions by firing at high-flying birds moving into a sanctuary.

The geese may know there are hunters below them, but so long as the birds stay high, they are safe, and once they are within the sanctuary, the birds know they are safer still. The geese are assured of water and disturbance-free rest. After a few hours, however, their empty gizzards are no longer satisfied to grind gravel without food, and the birds must move out to forage over neighboring fields. Geese are heavy, and they are unable to control the atmospheric conditions that may make them labor against a stiff wind or fly low in heavy overcast or fog. The same birds that sailed in yesterday 300 yards high are now straining on their way out—one-tenth the previous day's altitude. If geese could think ahead, they might never visit Remington Farms or a national wildlife refuge.

Although Canada geese are shot over water, such gunning is increasingly a matter of chance. Due to the mechanical corn harvester, decoy hunting for geese has become mostly a matter of pits and rush panels in corn fields, often several miles from the nearest river or sanctuary pond. Some field decoys are so huge, they can be used as blinds with the hunter either digging a shallow pit for his legs beneath the hollow shells or lying within or alongside the decoys. When geese fly within range, the decoy is either thrown off entirely, or one side drops down to reveal the shooter inside.

Floating goose decoys are still manufactured, but they are usually bought by duck hunters who put out half a dozen as much to attract the attention of passing ducks as to attract a single goose. A New Jersey hunter I know always sets out a pair of Canada geese decoys regardless of the type of waterfowling he is doing. He says the fact that all other geese and ducks

Some old-timers say that when you see the white chin-straps on a Canada goose, that's the time to shoot. However, on a clear day, you can see the birds' chin-straps nearly a quarter mile away. Far better that you wait until you hear the creak of their wings or see their individual flight feathers to take your shot than feel remorse for crippling a bird which sails out of sight to a lingering death. *(Photograph by Clark G. Webster)*

know Canadas are smarter than they are, causes them to trust his rig. Some hunters use gull or even heron decoys as "confidence birds," but my friend reasons he would just as soon attract a passing flight of geese than a gull or a heron! Furthermore, nearly every season he manages to take at least one stray goose. He claims to have shot one while scoter hunting half a mile off an Atlantic beach. You can find Canada geese just about anywhere!

SNOW AND WHITE-FRONTED GEESE

The snow represents our second most commonly seen color variety of North American goose. And with it we encounter a conundrum of the avian world. Why is it that several completely unrelated species of large birds have all-white bodies and wings with only black wing tips? What evolutionary advantage is there in adult snow geese, whooping cranes, white pelicans, gannets, white ibises, and (although there is more black on the wings and head than in the other species named) wood ibises sharing the same color pattern?

One answer has it that white is characteristic of birds which evolved along the fringes of the periodic ice sheets. However, how does this involve ibises, which apparently never associated with ice sheets? Another concept says that since all the birds which possess this pattern have more or less permanent pair bonds, and since complex plumage patterns are not important to such species, white with black wing tips is about as "uncomplex" a pattern as nature could evolve. Yet would not an all-white plumage, as in swans, or an all-black plumage, as in vultures, be simpler still? The mystery remains.

The snow goose also raises questions about how to classify birds with broad breeding ranges, which inevitably develop several races and subspecies. While there is intense rivalry between taxonomists who "split" and those who "lump" species of wildlife, the "lumpers" seemed to have gained the day over the past 25 years. The turn-of-the-century trend to find new subspecies under every bush has reversed itself to the point that the rare trumpeter swan is considered to be only a race of the Eurasian whooper swan, and the whistling swan has been downgraded in status as the American version of the Bewick swan.

Whereas F. H. Kortright once described in his seminal *Ducks, Geese & Swans of North America* a common Canada goose *(Branta canadensis canadensis)*, a western Canada goose *(B. c. occidentalis)*, a lesser Canada goose *(B. c. leuccopareia)*, a Richardson's goose *(B. c. hutchinsi)*, a cackling goose *(B. c. minima)*, and speculated about the existence of a giant Canada goose *(B. c. maxima)*—which we now know exists—Paul A. Johnsgard in the recently published *Waterfowl of North America* describes only one Canada goose *(Branta canadensis)*, period. Interestingly, the only Canada goose subspecies still held as such is the one ranked as "endangered" by the U.S. Department of the Interior. Furthermore, the Aleutian Canada goose, *(B. c. leucopareia)*, has borrowed its scientific name from Kortright's lesser Canada goose.

A similar lumping process has overwhelmed the snow goose and its allies. Gone are Kortright's lesser snow goose *(Chen hyperborea hyperborea)*, greater snow goose *(C. h. atlantica)*, and blue goose *(C. caerulescens)*. Their place has been taken by a single species: *Anser caerulescens*. However, so as not to simplify things too much, the diminutive Ross goose *(Anser rossii,* although it once bore *Chen* as its generic name) is still maintained as a separate species, even though field identification consists largely of seeing this winter visitor to central California in the company of other geese or ducks so the observer can note how small the Ross goose is. This bird is also maintained as an "endangered species" even though it frequently interbreeds with the snow goose, compounding our taxonomic problems. Since such hybrids are fertile, "snow geese" now range from the size of a mallard duck (a pure-blood Ross) to the 10½-pound birds (greater snow geese) found along the Atlantic coast.

Splitters may be down, but they are not out. Although Johnsgard does away with Kortright's old distinctions between the white-fronted goose *(Anser albifrons albifrons)* and the larger tule goose *(Anser albifrons gambelli)*

The lesser snow goose is an uncommon prize in Minnesota at the headwaters of the Mississippi River. By contrast, further west and south, the species is almost taken for granted, and some hunters let snow geese pass by while waiting for white-fronts and Canadas. *(Photograph by George Reiger)*

by merging the birds and dropping the subspecific names, an article in *American Birds* (March, 1978) by Bruce Krogman advises that the tule goose is alive and well and wintering in the Central Valley of California.

In a field study funded by a local sportsman's club and conducted largely at the Sacramento National Wildlife Refuge, Krogman checked hunters' bags and determined that unique physical characteristics which set apart the tule subspecies were to be found in a significant sample of immature and mature male and female "white-fronted geese" brought to the checking station. The irony of this is that hunters are usually the first people to perceive such subspecific differences, and observant waterfowlers have never wavered in their faith that while taxonomists may *think* that tule geese were simply larger, older white-fronted geese, or that lesser snow geese and greater snow geese are the same bird, hunters *knew* there were major differences between such birds. Hunters do not always measure such distinctions by relative size, color of eye-rings, number of tail feathers, and other related minutiae which, as far as many sportsmen are concerned, confuse the forest with the trees. Instead, hunters base their perceived distinctions on behavioral differences in the related waterfowl that makes it necessary, for example, to hunt lesser and greater snow geese, or white-fronted and tule geese, by very different methods.

California hunters have known for more than seventy-five years that tule, or "timber geese," as they are sometimes called, prefer the more secluded areas of a marsh where ponds and sloughs are surrounded by tules and willow trees. In order to reach such birds, you had to make special efforts to get where they "used." Thus, the tule goose, even before it became a scientifically acknowledged subspecies in 1917, was a superior trophy for California waterfowlers due to the bird's larger size, greater difficulty in reaching its preferred habitat, and its increased shyness (call it, wariness) compared to the white-fronted goose.

The lesser versus greater snow goose distinctions are even older. Long before biologists discovered that greater snow geese nest in areas generally east and north of the lesser snow goose's preferred reproductive grounds, hunters had surmised as much from the fact that the greater snow goose is an Atlantic Flyway bird while the lesser snow goose is found inland and to the west. Not only was the greater snow goose considerably larger than his lesser relatives, this subspecies is peculiarly at home on coastal salt marshes and rarely forages in fields, unlike his lesser cousin. The greater snow goose prefers cordgrass roots to domestic grains, and once it was restored to the game lists several years ago, hunters found this snow goose subspecies far less susceptible to such basic tricks as bleach-bottle and diaper decoys than the lesser snow goose. Taxonomists can argue all they like about the relationship between lesser and greater snow geese: for one hundred fifty years—or as long as Eastern seaboard waterfowlers have been aware there was a smaller snow goose in the West—sportsmen have known the two birds had to be hunted differently and that the greater snow goose was the greater trophy.

As for the blue goose/snow goose taxonomic controversy, the best common sense on this nondebate was spoken by a midwestern taxidermist when he complained he had never seen a blue goose colored precisely the way this "species" was illustrated in bird identification books. Since blue geese and lesser snow geese fly in the same flocks, feed in the same fields, and regularly breed with one another, what makes them different? he asked.

"Nothing," taxonomists finally replied just a few years ago. This pronouncement caused a mild hue and cry from some birders who felt they had been cheated of another species for their life lists, but waterfowlers showed very little reaction. They knew they used the same techniques for hunting lesser snows and blue geese. The only distinction they had ever made was that in areas where blue geese are more prevalent, snows are the greater trophy, and in areas where the white birds are more common, blues are the special prize. However, hunters are not about to stop calling the two varieties snow geese and blue geese. After all, they were doing that long before the concept of taxonomy was devised,[2] and as history shows, it is much easier to change a scientific name than a popular one.

On the other hand, for some Pacific Flyway waterfowlers, the continued listing of the Ross goose as a separate species when the equally diminutive cackling goose is no longer distinguished as even a subspecies of the Canada goose, offers less of a taxonomic question than a political one. They suggest the Ross goose is exempted by the "lumpers" because it is commonly regarded as an endangered species, while the cackling goose is not. Cynics assert that should the cackling goose, the greater snow goose, or any other variety now classified as a race of a dominant species, ever again decline to the point where it should no longer be hunted, taxonomists will provide the rationale for protection by "rediscovering significant genetic differences" between such birds and the larger species in which they are currently submerged.

BRANT

The last category of commonly hunted North American goose is the brant. The Atlantic Flyway subspecies, *Branta bernicla hrota,* and the Pacific form, *B. b. nigricans,* are today simply cited as *Branta bernicla.*

The brant occupies a special place in my memory, for it was the first goose I ever shot. Not far into my teens, my older brother and I had rigged a plywood boat as a combination decoy barge and floating blind for shoot-

---

[2] Thomas Henry Huxley (1825–1895) was possibly the first biologist to stress the difference between "the facts which constitute the subject matter of classification" and "the modes of generalizing them which are expressed in taxonomic systems." He did so in his *Manual of the Comparative Anatomy of Invertebrated Animals,* published in 1877, many decades after American hunters had started calling certain familiar birds "snow geese" and "blue geese."

The Pacific brant is distinguished from its Atlantic cousin by the generally darker body and the greater amount of white seen in the collar of the Pacific brant. This race winters as far north as southeastern Alaska and British Columbia, but more than 60 percent of the population flies to Scammon Lagoon and San Ignacio Bay in Baja California where some years up to 100,000 birds may be found feeding in the shallows near schools of breeding gray whales. *(Photograph courtesy U.S. Fish and Wildlife Service)*

ing in the Great South Bay, Long Island. Greater scaup were our target species, but among the more than one hundred decoys we had made, bought, found, or had been given were a dozen red cedar brant facsimiles that must have weighed 15 pounds apiece. The decoys had originally been made in the 1910s for a hunting club at Bellport, Long Island, and they should have been stashed away in the attic to gather dust against the day we could have traded them for their weight in gold. However, from our first day in the marsh, we used them religiously, as much for their romantic associations as for the practical fact they were all we had in the way of brant decoys.

The many hours of actual preparation for opening day were well padded by a far greater number of hours of planning and daydreaming about what it would be like. We lived more than an hour's drive from where we were to hunt, and we knew that putting out all our decoys would take still another hour. Consequently we were on the road just after midnight and completely stooled out beneath a starry sky by 4 A.M. Tony and I sat back to back, looking over the rush-covered gunwales of the boat without being able to see the outline of the nearst decoy. The lights of Manhattan illuminated the western horizon.

I must have fallen asleep, for I was suddenly startled by my brother's admonition to "stay low!" Since I could not have gotten much lower without going overboard, I said nothing and stared into the graying sky. We were anchored at the edge of a marshy island and behind me, facing my brother, I could hear the mysterious murmur of approaching birds. I could make out 40 or more decoys on my side of the boat, but nothing was flying in my field of vision. Although I very much wanted to turn to see what was coming, I didn't move, less because I was such a crafty, patient hunter than because I knew my brother would punch me if I turned.

The muttering birds drew closer and their strange sounds were captured and enhanced by the parabolic shape of the boat. I began to wonder whether my brother's strategy was to let the birds land on us when his American Gun Company side-by-side fired once, twice. I swiveled about and was amazed by the spectacle of more than 300 brant filling every niche of available air space in half of the sky. The birds babbled and complained as their wings churned furiously, climbing from 20 to 30 to 40 yards distance in about the time that it took you to read these few words.

I fired into the flock with my grandfather's Browning that was as old as the brant decoys. I hit nothing. I fired again and heard my brother yell, "Lead 'im! Lead 'im!" I figured if I didn't "lead 'im," I'd hear about it the rest of the day, so I picked one bird from the swarm, swung well ahead of it, and pulled the trigger. A brant angled down ten yards behind the one at which I shot. I was so awestruck, I sat for a moment more watching the huge skein of birds condense into smoke and dissolve in the fiery haze of dawn.

My brother was thrilled by my shot and shared my pride in this, our first, brant. However, he masked his fond fraternal feelings with the words, "Pick up your bird, dummy!"

We sat the rest of that bluebird morning without another brant or duck coming within half a mile of us. I had put the brant between my knees where I could watch it and reach down surreptitiously from time to time to stroke its charcoal plumage and to reassure myself the bird was real and truly mine. Tony remembers the day as generally dull and uneventful. I can recall details like the bow seat in front of me which had a crazed design where the layer of paint had begun to fracture before peeling.

The brant is probably our fastest flying goose. In 1965, A. S. Einarsen published a study of black brant in which he had clocked these birds at ground speeds of up to 62 miles per hour. This compares to clocked speeds of 36 to 40 miles per hour for Canada geese. One calm day, I paced five Canada geese with my car at nearly 45 miles per hour for over a mile on the Chesapeake Bay Bridge. However, even if they had flown 50 miles per hour, the speed of the heavier Canada goose is no match for the more streamlined and lighter-weight body with faster wing beats (three to four per second) of the brant.

Since my first experience I have shot many brant under a variety of conditions. I have stalked them over the shallow lagoons of Baja, California, and called them over the winter-darkened waters of the Chesapeake. On several occasions, I have killed more than one bird with one round, and I once watched *six* (a daily limit at that time) eventually fall out of a flock after two of my younger brother's shots. Yet the details of those hunts blur and grow anonymous with age, and there is only one other brant episode etched in memory as keenly as my first.

On that occasion, my younger brother and I had kneeled for nearly two hours in the salt grass on a sod point thrust between a shallow cove and the channel running just inside the south shore of Long Island. The day was damply overcast, and faint flurries of snow swirled out of the east on indecisive winds. Although we could hear brant in the distance, they did not seem to be moving, and John decided to see if he could walk them up. He was still a discernible silhouette on the horizon when a tugboat came out of the mist, pushing a low wall of water onto the flats and against the marshlands on both sides of the channel. A dozen brant displaced by the suck and surge of water beneath them clamored into the air, swung ahead of the tug, and started down the channel to where our ungainly Bellport decoys rocked gently in the breeze.

I kneeled with my gun supported by cordgrass stubble and called repeatedly, varying the pitch in an effort to make my one voice sound like several. The brant called and passed, then swung well downwind before beating back to the stool. When they were over the decoys with two birds already settled in the water, I picked up my gun and killed the only bird that had turned and was heading away. I swung on another bird and dropped it precisely where it had intended to land. I swung on still another bird flailing to catch the wind and squeezed the trigger. Nothing. Again. Nothing. I glanced down and saw an empty hull hung in the ejector port

Trying to get *Field & Stream* editors Ed Zern (left) and Gene Hill to pose while geese are flying is like trying to get kids to sit still in an ice-cream parlor. The conversation could have gone something like this: ZERN "Since you're not sure what to do with that gun, Gene, hold this goose for me so I can collect another." HILL "Quiet, son, I'm concentrating." *(Photograph by Clark G. Webster)*

of my semiautoloader. I snatched it out, heard the bolt slam forward, and made a hasty shot at one last brant which had swung far into the cove and was now rushing to catch up with its disappearing kin. Incredibly, the bird rolled forward and skidded to a halt in the water. Three up, three down. My brother slogged back in time for the bows, but there were no encores.

Both these anecdotes have their morals. For one thing, if you allow yourself to be swept away by the spectacle of hunting, you won't take home many birds. While you may sometimes kill more than one bird with one shot when a flock is bunched over the decoys, you will rarely kill even one bird by shooting at the flock. Common sense and all good hunting textbooks tell you this, but at least once each season, every hunter disconnects his brain when a flock of birds appears over the decoys, and he blazes away, sure he can't miss, and swears later his shells must have been blanks.

Next, while flexibility is a virtue in hunting, impatience is not. Once your best day-before planning has you located at a spot with good prospects, give it a fair showing. If the birds are not flying, you really only have two choices: Wait it out or pack it up. You might be warmer pulling decoys and putting them out somewhere else or walking the marsh with the hope of getting a jump shot. However, unless you actually see birds using the area to which you plan to go, your efforts will be wasted. Or worse. For how often have you decided to walk across a field only to look back when a few hundred yards from your abandoned blind to see geese coming into the decoys?

On the other hand, if you do see birds trading over a particular point or up a gut some distance from where you sit, don't be so loyal to preconceived notions you cannot adapt to unexpected opportunity. This is the third lesson of waterfowling and, perhaps, the most important one. You must go where the birds are or will be "using." Do not expect them to come to just any "likely-looking" spot. All successful hunters spend twice as many hours scouting a territory, locating birds, insuring access, and building blinds than they spend hunting geese.

Finally, remember that everything happens fast in hunting. Each flock of geese could be the last for that day, that season, or (the usual feeling) forever. This day you are there to kill geese, not to take pictures or read books. If you have the leisure to photograph birds, it means you already have your limit or the birds are out of range.

If you see no birds, sorry about that. However, if you see them using a distant, but accessible, flyway, and you are too inert to move—that's okay—you may still get a shot. But you have no one to blame but yourself if you end up eating domestic turkey for Christmas dinner.

Speaking of dinner, the brant epitomizes the expression, "You are what you eat." Prior to 1931, when an unknown plague swept through most beds of *Zostera marina,* or eelgrass, on both sides of the Atlantic, brant were both abundant and succulent. They were undoubtedly the Atlantic Flyway's premier game bird—Canada geese being neither so plentiful nor cornfed in those days.

Within two years, the population of brant collapsed, and by 1935, there were fewer than ten percent of their former numbers on wintering grounds from Long Island to North Carolina. Just as *Zostera* has never fully recovered, neither has the brant. Atlantic coast birds subsist principally on *Ulva lactuca,* or sea lettuce, a leaflike alga rich in iron, iodine, and several vitamins, but apparently poor in certain other ingredients essential to the nutritional well-being of brant. As a result, many wintering birds are in mediocre condition, rarely build up fat reserves for the spring migration, and are frequently so rank in flavor, you must reluctantly abandon all hope of eating them.

During the past decade, Atlantic brant have been legal game only three seasons. There is no way to improve such percentages even if we quintupled the number of U.S. dollars spent in Canada on waterfowl habitat enhancement. The truth is most geese nest so far north along the Arctic Circle, they are beyond the reach of man's management. Either brant fly north to

Greenland and find suitable ice-free nesting sites and get their young on the wing before the snow starts flying again in August, or they don't produce a potential harvest of juvenile birds. If winter is delayed at one end of the arctic nesting season or comes early at the other, the U.S. Fish and Wildlife Service does not open a season on brant.

Brant may gather by the hundreds in the seaside marshes near our home, but our melancholy is in knowing that they used to concentrate there by the tens of thousands. Every October we look forward to seeing family groups of brant trading about the marsh while we work on blinds for the season ahead. Brant keep us company throughout the winter, sometimes swinging in over the decoys in response to our calling or their own curiosity. They will land among the wooden ducks and geese and pick daintily at the strands of *Ulva* caught on broken stalks of cordgrass or drifting on the falling tides.

Although brant are behaviorally less flexible—hence, less abundant—than Canada geese, and less tasty when feeding heavily on *Ulva* [3] than goldeneyes or greater scaup, this inflexibility—call it "wildness"—has a special appeal to wildfowlers. Brant do not flourish in captivity, and they and snows are the only North American geese to nest regularly on islands north of this continent and within the Arctic Circle. Brant make loyal parents, and the males will defend a nest from attacking gulls and jaegers even as the larger Canada goose gander will flail aside attacking foxes and raccoons.

Finally, the brant is a bird of the moody and magnificent ocean coasts. Except for the night migrations of Atlantic brant across the breadth of Quebec, this species rarely flys far from waters flavored with salt. A skein of brant undulating across the wave tops of a foam-crested sea is a sight that stirs the soul of any ardent waterfowler and makes him long to hunt these birds. Although the brant is no larger than a mallard, the sea goose is one of the supreme trophies of wildfowling.

---

[3] During the long winter freeze of 1976–77, brant, along with greater snow geese, appeared in fields of winter wheat and rye on seaside farms along the lower Delmarva peninsula. This previously undocumented behavior was the result of extreme hunger and desperation, since their normal foods were locked in the iron-hard marsh and below the ice found everywhere behind the seaside islands. Whether a significant number of birds will retain a memory of such food and begin foraging more regularly in upland fields remains to be seen. (Small flocks of greater snow geese have been seen feeding in winter wheat and corn stubble during the past two winters.) If brant and greater snow geese adapt to feeding on agricultural crops, their winter survival rates may increase, and the flavor of the brant may improve.

FIVE: PERCHERS AND DABBLERS

Two young fellows pulled a couple of snags together on a
Mississippi sandbar and waited for their first shots at
ducks. Suddenly a dozen teal swooshed out of nowhere
and were gone before either youngster could react.

"Stay down!" hissed the older boy.

"What for?"

"The world's round, ain't it? Those ducks will be
back in a couple of minutes."

TWO TRIBES of waterfowl, Cairinini and Anatini, contain the most eagerly sought-after ducks in North America. This is partly a result of their beauty (the gorgeous male wood duck is a member of the Cairinini, or perching clan), their abundance (over 5½ million mallards are harvested every year in this continent without in the least inhibiting the continuing expansion of this species into new habitat), and their generally excellent flavor (with the exception of shovelers that have been feeding in the coastal marshes of Louisiana or Virginia).

Wood Duck

The wood duck *(Aix sponsa)* has a close Asiatic relative, the mandarin duck, whose drake is comparably gorgeous and frequently found on zoo ponds or in private collections. Both species prefer to nest in tree cavities, have sharp claws on their webbed feet for gripping limbs and fluttering up the sides of the nesting cavity when newly hatched, and both species use their long tails for weaving, dodging, and making sudden stops as they hurl like grouse through the forest overstory.

At one time the wood duck was believed to be on its way to extinction. George Bird Grinnell noted in 1901 that "being shot at all seasons of the year, they are becoming very scarce and are likely to be exterminated before long." However, total protection gave them time to recover, and the construction and placement of literally hundreds of thousands of nesting boxes during the past half century has helped rebuild populations to precolonial numbers and, in some areas of its range, possibly to exceed even those lush statistics.

Today the wood duck is the fifth most commonly found duck in hunters' bags in the United States and Canada. More than a million are killed annually with some 85 percent of the total taken in the Mississippi and Atlantic Flyways. Split seasons have been specially created in some eastern states to take advantage of the tendency of wood ducks to move south sooner than many other waterfowl. Early blue-winged teal seasons have not been as successful as wood duck seasons, because blue-winged teal move south earlier than woodies and through areas where other waterfowl will pass. Thus, "teal seasons" have sometimes resulted in inordinate pressure being put on locally produced and barely fledged mallards and black ducks, while special wood duck seasons provide up-country hunters with, perhaps, the only waterfowl shots they may get all year.

Old-timers remember when wood ducks were scarce and no hunting of the species was allowed. Elderly waterfowlers often look on woodies with a special protective concern, and many feel the bird is too beautiful to be shot. However, there is no crime in harvesting such an abundant crop, but there is one in wasting a notable feature of this bird: the drake's plumage. Visible pain is scrawled across the expression of fly fishermen who learn that duck hunters in the piedmont or coastal sections of the country will frequently pluck and throw away the feathers of wood ducks and green-winged teal because such regional sportsmen have no use for dry flies when summertime rolls around. If you fall into this category, think of a fisher-friend who lives in the mountains and make him an ecstatic man next Christmas with a gift parcel of flank feathers from the more handsome drakes you shoot, including mallards. If you don't know any fly fishermen, gain the goodwill of and possibly a little credit at Orvis (Manchester, Vermont 05254) by sending them the feathers. Quality fly-tying materials are in desperately short supply.

This may as well be the time to mention it, for another wasted resource in waterfowling is the giblets: the hearts, gizzards, and livers of the birds you shoot. Incredibly, most hunters throw such tasty protein away. Even at Remington Farms, where as many as 1,200 geese are killed and processed annually, the giblets are never saved unless a guest makes a specific request to have them set aside. Quality protein, like quality fly-tying materials, is increasingly hard to find, and a side dish of diced and sautéed giblets spread in a buttery gravy over wild or domestic rice provides almost as much satisfaction to the tongue's taste buds as a roasted-rare wood duck in orange sauce.

If you are concerned about heavy metal or chemical concentrations in the duck's internal organs—more of a worry in mollusk and fish-eating ducks than in dabblers—you can still save the giblets to be stewed as a treat for your dog. The retriever will adore you for it, and, who knows, the exotic chemicals may prevent worms!

Although wood-duck decoys are available, this species is principally hunted by jump shooting, either by walking down shallow streams, cutting across oxbows and ambushing the birds from the bank above, or by canoeing down winding rivers with a shooter always ready in the bow. In the mid-Atlantic, the canoe or small skiff is camouflaged, and the art of the hunt, as in English punt gunning, is to see how close you can get to the swimming or resting birds before they become suspicious and take flight.

Twenty years ago, I enjoyed floating down New Jersey rivers in a rubber-and-canvas kayak, taking turns with a companion in jumping and shooting wood ducks and mallards. While there was something approaching luxury in this style of hunting, since the birds were killed from a nearly horizontal position, in reality, the ability to kill ducks consistently while practically lying on your back with absolutely no ability to swing right (if you shoot off your right shoulder) may categorize such gunning as a feat rather than a sport!

Muscovy

The muscovy duck *(Cairina moschata)* is the wood duck's nearest relative in North America. This may come as a compound surprise to many people who either thought the muscovy duck was a domestic form of mallard (just as Embden, Toulouse, and Sebastopol geese are domestic varieties of the greylag goose) or that the muscovy duck was just that, a Russian bird.

Actually this large duck (males weigh nearly nine pounds) is a native of Mexico, Central America, and much of South America as far south as Argentina. The species was domesticated by several Amerind tribes, and most European birds are descended from muscovies taken to Spain following the conquest of the Incas. When domesticated varieties were introduced to England from the continent in the sixteenth century, the English called the bird "muscovy" in the mistaken belief it came from Eastern Europe. The English made a similar error when they named another North American native the "turkey." A small irony of both these birds' association with man is that neither the domestic turkey nor the domesticated muscovy duck is as popular in its native hemisphere as chickens and white mallards originally introduced to America by way of Europe from Asia.

Muscovies are nonmigratory and unadventurous as a species. They

The author has spent many hours watching widgeon and canvasback feeding together, but never saw a widgeon rob a diver of his dinner. Scavenge scraps, yes—outright thievery, no. *(Photograph by George Reiger)*

rarely stray even as far north as Texas, and most attempts to establish the species in Florida, using the offspring of wild stock from South America, have met with failure. Today the trend in wildlife management is away from exotic introductions, and waterfowlers may never have the curious opportunity to hunt these strange birds in the United States.

Several season ago, I was hunting mallards and Canada geese on a tidal marsh in Virginia when a huge, noisily flapping waterfowl came winging down the creek.

"What the devil is that?" I asked my scientific companion.

"Beats me," he said. "Let's collect it and find out."

He started to rise but sat down again. "It's a muscovy."

"If it is, it's either feral or an escapee from a collection. Let's get it!"

Unfortunately, by the time we had intellectualized the situation, the bird was gone—a swift, strong flyer exhibiting not the slightest interest in mallard or Canada goose decoys.

Widgeon

The Anatini—surface-feeding, dabbling, or puddle ducks—feature relatively few species unique to North America. However, the American baldpate or widgeon *(Anas americana)*—some authorities spell this *wigeon*—is a handsome exception. Although most dabblers feed in shallow water, tipping for their food rather than submerging for it, the baldpate prefers deep-

Being able to distinguish the two widgeons—American, *left,* European, *right*—is of increasing interest to waterfowlers as the European widgeon continues to expand its range in North America. Besides regular appearances in the Atlantic Flyway, "sightings in northern California of this species," says the May 1979 issue of *American Birds,* "have increased in recent years to the point they are no longer newsworthy." In addition, during the winter of 1978–79, European widgeon showed up in Arizona, Colorado, Texas, and far-flung Hawaii. *(Left photograph by Glen Smart. Right by George Reiger)*

water plants, which it cannot easily reach. However, the American baldpate and its close European relative solved the conflict between their desired diets and their diving inadequacies by evolving a commensal relationship with skilled divers of the tribe Aythyini. These latter birds, collectively known as pochards or freshwater diving ducks, include on this continent the canvasback, redhead, ring-necked duck, and the scaups. The arrangement seems to be that in exchange for a wary watch for enemies provided by the baldpates, the pochards yield some of the food they bring up from the bottom. There is some conflict of opinion about how this yielding is done. Tradition and popular illustrations depict the baldpate actually robbing reluctant canvasbacks. However, during two winter weeks spent in a photographic blind overlooking a freshwater pond in coastal Virginia and filming these two species together, I never saw a single incident in which one duck robbed another—and food was in sufficiently short supply to justify such behavior. More often, a canvasback would bob to the surface with a weed in its bill, shake its head to align the plant for easy swallowing, and inadvertently toss part of it away. Meanwhile, the baldpate, sitting high and alert on the water, quickly paddled over and consumed the root or leafy fragment.

This ancient relationship may be deteriorating over significant portions of the overlapping winter range of divers and widgeon. Whereas canvasbacks and redheads once fed over the *Vallisneria* beds, which were the reason the Susquehanna Flats and Currituck Sound became fabled names in waterfowling, the availability of preferred duck food is diminishing due to damming, pollution, silting, salt incursion, or combinations of all four. As a result, wintering canvasbacks and redheads consume more animal matter, especially clams, than they once did and taste little different from the greater scaup which used to fetch less than half as much money in market gunning days. Meanwhile, widgeon, frustrated by a lack of free green lunches served by pochards, seek out swans to bring up food or move into upland fields to browse. Widgeon, also, mingle with other dabblers feeding along the margins of ponds and rivers.

Perhaps exotics will always appeal more than native species to certain people, and the drake European widgeon *(Anas penelope)*—with his apricot-hued head and neck and creamy crown—strikes many observers as a prettier species than our native bird with his green face patch and white crown. The European widgeon may be a more common visitor to American shores than was once believed. George Bird Grinnell recalls shooting a male "English widgeon," and when his guide picked it up, he called it a cross between a redhead and a widgeon, as though such an unlikely arrangement had been seen before. Every Audubon Christmas bird count through the Atlantic Flyway yields several European widgeon (presumably drakes for certain identification), and, to quote the May 1979 issue of *American Birds,* "sightings in northern California of this species have increased in recent years to the point where they are no longer considered newsworthy."

The European widgeon is a handsome bird, but as our native baldpate grows older, his crown turns yellow, his tail becomes more spikelike, and he assumes a more distinguished appearance than his juvenile progeny. The two middle tail feathers on a specimen I collected near Annapolis, Maryland, projected two full inches beyond the ends of the other tail feathers, making this veteran drake widgeon competitive with a pintail.

Hunting widgeon can be a frustrating business. Over much of their wintering range, they are taken incidentally with other dabblers, and for some waterfowlers, their appearance is disappointing since, for all their vegetarian habits, baldpate are not always as tasty as mallards and pintail. However, no duck can more effectively drive a sportsman to distraction!

Widgeon like to circle—and circle—and circle—then start to slide down toward the blind—and, perhaps, one or two will—before the rest climb back

The gadwall has one of the most peculiar breeding ranges of any duck in North America. You will find some nesting in Alaska's Mount McKinley National Park; others along the Colorado River separating Arizona and California; still others in the suburbs of Lincoln, Nebraska; and a few near the parking lots at Jones Beach State Park on Long Island, New York. Nowhere as abundant as the mallard, the gadwall is nearly as widely distributed. *(Photograph by Glen Smart)*

out of gun range to circle and circle all over again. By comparison, suspicious widgeon will make a wary mallard seem downright foolish. Perhaps, widgeon are playing the waterfowl's equivalent of "chicken" with the first birds over the stool, the winners—or the losers, if the hunter's reflexes have not been completely discombobulated by the time the birds slip within range.

Surprising to many eastern gunners, the widgeon is the fourth most commonly found duck in hunters' bags across Canada and the United States. Over one million are shot annually in North America, with the Pacific Flyway alone accounting for half the total. By contrast, the Atlantic Flyway sees fewer than 80,000 killed annually. Obviously, the American widgeon is in good supply and with a cautious but adaptable disposition, this species is likely to be one of our most important game birds for many generations to come.

Gadwall

Although nowhere very abundant in its range, the gadwall *(Anas strepera)* was formerly the most widely distributed waterfowl in the world. However, mallards have been introduced or introduced themselves to so many new, and once exotic, habitats, the gadwall has slipped to second place, but still far ahead of the pintail, as the earth's most cosmopolitan duck.

Depending on where you hunt in this continent, the gadwall is either a pleasant surprise or an expected part of the day's action. Although the gadwall is the seventh most commonly found species in hunters' bags in the U.S. and Canada, almost the entire kill takes place west of that extensive spine of mountains known variously as the Catskills, the Blue Ridge, or the Allegheny. Thus, although the annual continental kill is approximately three-quarters of a million birds, fewer than 40,000 are shot in the Atlantic Flyway.

That latter figure might be even smaller, except that beginning just after World War II, pairs of gadwall started breeding along the south shore of Long Island, especially at Jones Beach. During the past three decades, while the New York colony has peaked and mysteriously declined, gadwall have begun reproducing in the freshwater sloughs of barrier islands from New Jersey south to the Carolinas and on marsh islands dotting the eastern shores of the Chesapeake. Furthermore, releases of immature gadwall in New England and Florida may account for recent nesting records from these parts of the country.

The gadwall is not an easy bird to identify in flight, particularly in the Atlantic Flyway where its appearance is always unexpected—a little like bobwhite whirring away before a Minnesota grouse hunter. Although most gadwall breed within the parameters of the Central Flyway, the majority of birds appear to drift east, where the greatest U.S. kill (more than 385,000) occurs in the Mississippi Flyway. Hunters in Minnesota or Arkansas might see gadwall often enough to become expert at identifying them on the wing. However, the last one I shot I would have sworn was a hen baldpate—well, maybe a pintail—until my retriever brought in a handsome drake "grey duck."

Once in hand, there can be no mistake. Even the hen gadwall, with her general resemblance to the hen pintail, has the distinctive white speculum which separates this species from all other puddle ducks. In addition, neither the pintail nor the baldpate have the lovely yellow legs and feet of the adult gadwall. In both appearance and taste, this species is a prize of waterfowling, and especially appreciated as such in the East because the species is scarce. I've jumped numerous gadwall off South Dakota stock ponds and gunned down several daily limits in that manner. However, I cannot remember the particulars from any one of those raids. On the other hand, I can recall even the mood of the day when I have taken gadwall in the Atlantic Flyway. Uniqueness, as well as variety, provides the spice in life.

Green-Winged Teal

Astonishing as it may seem to Pacific Flyway hunters, the green-winged teal *(Anas crecca),* not the pintail, is the second most commonly harvested waterfowl species in North America after the mallard. In some recent seasons, more than 1.9 million green-winged teal have been killed in all four flyways of the continent, while the figure for pintail barely exceeded 1.3 million.

Other hunters are astonished that teal can be harvested at all. They are such swift flyers, more like supercharged shorebirds than ducks in their twisting flight, early authorities rated their progress at better than 100 miles per hour. Some better-than-average shots still insist teal have to be killed on the water or not at all.

In reality, teal rarely exceed 50 miles per hour, and when they brake over the decoys or first jump into the air on takeoff, they are doing half that. Physiologically speaking, green-winged teal are handicapped in their efforts to fly much faster than about 50 because of their tiny size. Although brant are exceptional in being swifter than most larger geese, a rule of thumb is that the largest species of related avian forms will fly faster than its cousins, just as long-legged runners generally outdistance their shorter rivals. This is a peculiarly hard fact for many hunters to digest. There is no way you can convince the ordinary dove shooter, for example, that the larger, clumsier-looking pigeon, alias rock dove, alias *Columba livia,* can fly faster than his sleek and beloved mourning dove *(Zenaidura machoura).* Yet racing pigeons are among the fastest birds on earth, with one mounted specien in the Smithsonian having been clocked on a still day over a course of several miles at 92 miles per hour. Dove hunters may think their targets fly as fast as that, but a mourning dove needs a tail wind to reach even 60 miles per hour. Having made the point, we must now acknowledge that the small size of green-winged teal (a big drake doesn't weigh a pound) and the proximity of the birds to the gunner when they buzz the decoys or make touch-and-go landings in the stool reminds us of bees, not ducks—and how do you figure the proper lead for a bee?

In bygone days when the "splitters" still held sway, there were two green-winged teals: the American version, *Nettion carolineuse,* and the European edition, *Nettion crecca.* The European teal nested across northern Europe and Asia and as far west (or east, depending on your perspective) as the Aleutian Islands. Therefore, an American gunner had just as much chance on the West Coast as in the East to bag one of these exotic fowl.

European teal behaved like green-winged teal, and the only discernible difference was that when the two varieties were in hand or on the water close by, you could see that the drake European teal had a prominent white line along each side of its back (which the American teal drake lacked). Meanwhile our native drake had a white crescent in front of its folded wing, which the European variety did not have. Small differences, perhaps, but they used to offer wonderful grist for debate in duck blinds on cold, slow mornings, and my younger brother was insufferable for a brief period following his shooting of the only European teal recorded in our family hunting logs.

The triumphant "lumpers" have now thrown John's rarity out the window, and more than one waterfowler is melancholy about the entire business. All birds offer the mystery of where they were born, where they have traveled, and where they were going when the paths of hunter and hunted crossed. The European teal was and is as distinctive a visitor to the mainland of this continent as the European widgeon, the Baikal teal, the falcated duck, or the Bahama pintail—just to list four other unusual puddle duck visitors to North America. The dash of white across the back and the absence of the white crescent in front of the wing were significant proof the bird was a foreigner—certainly as significant as if it sported the ornamental chestnut-striped scapulars of the Baikal teal. The European teal evokes visions of Scandinavian meadows and streams just as the Baikal teal evokes pictures of misty Siberian forests and lakes. To lump into a single species the various subspecies of a bird with a worldwide distribution, such as the green-winged teal, is to eliminate something of the wonder of waterfowling for a hunter who may never see an Icelandic sunrise, but who can hold a fragment of its meaning in his hands.

Teal are small enough to fly through a pattern of number 4 or 5 shot at 40 yards so that only one or two pellets strike the bird—enough to knock it down, perhaps, but not enough to kill it. A good retriever is as essential in areas where teal are found—and what swamp, river bend, or coastal pond in the country doesn't host the potential of teal—as where larger ducks are hunted. Indeed, a teal often relies on cunning and what amounts to reason to escape pursuit since it lacks the diving capacity of a canvasback or the stamina of a mallard. I once retrieved a teal from beneath a floating branch where only the bird's bill gave its hiding place away; and I have found crippled teal tucked into clumps of grass so small a handkerchief would have easily covered both grass and bird. A large part of the green-winged teal success story is based on the fact that they conceal their nests better than most other species of waterfowl, and that mother teal are especially staunch defenders of their broods. Thus, their ability to hide and their will to elude capture make them particularly tricky ducks to recover as cripples. A strong dog with a good nose will be on top of stunned birds, or in such hot pusuit of running or swimming cripples, that they never have the fatal opportunity to orient themselves and make good their escape.

The Mallard

The mallard *(Anas platyrhynchos)* is everybody's waterfowl. The olive-billed and green-headed drake with the white neck ring and chestnut chest is as familiar to fanciers of Oriental or Occidental wildlife art as it is to kids anywhere watching the rerun antics of Daffy Duck. Whether the writer is playwright Henrik Ibsen or poet Henry Gibson, the mallard makes a significant impact on culture and reflexively comes to mind whenever the phrase "wild duck" is heard.

In North America, even though 5.5 million mallards are killed annually by hunters, by season's end there are still nearly 7 million mallards wintering across the continent, acquiring fat reserves for the spring migration and the rigors of reproduction so that another 13 million mallards will move down the four flyways the following fall, providing food, and esthetical and recreational enjoyment for people wherever they go.

Although the mallard's traditional North American nesting range spans the upper Midwest to Alaska, any roadside ditch, borrow pit, or farm pond is liable to nurture a hen mallard and her insect-eating brood of ducklings. The adaptability of this species is legendary, and some birds have been known to nest in the flower beds of busy urban parks and to feed in the swill of hog troughs which may include such delicacies as rotting vegetables and chicken guts.

Every winter evening at the Bronx Zoo in New York City or the National Zoo in Washington, D.C., wild mallards fly in to share the food and security of their pinioned cousins and leave again at first light. If a landowner constructs a pond and is impatient to let nature take its course,

Sears, Roebuck and Montgomery Ward will sell newly hatched mallards—"as near wild as possible"—for less than a dollar apiece.

The ease and reliability with which mallards can be raised has led to some harebrained "stocking" stunts in the past and only slightly more sophisticated variations in the present. Once it was learned that trout could be successfully planted in remote mountain lakes by flying low over the surface and pouring thousands of fingerlings out the aircraft door, several private and even public agencies tried doing the same thing with mallard ducklings. The physiological and behavioral needs of the species were utterly ignored as different donors (including unknowing taxpayers) rushed to outdo one another in throwing ducks (and dollars) out the window.

Today mallard "stocking" continues in many states, but plane releases have thankfully been abandoned. Instead, officials in Maryland use state duck-stamp revenue to buy and release tens of thousands of mallards annually on "suitable," often meaning, roadside, waters. Maine finally terminated its more modest program run by sportsmen's clubs and supported by the state fish and wildlife department in which mallards were bought from a game farm in Wisconsin and put out wherever the birds appeared to receive the least harassment from outboard motor boaters, poachers, and kindly people who thought they were doing the mallards a favor by feeding them. In addition, sponsors of the Maine effort admitted that "big turtles and eagles negated our stocking in some areas."

A major problem with stocking mallards in northern waters is that a parasite, leucocytzoan, whose intermediate host is the blackfly, frequently wipes out entire broods of mallard ducklings. Native black ducks appear to be less susceptible to the infestation, but stocked mallards are hybridizing with native blacks and possibly reducing their resistance to the parasite. State spokesmen for Maryland and Pennsylvania,[1] the two major stockers of mallards in the Atlantic Flyway, tend to disparage the hybridization issue. They point out that as far back as the nineteenth century, George Bird Grinnell reported killing several black duck-mallard hybrids in North Carolina, and that Francis H. Kortright reported the young of such crosses

[1] On December 27, 1978, hunting license buyers in Pennsylvania made a contribution to my Virginia recreation and diet when I shot a hen mallard wearing a Game Commission band which had been put on the bird 5 months earlier in Wayne County, 350 miles away. Of course, that's nothing. Pennsylvania pen-raised mallards have been recovered from 38 states, including Alaska, most Canadian provinces, and Jamaica in the West Indies. Pennsylvanians even shoot a few.

have "normal sex ratios and the usual fertility." However, the issue has never been over breeding success in numbers, but in genetic quality. Maryland politicians claim that since relatively few of their stocked birds survive the first winter (a majority presumably going into the game bags of Maryland hunters), and since relatively few black ducks breed in Maryland (anymore), the impact of that state's annual stocking of as many as 70,000 mallards is minimal.

The only measurable data in this controversy comes from wing samples sent in by participating hunters to the Laurel, Maryland, laboratories of the U.S. Fish and Wildlife Service. By 1970, projections of more than 12,000 mallard x black duck crosses were showing up annually in the wing survey, and the most recent figure is almost 15,600.

However, scientists within the service appear divided over the implications of the miscegenation problem, or, indeed, since less than one percent of all the ducks killed in North America are hybrids, whether there is a miscegenation "problem" in the first place. One researcher questions whether the black duck is sufficiently different from the mallard even to constitute a separate species, proving that "lumpers" continue to expand their range along with the mallard. Because of so many different opinions, there is no significant federal pressure on the states to do something wiser with their duck stamp and other waterfowl conservation funds than to throw ducks out the proverbial window.

Several years ago, at the Delta Waterfowl Research Station in Manitoba, an experiment was conducted to determine the long-term value of stocking mallards. Two areas were selected adjacent to one another in which there were normally about 16 nesting mallard hens per square mile. Each area was four square miles and shared comparable habitat. Into the test area, many hundreds of additional mallard ducklings were released; no birds were introduced into the control area.

The following spring, the survivors of the release program returned, and the number of nesting hens shot up to 66 per square mile, far above the previous record for the area of 36 breeding pairs. So far so good. Yet when no further artificial introductions were made, the average number of nesting pairs in the test area fell back to that averaged by the control area throughout the three-year period: namely, 16 breeding pairs per square mile. To put such test results in a nutshell, you get more ducks for the dollar by preserving or enhancing nesting habitat than by investing in incubators, brooders, and tons of cracked corn.

The pressure for mallard release programs is most intense in the Atlantic Flyway, because with low or nonexistent limits on brant, wood ducks, black ducks, canvasbacks, and redheads, the Atlantic Flyway hunter has relatively few preferred waterfowl species of which he can take more than two a day. Although pintail and gadwall are 10-point birds under the point system selected by several Atlantic Flyway states, these ducks are 10-pointers large in part, because they are uncommon in that flyway. If a hunter kills ten a season, much less ten a day, he has had an exceptional year.

All this sounds very remote to farmers in the upper midwestern US. and prairie provinces of Canada, where flights of 10,000 mallards (a not uncommon fall phenomenon in prime farming country) can consume or trample beyond harvest 50 tons of grain a day. Some unlucky farmers have watched an entire year's profit go up in feathers within a week. Farming is a billion dollar business in Canada, and crop depredations in recent years have amounted to over $100 million annually. Although many Canadians hunt ducks and some Americans cross the border each year to hunt waterfowl as they begin the fall flight, fewer than one million of the 5.5 million mallards harvested each year in North America are shot in Canada. Even if we added the other two million ducks and geese killed and retrieved every year throughout the breadth of Canada (and not just those taken on the prairies), this does not qualify Canadian waterfowling as a $100 million activity which could justify a comparable loss in exportable crops. Thus, despite justifications by American biologists, we can sympathize with Canadian farmers who watch state duck-stocking efforts with unqualified horror.

However, the mallard's vices as a field feeder are its virtues as a table bird. Whether its flavor is derived from wheat gleaned in Alberta, corn in Kansas, peanuts in the Carolinas, soybeans in Mississippi, or rice in California, the mallard is probably the most dependably tasty duck that can be set before a gourmet. Considering the competition, that fact alone would make the mallard North America's favorite waterfowl.

However, there is still another, and possibly more important reason, and it has to do with the mallard's responsiveness to traditional hunting techniques, especially the art of duck calling. No other waterfowl is so receptive to persuasive calling and so wary of careless quacking. Geese are sometimes lulled by sounds only the least bit reminiscent of a flock's clamor, and diving ducks already committed to landing can be reassured with some muttered imitations of their kind. But mallards with no apparent desire to visit a set of decoys can be turned from their previous course and patiently "talked down" within gun range by an experienced caller. Nothing, except good retrieving, in the entire realm of waterfowling is more beautiful to behold or more prideful to enact than to encourage a high-flying trio of mallards to abandon their previous plans and, with much circling and suspicious chatter, come visit your humble spread of mallard decoys tucked in a corner of the marsh or in an opening of the flooded timber.

Like fine piano playing, duck calling is about 3 percent talent, 5 percent the instrument itself, and 92 percent practice. It is amazing how many hunters spend dozens of hours discussing the pros and cons of different decoys and shotguns before making the necessary purchase, but will pick out the prettiest or cheapest duck call in the display case, give it a tentative toot to see that it quacks, then plunge into the marsh and frighten every duck within earshot with what sounds like a territorial fight between a great blue heron and a flock of crows with laryngitis!

If your companion has purchased an inferior call (and there are many), or if he doesn't know how to use a double-reeded Yentzen, don't be polite—don't stand on ceremony and friendship—get the call out of his mouth and encourage him to chew gum if he must be orally compulsive. On the other hand, when you run into another hunter at the public landing after a morning of listening to his agonizing imitations of an egg-bound hen, be sure to compliment him on his superb calling, for each sour note from another blind will keep the birds moving to you.

Having judged a couple of duck-calling contests, I find it difficult to recommend one call above all others, particlarly because different mallards appear to have different accents in different parts of the country. I kid you not. A master mallard caller from the Arkansas bottomlands may scare the pinfeathers off a mallard in the Sacramento Delta. That is why the notion of a "World Championship Duck Calling Contest" is wonderful public relations, a lot of fun, and impossible. While such self-styled "world championships" rarely solicit participation by skilled callers from outside the host state, the real point is that what sounds good to a panel of human judges may sound awful to a panel of ducks.

A while back I ran into outdoor writer Gene Hill in Easton, Maryland, where he was about to judge a duck-calling contest. I asked him how this was possible since Gene is hard of hearing. "I read lips," he replied, revealing his complete understanding of the motives and tradition of world-championship duck-calling contests.

Southern Mallards

Three birds—the Mexican, mottled, and Florida ducks—are variously treated as separate species, subspecies, or races of the common mallard. The drakes of all three populations, like the male black duck, resemble the female mallard, but are darker overall. Probably the most significant field difference between the common mallard and its southern kin is that female common mallards have orangish-yellow bills frequently spotted with black, while both sexes of Mexican, mottled, and Florida ducks have yellow or olive bills with little or no spotting. (No wonder positive identification of the mottled duck is muddled!)

The Florida duck ranges throughout the lower half of that peninsula from Gainesville in the north to Key Largo in the south. The estimated total population of 50,000 birds is concentrated west of Lake Okeechobee. The mottled duck ranges from Alabama along the Gulf Coast into Mexico. Its estimated total population is 100,000 birds, and the majority are found in Louisiana.

Finally, the Mexican duck once ranged from southeastern Arizona and northcentral New Mexico southward into the Valley of Mexico. Its present range is much reduced, especially in the north. A couple of years ago, waterfowling was curtailed in parts of Arizona, New Mexico, and west Texas to comply with the requirements of the Endangered Species Act, under which *Anas diazi* is listed. A national brouhaha resulted over this closed season with southwestern waterfowlers convinced it was the first federal step in the eventual closing of all duck hunting. One writer in Phoenix charged that the closure was "proof positive" the U.S. Fish and Wildlife Service was trying to emasculate the hunter—overlooking the fact that two years before the Mexican duck affair, that same Fish and Wildlife Service had restored the greater snow goose to American game lists after half a century's absence.

The protesting waterfowlers made one interesting point: Since mallard x Mexican duck hybridization is a more serious threat than hunting pressure to the remaining Mexican duck populations within the United States, by eliminating the annual harvest of drake mallards wintering in Mexican duck habitat, the Fish and Wildlife Service was indirectly sponsoring the continued decline of pure strains of Mexican ducks.

The federal government pooh-poohed such reasoning, but it did concede it had no information on how many pure-blooded Mexican ducks were left in the United States. A hurried survey could turn up only a few questionable individuals. As a result, the Mexican duck was reclassified from "endangered" to "threatened," which means that under certain circumstances, the birds can be hunted.[2]

The controversy over the precise taxonomy of southern mallards, the common mallard, and the black duck has masked an interesting physiological and behavioral anomaly having to do with pair-bond formations and family loyalties. Said more simply, waterfowl in which both sexes look alike—that is, whistling ducks, geese, and swans—normally have strong pair bonds, and the males regularly assist in the rearing of the young. Waterfowl in which the male is more colorful than the female normally have weak pair bonds, and the male rarely assists in the rearing of the young.

The common mallard usually creates new pair bonds every year. When an incubating female loses her clutch of eggs, she will remate with any available male if her original mate has already abandoned her. Furthermore, unpaired males frequently rape unguarded females which have already begun to nest. Similar behavior is found among southern mallards and the black duck, although in the latter species, the female has been observed to take the same mate following their summer moult, and the drake will attend his hen for up to twenty-two days after she starts to incubate.

In the case of mature black ducks or southern mallards that take the same mate twice, there is generally no ceremony or aquatic displays accompanying the renewal of such pair bonds. However, newly mature females or

[2] As we go to press, the American Ornithological Union (A.O.U.) has just declared the Mexican duck to be a mere race of the mallard. The mottled and Florida ducks will probably be similarly reclassified. The lumpers continue indomitable.

those which do not encounter their previous mates following the summer moult will incite males against one another just as the hen common mallard does. Furthermore, male black ducks display the backs of their heads to females just as mallard drakes do, which may suggest why green highlights in the head plumage of drakes is the dominant color characteristic passed along in mallard x black duck hybrids. The head display, ritualized preening, are important behavioral holdovers from a period of several million years ago when black ducks were evolving from mallards. Once upon a time, black duck drakes had more colors to display than their modern descendants, who may be evolving toward a more permanent pair-bond relationship with their hens than the compulsively polygamous mallard drakes.

Black Duck

There are certain birds that will always carry special and even mystical associations for man. Among falconers, the gyrfalcon, even above the princely peregrine, has more awe-inspiring tales told about it than, perhaps, there were ever captive specimens. Among waterfowlers, even those in western flyways where the species rarely strays,[3] the black duck *(Anas rubripes)* arouses the greatest awe. Worshippers will insist that black ducks can smell a man tucked inside a blind half a mile away (not true), that their eyesight is equal to the eagle's (probably not), and that a giant race of 4- and even 5-pound birds winters along the Canadian and New England coasts (yes).

The black duck is the environmental standard of the Atlantic Flyway. More than any other waterfowl species, the fall flight of black ducks is symptomatic of the ecological well-being of the entire eastern half of the continent. Thus, that there has been a steady decline of this species since about 1950 is depressing news, which more than offsets the wonderful recovery of the wood duck and the phenomenal growth of Atlantic and Mississippi Flyway Canada goose populations. After all, wood ducks are as adaptable as mallards, and geese normally nest in the arctic and subarctic regions of Canada and Alaska where they have been, until very recent years,

---

[3] More than a century ago, the amazing Mr. Grinnell shot a black duck x pintail hybrid in Wyoming.

Black ducks have never taken kindly to captivity. When waterfowlers familiar with the species hear of individuals that have been tamed, they know it can only be true if that particular "black duck" is three-quarters mallard! *(Photograph by George Reiger)*

little affected by man's development and alterations of the environment. Black ducks, however, breed from Manitoba east to Newfoundland and south to North Carolina. Fully half of their ancestral nesting range lies within the heavily settled and industrialized corridors of the northeastern United States and Canada. The flesh and organs of many specimens are loaded with the residues of heavy metals and pesticides, and that the species is not more seriously affected by pollution, overshooting, and hybridization with semidomestic mallards is excellent testimony to its tenacity.

For many hunters, the black duck is only a shadow against a star-spotted sky, a hen quacking in the night, as birds leave the salt marsh well before dawn to fly offshore to sleep away the day at sea before returning to the coast at night, long after the last legal gunner has pulled his decoys. In some respects, black ducks appear more sagacious than the most admiring stories told about them. In addition to being more critical of sloppy calling than geese or even seasoned drake mallards, black ducks are frequently indifferent to even the very best calling. Furthermore, black ducks are not so dominated by courtship ties that if one of a pair of blacks decides to visit a stool, and the other bird is suspicious of the setup, the more wary of the two will let the more trusting take his or her chances. This may occur even in January when pair bonds are generally well established.

In contrast, if one of a pair of Canada geese decides to land, even if such birds are unmated young of the year, the social cohesion of this species is such that when one goes in, both go in. This is even more true of family groups involving four to six birds. The adults may be leery of the situation below, but they are indulgent parents, for if the yearlings commit themselves, so will their reluctant elders.

Black ducks are found almost entirely in the Atlantic and Mississippi Flyways, and they are either shot incidentally on jump shooting expeditions in which the mallard is the target species, collected from river or salt marsh blinds where most anything that flies by is fair game, or selectively hunted by a devoted breed of waterfowler found principally along the Atlantic coast.

The usual technique involves a layout boat and not more than half a dozen decoys. Some purists use only three, but the precise number is determined more by whether you plan to shoot over a spacious pond or in a narrow creek and not by any rigid formula passed down from father to son. The layout boat is specially constructed for one or two shooters and a dog. It is sometimes broad in the beam in order to accommodate two reclining gunners, but its essential ingredients are a low profile and short length— never more than 10 feet.

Permanent blinds can account for their share of sport with black ducks, but not to the degree represented by layout boats. By the time black ducks filter down to the middle states, they have been educated so that many avoid on principle any conspicuous structure on the marsh. Unfortunately, black ducks are suckers for bait, and a good deal of hunter success from permanent blinds south of Long Island, New York is based on corn. Not only must the layout boater seek his recreation away from such well "sugared" spots, he must hope there will be enough survivors from the overkill normally associated with baiting to ensure him some recreation.

If a man is serious about black duck hunting, sooner or later he must build or buy a layout boat that can be moved from point to cove to creek even as the wary birds themselves move about. *(Photograph by David W. Corson)*

However, if the layout hunter does his homework, there should be no great difficulty in putting himself in position to obtain a legal limit of one or two black ducks. (The limit in Canada is four to six, depending on the province.) This homework consists of scouting the marsh creeks and coves the afternoon before a morning hunt to discover where the birds are "using." At dawn along the coast, particularly if there is a northeast wind and a rising tide or, second best, a clear morning with a falling tide, the flighting black ducks coming into the creeks and salt ponds to feed should provide ample opportunity for a limit within the first hour of legal shooting time.

When a layout hunter moves into a secluded pond or the upper reaches of a marsh before dawn, he may move out birds that have been feeding or resting there during the night. In many cases, the birds will not know what startled them into flight, having heard only the takeoff or alarmed quacking of another duck. If the hunter can control himself and not attempt to take (illegally) these departing shadows, odds are they will be back within an hour—when the hunter is more properly set up to receive them.

This rule of thumb is equally true of any puddle duck that moves into the marsh after you have put out your decoys. If the bird flares over your rig because you moved too soon, don't be so foolish as to fire a departing, out-of-range shot. You will only cripple the bird and, perhaps, not find it in the tall grass and mud. Or you will miss and ruin your chance of that particular bird returning later in the day. Even flared black ducks will often return within an hour if you are stooled out where they have been "using."

This is also why, if you can control yourself, you will let sizable flocks of black ducks come and go. Even if you should kill a double of black ducks (in many states, the legal maximum), you will have taught the survivors something you would prefer their not knowing—especially if you hope to see those same birds over the same marsh again that season.

Concentrate on singletons and doubletons for layout shooting. Wait until the birds are within easy range, even if it means popping a vein while they circle several times, looking over the decoys and the surrounding marsh. Then sit up and kill cleanly. In tall-grass country, a good conservation rule of thumb is to ignore potential doubles and concentrate on killing one bird at a time. When I am shooting a marsh surrounded by phragmites or chest-high spartina, I fire a second and a third shot at a duck only if I have hit, but not killed, the bird with the first shot. Furthermore, I try to fold ducks over the stream or tidal gut where I can see whether I need another quick shot to finish a heads-up cripple. Even with a dog, I still lose occasional black ducks, especially those that hit the water and dive in one, almost simultaneous, motion.

Fish and Wildlife Service data indicate that 10.3 percent of the Atlantic Flyway black duck harvest and 7.4 percent of the Mississippi Flyway black duck harvest is made during the 30 minutes of legal shooting time before sunrise. Similar percentages (10.7 and 7.4) represent the black duck harvest during the legal *hour* before sunset.

Besides the advantage of having as much action in the first half hour as the afternoon shooter has in the last hour, a dawn hunter has several additional things going for him. First, and perhaps most important, rarely can you kill ducks in the early morning before you can see them to determine species, if not sex. A predawn glow suffuses the land and waterscape with sufficient light in the half hour before official sunrise to enable you to make all necessary identifications. If overcast or fog delay your ability to discern birds, you won't be breaking any laws by waiting for poor visibility to clear. However, at sunset, particularly on a clear day, you may still have 45 minutes of good light to gun by, but which should properly be used to gather decoys and make a start for home. Unfortunately, the temptation to wait for birds still loafing on open water or sandbars is great—and illegal.

Next, if you knock a bird down at sunset, you will be rushed to find it, both because of the growing darkness and because you may still need to pull in your decoys and make a possibly long boat ride through the gloom to reach home. On the other hand, at dawn, each passing minute gives you better light by which to search for a cripple. With an entire morning ahead of you and being generally more alert at dawn than after a long day of sitting and staring into space, most hunters are more successful in retrieving cripples at dawn than at dusk.

Finally, sunrise hunting is more exciting because more wildlife of all kinds is out at first light than at dusk, when different species have different schedules for calling it a day. Sunrise is a more active, even cheerful, time to hunt. Since a large part of the pleasure of waterfowling is in being alive to see and hear the sights and sounds of marsh birds and mammals, dawn is a more stimulating time of day to hunt than dusk. The ultimate bonus occurs when you take a limit of black ducks and are back home in time for a breakfast or brunch with the family with still most of the day ahead of you for work or more play.

In the 1950s, the preseason continental population of black ducks was possibly more than 4 million birds. In the 1970s, the preseason population has fallen to less than 3 million birds. Both the preseason and winter surveys indicate a significant 2½ percent per year decrease in black ducks over the past twenty-five years.

Most hunters and wildlife biologists are unhappy about these statistics, but we spend a pathetic amount of time disputing their reliability. Some hunters point out that in 1971, the estimated black duck bag, plus crippling, came to nearly one million birds, while the winter survey following the season totaled only 414,000 birds. Since you cannot subtract one million birds from a breeding population less than half that size and expect the species to provide any hunting the following year—which it did, yielding a harvest only slightly less than the year before—the survey statistics must be out of line and accounting for far less than half of the actual number of surviving black ducks.

Yet are perfect numbers more important than what trends indicate about the resource itself? While we quibble, every indicator points to the continuing decline of the black duck.[4] In 1955, the daily bag limit in all states was four birds, and the season was 70 days long. Today the daily bag limit is one or two black ducks, and the season has been reduced to 45 or 50 days, depending on which state you hunt. During this same time span, hunter success has dropped in the Atlantic Flyway from more than two black ducks per hunter per season to less than one. And while the seasonal black duck bag of one bird per four active hunters in the Mississippi Flyway has remained more or less constant over the past decade, hunting effort has increased from fewer than five days afield per hunter in 1955 to nearly eight days afield, with additional pressure represented by a doubling of the total number of waterfowlers in both flyways since 1960.

Until 1969, the black duck headed the harvest list for waterfowl in the Atlantic Flyway. That year it was replaced by the mallard, and the following year, the black duck dropped to third place behind the wood duck. Although habitat deterioration and the replacement of the black duck by the mallard along the fringes of the black duck's formerly expanding breeding range are cited as the principal factors in the black duck's decline, biologist Walter F. Crissey has shown that the black duck's high survival rate (based on winter bandings and, in fact, higher than the mallard's) and the black

---

[4] In the past five years, hunter harvest has fallen dramatically. In 1977, the total U.S. kill was fewer than 300,000 birds, and that figure includes approximately 14,000 black x mallard hybrids. The Canadian harvest may be greater than the American, but that still doesn't begin to total a million birds.

duck's high average reproductive rate (again, higher than the mallard's) suggest the species has adequate habitat and can more than hold its own with the mallard without its having to resort to agriculturally destructive field-feeding practices, all, if hunting regulations give the black duck an even chance.

Recreational hunting activity, and not daily bag limit, seems to be the crucial element in determining black duck numbers. While duck trapping and other forms of illegal harvest coninue to be corrosive of proper management—particularly in the mid-Atlantic area of this species's range—the ever-increasing pressure from recreational hunters, especially in Canada, where more than half the black duck harvest is presently made, appears to be affecting the species far more than the relative handful of duck poachers operating in both eastern flyways.

Aelred D. Geis, Robert I. Smith, and John P. Rogers discovered that black duck mortality is highest in a region composed of southern Ontario, southern Quebec, the Maritime Provinces, and the northern tier of Atlantic and Mississippi Flyway states. Walt Crissey points out that this region is precisely the most productive portion of the black duck's breeding range, and that within the region the indigenous population is being over harvested.

Crissey writes: "It must be remembered that banding studies have shown that there is a strong instinct for birds to home to their natal areas when they return in the spring. This is especially true for adult females, but it is true also for immature females and males to a lesser degree. They will home, that is, providing they are still alive to do so."

What is the solution? Simple, if we want to justify our role as responsible sportsmen and agents of scientific waterfowl management: Reduce the length of the black duck season in those areas where the birds are currently overharvested to a minimum of 20 days or a maximum of 30 days. Many hunters in the eastern flyways recognize the black duck on the wing and are able to differentiate it from the hen mallard. Therefore, other waterfowl can still be hunted during the currently recommended 45- or 50-day season. However, so as not to make the ordinary gunner an outlaw if he inadvertently kills a black duck during its closed season, a mild penalty of 100 points per day (that is, kill a black duck, and you're done hunting for the day) should be imposed.

If this plan still does not work, even more bitter medicine should be taken. The eastern flyway councils will have no choice but to close black duck hunting entirely in the northern states and those parts of Canada found by Geis, et al., to be where the heaviest harvest is made. Canadian cooperation is imperative, both for the continued well-being of the black duck as well as for the continued well-being of those laws and treaties which bind our two nations together in a common regard for migratory wildfowl.

Pintail

Every year more than twice as many pintail *(Anas acuta)* as black duck are killed by North American waterfowlers. Although the pintail harvest seems huge, surveys made after most of the shooting is over find more than 3.3 million pintail happily ensconced on their wintering grounds, with approximately one million of those birds resting on the creeks and lagoons of Mexico.

As a Canadian Wildlife Service official asked the visiting California Department of Fish and Game representative, "Even if we could produce more pintails, where in the world would you put them?"

Eastern hunters have an answer. Despite the enormous continental harvest, Atlantic Flyway gunners account for fewer than 50,000 pintails annually, and the huge hunter population in the Mississippi Flyway takes just five times that number. Well over a million pintails fall to gunners in the Central and especially the Pacific flyways.

However, there is nothing any individual or governmental agency can do about the distribution of waterfowl. Opportunities in hunting, like much else in life, are not evenly apportioned, and human whim or law won't make the slightest difference. If you want to shoot pintail in quantity, you must go west, young man, and if you want to shoot black ducks at all, you must go east.

The pintail is most abundant as a breeding species from the Great Plains north and west to Alaska. Within an hour of my first visit to Anchorage, I discovered a pintail nest not far from the busy international airport—just after a stray dog had destroyed it. Elsewhere throughout the subarctic from the Aleutian Islands to Ellesmere Island (where in 1968 a pintail nest was discovered 700 miles north of any previously known breeding site), pintails are more likely to be harassed by wild canines than the domestic kind.

In some respects, pintail are the most upland of waterfowl. This designation refers to their breeding habits, which often finds pintail nests many hundreds of yards from the nearest water, as well as the fact that pintail are more often responsible for damage to farmers' crops than even mallards or geese. Pintail prefer wheat to corn, and they would be an even greater nuisance, particularly in the prairie states and provinces, except that the species is impatient to be south once its family-raising chores are over. Both sexes migrate early, but often separately, and one October morning I saw a flock of about 700 birds near Chestertown, Maryland, with nary a hen in the formation.

Pintail are good flyers, and they seem to know and enjoy this element of existence. Perhaps, youthful exuberance is the motive behind some truly remarkable migrations which may take a juvenile bird from its birthplace in Alaska to the interior of the Soviet Union, South America, or even Hawaii. Like black ducks, hard-hunted pintail learn to raft up on open water by day and to fly inland to feed at night. Even when they move about from field to field, pintail will sometimes fly so high, only their distinctive silhouettes reveal their identity. Pintail look so much like streamlined aircraft that with their wings barely trembling in the frosty dawn—the rising sun staining their white bellies a soft metallic rose—a ground observer could be excused for imagining the birds were leaving vapor trails!

Wariness is only one reason for this species' success. Nesting pintail hens have a remarkable tolerance for the proximity of their own kind, and while such behavior doesn't approach the colonial nesting tendencies of sea ducks, it does lead to maximum utilization of available habitat. In addition, hen pintails are persistent defenders of their broods, and long after a hen mallard will have abandoned her young to their fate, a female pintail will still be buffeting a marauding skunk.

About 75 percent of all the pintails in the Pacific Flyway winter in California. Their depredations on crops in the Imperial Valley led to special hunting regulations nearly four decades ago which permit what amounts to legalized baiting of waterfowl. Periodically the Fish and Wildlife Service gets a pang of conscience, reviews the situation, and tries to amend this contradiction in federal law. They are urged on in this effort by hunters and conservation officials in other states, either outraged by this legal exception that Californian courts now insist is a "tradition," or plainly jealous of what amounts to some of the fastest waterfowl shooting and most generous limits left in the United States.

Rather than gnash their teeth in envy, eastern gunners should adopt a more positive attitude toward their pintail-scarce skies. Since nothing can be done to change the local situation, each sprig killed becomes a more memorable trophy for the individual hunter. Like a bottle of wine with a good meal, a pintail makes a beautiful outing more memorable. Some of my best pintail shooting has occurred during the brilliantly clear weather that follows a sustained spell of wind and rain. This species seems to rejoice in its ability to be up and on the wing again, and practically all the pintail I have shot in eastern flyways have been taken under such splendid conditions.

One day a quarter century ago, I lost the last decoy my grandfather had carved, plus 20 other nondescript wooden blocks, when my small punt sank in a vicious northeaster that drowned every marsh island on Long Island's Great South Bay. The next morning was calm and crystal clear, and I returned to the marshes to spend the day searching for the missing decoys. Although I found half a dozen, I never found the one that meant most to me. In the afternoon, while resting on a massive timber that had been swept up by the storm and contemplating my stupidity for having gone hunting with an heirloom, a trio of pintail came chasing over the marsh and towered when they saw me a few yards away. Had they kept flying on a natural course, I might have been too absorbed by my mood to take a shot. However, their frantic reach for the sky aroused me, and I toppled the drake at extreme gun range.

It was a clean kill, and it was the first pintail I ever shot. I should have

Pintail are often taken in clear weather. But you have to be well concealed before the birds will come within range. However, dogs don't matter. In fact, dogs sitting out in plain view sometimes seem to do more to attract waterfowl than to frighten the birds. *(Photograph by Curtis Badger)*

Artist Bob Kuhn knows that teal hang around the marsh waiting precisely for that moment when you are busy with something else in order to buzz the decoys. However, if the dapper little ducks ever gave us a chance to get ready, they wouldn't be teal, and we wouldn't love them as part of the experience of waterfowling half so much. *(Reproduction courtesy Remington Arms Collection of Game Art)*

been pleased and proud. Instead I stood with the lovely bird in my hands and remembered an old man who never learned to speak English without a German accent and whose chief recreation was building boats and carving decoys and helping his grandchildren tack together bird houses. Tears welled from my eyes—for the missing decoy—for the missing man. I had made the wrong gesture in killing that pintail, and I am glad they are uncommon in the flyway where I do most of my hunting. The fragile beauty of the drake cannot be taken for granted; for me it is a compelling emblem of life's bittersweetness.

Blue-Winged and Cinnamon Teal

The blue-winged teal *(Anas discors)* and the cinnamon teal *(Anas cyanoptera)* are lumped together by the U.S. Fish and Wildlife Service for the purposes of winter survey, and so shall we, for the purposes of species comparison and summary. If you shoot a brownish bird with bluish upper wing coverts in the Atlantic or Mississippi Flyway, you have almost assuredly shot a blue-winged teal hen. If you shoot a similar bird in the Central or Pacific Flyway, a toss of the coin may settle the issue better than a field guide as to whether you have a blue-winged or cinnamon teal hen—unless you saw the bird flying with males in nuptial plumage. In that case, the drake with the white facial crescent and white rump spot is the blue-winged teal, and the bird with the rich red color, reddish eye, and lack of white anywhere on the body is the cinnamon teal.

How can you tell the hens apart? Well, one rather nebulous way is to compare cheeks. Female blue-winged teal have yellowish white cheeks whereas female cinnamon teal have whitish yellow cheeks. For more positive identification, let us quote Johnsgard quoting Spencer quoting Duval: "Twenty-six female blue-winged teal had a maximum exposed culmen length of 41 mm., while seventeen female cinnamon teal had a minimum exposed culmen length of 41 mm., with means of 38.7 and 43 mm., respectively."

Since that doesn't seem to offer the ordinary hunter much help, just remember that no matter where you shoot, both species are worth the same number of points or birds-per-day toward your limit, and that both species are predominantly seed-eaters and superb flyers, offering difficult shots and excellent eating.

What is remarkable from a taxonomist's standpoint is that there is far less hybridization between these two closely related and look-alike (at least, the hens) species than there is among the black duck and mallard. In the eastern half of Washington State, blue-winged teal and cinnamon teal nest in the same vicinity and feed on the same kinds of plants and insects. Yet a hybrid hatch is exceptional. Doubtless, this is because blue-winged and cinnamon teal do not share many of the same wintering grounds where pair bonds are formed.

The blue-winged teal nests from coast to coast—from Victoria, British Columbia to Pea Island National Wildlife Refuge in North Carolina—but the center of its breeding activity is the geographical center of the continent where, for example, it constitutes nearly half the breeding waterfowl of Minnesota and is Iowa's most common duck.

By August, however, most of the continent's blue-winged teal are on the move. Although egg incubation periods for mallards and teal are roughly the same length, it may take as long as two months for a mallard to

Since blue-winged teal start their trek south in August, special September teal seasons work better in more southerly latitudes than along the northern tier of the United States. In Missouri and Arkansas, flooded timber offers tricky shooting through branches often still carrying their complement of summer's leaves. *(Photograph courtesy Missouri Department of Conservation)*

fledge, but only about forty days for a blue-winged teal. Thus, it is less a dislike of cold weather (as old-timers believe) that sends blue-winged teal south sooner than other puddlers, than a restless disposition reinforced by an ability to move out sooner than other breeding duck which makes the blue-winged teal our earliest migrant.

Even with early or split seasons, the numerous blue-winged teal constitute little more than 700,000 of the more than 20 million ducks and geese shot every year in Canada and the United States. About 480,000 of these birds are killed in the Mississippi Flyway, where Louisiana's tally of 250,000 birds heads the harvest.

The overwhelming majority of blue-winged teal skip the country, where for example years ago in Batista's Cuba, visiting American sportsmen shot the birds on the Isle of Pines over decoys improvised from coconuts. Across the Caribbean in Nicaragua or Panama, native hunters use .22s or traps to take the birds, and, in parts of South America, blue-winged teal are still hunted from horseback much as naturalist/novelist W. H. Hudson did in the 1890s.

Cinnamon teal are not nearly so restless. Guatemala is about as far south as they winter. And although there is an attempted breeding record from near Ocean City, Maryland, cinnamon teal rarely stray even as far east as Nebraska. Utah seems to be the center of their breeding activity, and the Colorado River may be the principal pipeline for migrants moving between the United States and Mexico. Cinnamon teal are commonly seen in late summer by rafters on the Colorado River between lakes Powell and Mead. By the time opening day rolls around in the fall, the Colorado River border between California and Arizona and continuing into Mexico offers probably the best cinnamon teal shooting in the entire West.

While cinnamon teal will give any set of decoys composed of other species a buzz-by, you will improve your odds for action by painting a few teal-sized decoys a suitable cinnamon red. Blue-winged teal decoys are difficult enough to find, but green-winged teal decoys are somewhat more common and can be adapted with a latex (oil-based paints do not stick well on plastic-bodied decoys) blend of red and brown. Make sure the pattern approximates the bird, and the paint dries to a flat finish. Don't forget the red eyes. You may not create a collector's item, but you will possess a serviceable and unique decoy for a serviceable and unique bird.

Spoonbill or Northern Shoveler

When sportsmen hear the adjective "northern," they naturally wonder whether there is a southern edition of the same bird. And in this case, there are—three of them: the Cape shoveler of South Africa, the red shoveler of southern South America, and the Australian shoveler of Australia, Tasmania, and New Zealand. All shovelers have pale blue upper wing coverts and green speculums (just like blue-winged and cinnamon teal), but shovelers are readily distinguished from all other ducks by their spatulate (which means spoon-shaped) bill.

The northern shoveler *(Anas clypeata)* is one of five Holarctic surface-feeding ducks found in North America. (The others are the gadwall, green-winged teal, mallard, and pintail.) The northern shoveler possibly makes the longest regular migrations of any waterfowl. While blue-winged teal hold the record in North America with flights from the Canadian subarctic to south of the equator,[5] the northern shoveler breeds within the Arctic

[5] One blue-winged teal banded in Saskatchewan was recovered six months later in Peru, more than 7,000 direct air miles from the original banding site.

Although these shovelers were photographed in North Dakota, they were probably in another state or province by dawn. These are our greatest migrants among waterfowl, and northern shovelers have been known to fly 18,000 miles in a single year. *(Photograph by Dave McLauchlin)*

Circle north of Europe and Asia and winters as far south as central and southern Africa. Since such migrations are not directly north and south, and since there are many detours, switchbacks, and side excursions during such wanderings, an adult northern shoveler may travel as many as 18,000 miles within a single year.

Shovelers are busy birds. Because they have relatively small bodies (a 2-pounder is huge), they must work harder to keep their furnaces fueled than that other green-headed duck with which they are frequently and erroneously compared, the mallard. In one of those apparent contradictions of nature, smaller forms of the same kind of wildlife have to feed more constantly than larger forms, because larger wildlife have more energy reserves (due to their larger bodies) in relation to their energy-burning appendages. For this reason, the Arctic tern and common crow forage more widely and make longer seasonal migrations than their larger counterparts such as the royal tern and the raven. For this reason, too, shovelers and teal, not swans and geese, are North America's greatest waterfowl migrants.

All this helps explain why shovelers and teal are not "stupid," as some waterfowlers claim, just because these birds pitch more readily to a set of decoys than mallards or pintail. Shovelers and teal simply have no time to waste on preliminaries. Each winter day is short (which also explains why North American shovelers and teal stray into the southern hemisphere where summer is in full swing during the depths of our winter, and where daylight and foraging opportunities are consequently extended); and if a small and hungry duck sees what appears to be a gathering of waterfowl on a creek or cove below, its genetic programingknows that more of its kind will survive to reproduce to survive (hopefully, ad infinitum), if it places the gratification of its hunger above caution.

Rather than "stupid," I prefer the word "trusting," for it does not deny shovelers and teal knowledge of the continual risks they are running. Taxonomically, shovelers and blue-winged teal are more highly evolved than mallards and pintail, and the ancestors of all four species have been churning the air waves longer than our ancestors have been plodding through the muds below them. There is nothing "stupid," or by implication, unsuccessful, about any form of waterfowl.

The shoveler is the only puddle duck I normally let come and go over my decoys without firing a shot. When I was younger, I shot them because a boy beginning to be a hunter will kill everything that is legal. However, the large quantity of animal life the shoveler strains from the shallow, sometimes stagnant, pools this species prefers gives its flesh an unappetizing flavor which I find more repellent than any so-called "fish duck" I have ever eaten.

And while I have been waiting, lo, these many years for a drake in prime nuptial plumage to make his appearance over my decoys so I could attempt to add him to my collection of mounted birds, male shovelers acquire breeding colors so late in the hunting season—they are almost as extreme as male ruddy ducks in this regard—I still have that empty niche in the cabinet.

Yet the principal pleasure and wonder of this bird is in its existence. One of the most satisfying late afternoon hunts I can recall involved no shooting, but instead sitting and watching shovelers pitch to teal decoys and immediately begin to comb the shallow water and bottom for plankton. The sun was in my eyes, but its glare back-lit the busy fowl so that their silhouettes designed a fantastic water ballet with music provided by their rattling chatter and the wind rustling in the reeds.

As darkness fell, I stepped from the blind to collect my decoys, flushed the shovelers, and felt in that instant that hunting must be an acquired passion, and not an instinct. Much of our motivation to hunt, particularly as we grow older, is an attempt to recapture those sublime moments afield that shape our best memories. Of course, we can never experience again precisely what we enjoyed once, but the longing and the searching create fresh moments and additional memories.

"So we beat on, boats against the current, borne back ceaselessly into the past," said F. Scott Fitzgerald.

Recreation is not merely a gift of time, a diversion from work. It is essential to anyone's well-being. Recreation provides us with leisure in which to seek those singular experiences, those epiphanies of awareness, rarely found in the context of our daily labors.

Nonhunters often ridicule hunters about all the trouble we undergo just to acquire protein that could be purchased at a market for a fraction of the cost of any one of our many outings. Nonhunters use the word "work" to describe our activities, forgetting that work is only those things all of us must do which we would rather not do. Waterfowling is never work.

People who prefer watching a sport to playing it—who, therefore, extract no meaning from hunting and fishing as it is depicted on television—may never realize that the greatest value of outdoor recreation is in the time it gives us to think, to dream. If imagination is buried beneath routine, wisdom is buried with it, for both are products of leisure.

The beauty and the sorrow of waterfowling, the warmth and the chill of watching shovelers from a blind at sunset, is in knowing that existence is "the thing that hath been, it is that which shall be; and that which is done is that which shall be done; and there is no new thing under the sun."

SIX: DIVING DUCKS

*A former market hunter whose modern reputation was
more as a boozer than a shooter went out one dawn with
a young hunter who wanted to see all the skills of yesteryear in action. However, it was sunbathing, not waterfowling, weather, and the less it looked like the old
hunter would get a shot, the more he boasted about kills
he had made in the good old days. Since he punctuated
these stories with swigs from a pint flask, he quickly
mumbled himself to sleep.*

*A half hour passed when a solitary bluebill buzzed
the decoys. The boy jumped up, fired two shots, and
missed. The shooting woke the old-timer who leaped to his
feet, waved the barrel of his shotgun in the direction of
the fleeing duck, and pulled the trigger. The bluebill
tumbled belly up into the lake.*

*"That's the most amazing shot I ever hope to see!"
exclaimed the youngster.*

*"Shucks," said the old man, "when a flock that big
goes through, I usually knock down half a dozen."*

WHEN YOU think about it, "Diving Ducks" is a silly subdivision for waterfowl. All waterfowl are capable of diving. However, some only do so to escape danger, as when flightless swans and geese dive to avoid capture; some only do so to reach some particularly choice food, as when green-winged teal and widgeon dive for corn; but some do so habitually to feed—such as the birds to be covered in this chapter.

The first subsection of the subdivision "Diving Ducks" is the tribe Ayhyini, or freshwater diving ducks. In its original meaning, *Aythya* had nothing to do with either freshwater or diving ducks. It was merely the name which Aristotle applied in his *Natural History* to an unknown water bird and which modern taxonomists have used to describe the "pochards" (word origin unknown)—after recent authorities judged *Nyroca,* which means "diving duck" in Latinized Russian, and which had covered the genus for three-quarters of a century, to be no longer adequate. Perhaps, taxonomists settled on *Aythya* as sufficiently ancient and vague to cover every option. An additional element of confusion is provided by the fact that several species of freshwater diving ducks spend a significant segment of their lives on brackish and even salt waters.

Canvasback

The undisputed king of North American pochards is the canvasback, *Aythya valisineria.* This is the species that once made the reputation of the Chesapeake Bay as the waterfowlers' mecca of the United States. Over half of all the canvasbacks on earth still winter there. Unfortunately, today that means fewer than 150,000 birds, where centuries ago they may have numbered into the millions.

So much has been written about the canvasback, most anything I might add would be redundant. If the editor of any outdoor magazine wants to stroke the nostalgic nerve-endings of his readers, he can always count on a retrospect of the canvasback to turn the trick. In 1978, South

A peculiarly high mortality rate for female canvasbacks results in many late-winter flocks being composed almost entirely of males. Some hunters see those concentrations of drakes and, forgetting that it takes two to tango, come out with the thoughtless question: "Look at all the cans; why can't we shoot them like in the old days?" *(Photograph by George Reiger)*

Dakota devoted an entire issue of its *Conservation Digest* (Volume 45, Number 4) to "King Can," and I myself contributed to the trend with a short story entitled "The Last Canvasback" for the May 1974 issue of *Audubon.*

However, the definitive work on this species is still H. Albert Hochbaum's *The Canvasback on a Prairie Marsh.* It is less a biological monograph than a hymn sung in praise of this lordly bird. First published in 1944 by the American Wildlife Institute (later, the Wildlife Management Institute), copies are now nearly as scarce as broods of young canvasback.

Historical accounts generally turn the clock back no further than the fourth quarter of the nineteenth century to describe incidents from the market hunters' last hurrah. Yet one of the most perceptive renderings of the canvasback was written about 1810 by America's first birder, Alexander Wilson. In his *American Ornithology,* Wilson writes in and of a time when the United States was a freshly minted nation and the canvasback was both a symbol of its bounty and its future despoliation:

The Canvass-Back Duck arrives in the United States from the north about the middle of October; a few descend to the Hudson and Delaware, but the great body of these birds resort to the numerous rivers belonging to and in the neighborhood of the Chesapeake Bay, particularly the Susquehannah, the Patapsco, Potomac, and James Rivers, which appear to be their general winter rendezvous. Beyond this, to the south, I can find no certain accounts of them.

At the Susquehannah, they are called Canvass-Backs; on the Potomac, White-Backs; and on James River, Sheldrakes.[1] They are seldom found at a great distance up any of these rivers, or even in the salt-water bay; but in that particular part of tide water where a certain grasslike plant grows, on the roots of which they feed.

This plant, which is said to be a species of *valisineria,* grows on fresh-water shoals of from seven to nine feet [deep] (but never where these are occasionally dry), in long, narrow, grasslike blades, of four or five feet in length; the root is white, and has some resemblance to small celery.

This grass is in many places so thick that a boat can with difficulty be rowed through it, it so impedes the oars. The shores are lined with large quantities of it, torn up by the Ducks, and drifted up by the winds, lying, like hay, in windrows.

Wherever this plant grows in abundance, the Canvass-Backs may be expected, either to pay occasional visits or to make it their regular residence during the winter. It occurs in some parts of the Hudson; in the Delaware, near Gloucester, a few miles below Philadelphia; and in most of the rivers that fall into the Chesapeake, to each of which particular places these Ducks resort; while, in waters unprovided with this nutritive plant, they are altogether unknown.

On the first arrival of these birds in the Susquehannah, near Havre de Grace, they are generally lean; but such is the abundance of their favorite food that, toward the beginning of November, they are in pretty good order.

They are excellent divers, and swim with great speed and agility. They sometimes assemble in such multitudes as to cover several acres of the river, and, when they rise suddenly, produce a noise resembling thunder. They float about these shoals, diving, and tearing up the grass by the roots, which is the only part they eat. They are extremely shy, and can rarely be approached, unless by stratagem.

When wounded in the wing, they dive to such prodigious distances, and with such rapidity, continuing it so perseveringly, and with such cunning and active vigor, as almost always to render the pursuit hopeless.

From the great demand for these Ducks, and the high price they uniformly bring in market, various modes are practised to get within gun-shot of them. The most success-

---

[1] Wilson may be mistaken; since colonial days, *sheldrake* has been an American synonym for *merganser.* Incidentally, "sheldrake" has nothing to do with shells or mollusks; it merely means a drake marked with white.

ful way is said to be decoying them to the shore by means of a dog, while the gunner lies closely concealed in a proper situation. The dog, if properly trained, plays backwards and forwards along the margin of the water; and the Ducks, observing his maneuvers, enticed perhaps by curiosity, gradually approach the shore, until they are sometimes within twenty or thirty yards of the spot where the gunner lies concealed, and from which he rakes them, first on the water, and then as they rise. This method is called *tolling them in*. If the Ducks seem difficult to decoy, any glaring object, such as a red handkerchief, is fixed round the dog's middle, or to his tail; and this rarely fails to attract them.

Sometimes, by moonlight, the sportsman directs his skiff towards a flock whose position he had previously ascertained, keeping within the projecting shadow of some wood[s], bank, or headland, and paddles along so silently and imperceptibly as often to approach within fifteen or twenty yards of a flock of many thousands, among whom he generally makes great slaughter.

Many other stratagems are practised, and, indeed, every plan that the ingenuity of the experienced sportsman can suggest, to approach within gunshot of these birds; but, of all the modes pursued, none intimidate them so much as shooting them by night; and they soon abandon the place where they have been thus repeatedly shot at.

During the day, they are dispersed about; but towards evening, collect in large flocks, and come into the mouths of creeks, where they often ride as at anchor, with their head under their wing, asleep, there being always sentinels awake, ready to raise an alarm on the least appearance of danger. Even when feeding and diving in small parties, the whole never go down at one time, but some are still left above on the look-out.

When the winter sets in severely, and the river is frozen, the Canvass-Backs retreat to its confluence with the bay, occasionally frequenting airholes in the ice, which are sometimes made for the purpose, immediately above their favorite grass, to entice them within gunshot of the hut or bush which is usually fixed at a proper distance, and where the gunner lies concealed, ready to take advantage of their distress.

A Mr. Hill, who lives near James River, at a place called Herring Creek, informs me, that, one severe winter, he and another person broke a hole in the ice, about twenty by forty feet, immediately over a shoal of grass, and took their stand on the shore in a hut of brush, each having three guns well loaded with large shot. The Ducks, which were flying up and down the river, in great extremity, soon crowded to this place, so that the whole open space was not only covered with them, but vast numbers stood on the ice around it. They had three rounds, firing both at once, and picked up eighty-eight Canvass-Backs, and might have collected more, had they been able to get to the extremity of the ice after the wounded ones.

In the severe winter of 1779–80, the grass, on the roots of which these birds feed, was almost wholly destroyed in James River. In the month of January, the wind continued to blow from W.N.W. for twenty-one days, which caused such low tides in the river, that the grass froze to the ice everywhere; and, a thaw coming on suddenly, the whole was raised by the roots, and carried off by the fresh.

The next winter, a few of these Ducks were seen, but they soon went away again; and, for many years after, they continued to be scarce; and, even to the present day, in the opinion of my informant, have never been so plenty as before.

The Canvass-Back, in the rich, juicy tenderness of its flesh, and its delicacy of flavor, stands unrivalled by the whole of its tribe in this or perhaps any other quarter of the world. Those killed in the waters of the Chesapeake are generally esteemed superior to all others, doubtless from the great abundance of their favorite food which these rivers produce.

At our public dinners, hotels, and particular entertainments, the Canvass-Backs are universal favorites. They not only grace but dignify the table, and their very name conveys to the imagination of the eager epicure the most comfortable and exhilarating ideas. Hence, on such occasions, it has not been uncommon to pay from one to three dollars a pair for these Ducks; and, indeed, at such times, if they can, they must be had, whatever may be the price.

The Canvass-Back will feed readily on grain, especially wheat, and may be decoyed to particular places by baiting them with that grain for several successive days. Some few years since, a vessel loaded with wheat was wrecked near the entrance of Great Egg Harbor [New Jersey], in the autumn, and went to pieces. The wheat floated out in vast quantities, and the whole surface of the bay was in a few days covered with Ducks of a kind altogether unknown to the people of that quarter. The gunners of the neighborhood collected in boats, in every direction, shooting them; and so successful were they, that, as Mr. Beasley informs me, two hundred and forty were killed in one day, and sold among the neighbors, at twelve and a half cents apiece, without the feathers. The wounded ones were generally abandoned, as being too difficult to be come up with.

They continued for about three weeks, and during the greater part of that time a continual cannonading was heard from every quarter. The gunners called them Sea Ducks. They were all Canvass-Backs, at that time on their way from the north, when this floating feast attracted their attention, and for a while arrested them in their course. A pair of these very Ducks I myself bought in Philadelphia market at the time, from an Egg Harbor gunner, and never met with their superior, either in weight or excellence of flesh. When it was known among those people the loss they had sustained in selling for twenty-five cents what would have brought them from a dollar to a dollar and a half per pair, universal surprise and regret were naturally enough excited.

Wilson's narrative suggests that so far as the Chesapeake and canvasback hunting are concerned, the "good old days" were not the 1880s, but the 1700s, and perhaps even earlier.

The canvasback is a large (a big male will weigh 3½ pounds), swift-flying (cans have been clocked at speeds in excess of 55 miles per hour), and still succulent (when fed on its namesake, wild celery or *Vallisneria*) bird. Although tremendous gunning pressure from market and recreational hunters alike has done much to ravage the canvasback, its specialized breeding requirements (the can prefers shallow prairie potholes surrounded by cattails, without woods, and with sufficient open water for easy takeoffs and landings), its susceptibility to nest parasitism by redhead ducks (hatching rates decrease in parasitized nests, and female cans may abandon such nests), its staggeringly high juvenile mortality (approximately 77 percent *after fledging),* and the unusually high mortality of adult females (as much as 25 percent higher than males) are the main reasons this species may never recover its place as North America's premier diving duck.

This possibility makes the wording of the duck stamp law in Maryland—the state where most canvasbacks winter—all the more disheartening. This law stipulates that state duck stamp revenues can neither be spent on research, which could help save the canvasback, nor on wetlands acquisition, which may help save some of the beleaguered bird's equally beleaguered wintering habitat, but must be spent only on the release of mallards or other easily reared dabblers to give Maryland waterfowlers something to shoot at, since they can no longer hunt canvasbacks.

A little over a decade ago, when it was still legal to shoot cans, a group of fellow instructors at the U.S. Naval Academy and I leased some shoreline along the Choptank River on Maryland's Eastern Shore. We had excellent hunting, and although we shot occasional geese and puddle ducks of various denominations, our greatest thrill was in watching squadrons of canvasbacks, composed mostly of the handsome drakes with their chestnut heads and ruby eyes, speed upriver to our decoys, flare in concert as we stood to shoot, and then be swiftly out of range after we saluted the regal birds.

One wintry day in Annapolis, I ran into one of Maryland's better known Eastern Shore politicians, and, as hunters will, we began comparing notes on the season just past. When he found I hunted not far from the town of Secretary, he scoffed, "Nothing but diving ducks up there. Damned canvasback aren't fit to eat since they started eating clams, and since the feds got so particular about us feeding 'em corn. If we aren't allowed to bait 'em, I say to hell with 'em. The sooner the canvasback are gone, the better. We're going to replace them with mallards."

I was appalled. I didn't know where to begin a rebuttal—with the fact that all waterfowl don't fit the same ecological niche; with the suggestion that cans were still far more tasty and better sport than the pen-raised and chemically-enriched mallards the politician had in mind; or the thought that Maryland sportsmen have what amounts to a historical obligation to the canvasback.[2] Instead I said lamely, "I think you're wrong," and changed the subject. Several years later it didn't surprise me to learn that this influential ignoramus was one of the sponsors of the Maryland (mallard) duck stamp act. But it's our fault: Sportsmen should never allow politicians to control the purse string in wildlife management.

Redhead

The life history of the redhead *(Aythya americana)* helps prove that waterfowl have a sense of humor—not that there is anything funny about redheads, possibly as many as half the breeding hens laying their eggs in other ducks' nests. The funny part is that a broad assortment of other waterfowl, doubtless fed up with redheads trying to sneak into their nests every time their tails are turned, make a point of dropping their eggs in redhead nests! Such part-time parasites include the fulvous whistling duck, gadwall, mallard, pintail, cinnamon teal, shoveler, canvasback (revenge must be especially sweet for this species), lesser scaup, and ruddy duck.

Why the redhead is such a compulsive user of other duck nests is one of the mysteries of waterfowldom. This habit offers no apparent advantage to

[2] Maryland sportsmen once respected this obligation. Back in the early years of Ducks Unlimited, when Glenn L. Martin was a vice-president, trustee, and state chairman of that conservation organization, Baltimore and Eastern Shore contributors built a project in Manitoba called Lake Maryland specifically to increase the breeding potential of canvasback.

Up to 78 percent of all the redhead ducks in existence winter along the Gulf Coast straddling the Texas and Mexican borders. Thirty years ago, when this photograph was made, that meant millions of birds. Today concentrations of a few hundred thousand are rare. (Note pintail flying from left to right above redheads.) *(Photograph courtesy U.S. Fish and Wildlife Service)*

the species. And since what amounts to conscientious parenthood among redheads results in barely fledged young being abandoned by their mothers at seven weeks of age (before they are able to fly), it is a wonder the redhead still exists. When you .add the low hatching ratio of eggs laid in other species' nests to the very high mortality rate of the young (as much as 80 to 94 percent for the year following juvenile banding and averaging 50 percent per year thereafter), it is remarkable there are still enough redheads reproducing (haphazard, as they may be) to provide an annual hunting harvest for the U.S. and Canada of approximately 150,000 birds.

Biologist Milton W. Weller [3] believes the redhead evolved in the alkaline areas of the American Southwest. This theory helps explain why, after the center of this species' breeding range shifted to the upper prairie

[3] Incidentally, Weller contributed the chapter on "Molts and Plumages of Waterfowl" in Frank C. Bellrose's excellent revision and update of Francis H. Kortright's classic *The Ducks, Geese and Swans of North America.*

Redhead ducks are the worst of waterfowl parents. So little devotion does the hen show her eggs or young, it is a wonder the species evolved in the first place! *(Photograph by Glen Smart)*

pothole country of Canada and the upper midwestern United States, the redhead still prefers to migrate to the Texas coast for the winter instead of following its nesting neighbor, the canvasback, to the Atlantic and Pacific coasts. Up to 78 percent of all the redheads extant gather each winter in Laguna Madre from below Matagorda, Texas, to La Pesca, Mexico. About 12 percent winter from the Chesapeake to Pamlico Sound, 5 percent are found in coastal Florida, and the remaining 5 percent are scattered from the Great Lakes to California.

Even when a redhead hen decides to nest, no species of waterfowl is as lackadaisical about nest-building or protecting its young. Apparently, all a gull, crow, or magpie has to do to eat a redhead egg or duckling is to fly down and ask for it. The hen redhead waddles aside, seemingly happy to be rid of her additional responsibilities. About the only good thing to be said for such a casual attitude toward perpetuation of its kind is that when redheads find an optimum breeding area—which means lots of alkali and hardstem bulrushes—the tolerance of breeding pairs for one another is so great that as many as five nests may be found per acre.

Unfortunately, such optimum breeding habitat is in short supply, and one cannot but wonder whether the redhead's push north and east into more acidic environments was not an evolutionary error which the species is paying for today in generally declining numbers. Each spring, fewer than 700,000 birds are distributed over their scattered and shrinking breeding grounds, when just three decades ago close to two million birds made up the spring migration. Overshooting and man's alteration of the environment are the principal reasons for the redhead's decline, yet, surely, the confirmed indifference of the females toward reproduction has not helped the situation.

Ring-Necked Duck

When discussing the ring-necked duck *(Aythya collaris)*, I'm glad I'm not a taxonomist. For one thing, I prefer the popular names "blackjack" or "ringbill," because this species has all the adrenocorticotrophic connotations of "blackjack," and because "ringbill" offers no confusion with pheasants or mallards—the latter being the only proper "ring-necked duck," since the faint gold collar of the male ringbill duck in nuptial plumage is not always discernible but the white collar of the mature drake mallard always is. Furthermore, the pale whitish ring near the tip of the bill will separate both sexes of ringbill ducks from their most abundant look-alikes, the lesser and greater scaup. However, since *collaris* means "collared" in Latin, some scientists would rather fight than switch.

Furthermore, if I were merely an objective recorder of wing and culmen lengths, I could not say, as I will, that the ringbill is one of my very favorite waterfowl, going back to some well-spent days in my youth gunning from small boats along the south shore of Lake Okeechobee, Florida, with water hyacinth piled everywhere to make the cartopper look like just another floating island. Out in front were a dozen to twenty scaup and mallard decoys, made of wood when we first hunted out of Fisheating Creek in the late 1940s, and gradually evolving into wax-impregnated cardboard, then plastic as the 1950s progressed into the early 60s, by which time the U.S. Army Corps of Engineers had tampered enough with the levels of the lake to ruin forever what had been one of the finest waterfowling grounds in the South.

Until the mid-1950s, most every dawn was whispered in by the rush of air through ducks' wings as birds began trading in the rose-hallowed darkness. By full light, the skies overhead would be crossed with flights of birds at different altitudes, darting in different directions. Occasionally a smudge on the horizon would materialize into a flock of ringbills, which swooshed over the decoys, were greeted by a barrage of shot from my father's double, my older brother's semiautomatic, and my own bolt-action Mossberg, before racing on their way again, perhaps, leaving one or more of their number behind—dead, but not knowing it—paddling feebly at the sunrise.

Blackjack are small birds. Most weigh less than two pounds. However, one bright, windy day, after a flock swept over the decoys and we had spilled four, we found their combined weight was just about ten pounds. Sometimes there was skim ice on the creek at dawn. But by ten o'clock, we'd be stripped to shirt sleeves and tennis shoes for wading after coots and cripples. If we still didn't have our limits by noon, we went bass fishing or started home. Since opportunity and practice make for confirmed water-fowling habits in later years, I owe much of my love of duck huting to the ringbills of Lake Okeechobee.

Like the green-winged teal—known as "a pound of butter" in the mid-Atlantic—the little ringbill is one of the most delicious birds flying. Its largely vegetarian diet is one reason, but its small size is another. Like the tiny teal, the ringbill is tender as well as tasty, and as anyone can attest who has eaten a flavorful, but tough Canada goose, texture counts for much in the realm of culinary excellence.

The ringbill has a Eurasian cousin known as the tufted duck *(A. fuligula),* whose lack of a white vertical bar between the male's black back and chest and the presence of a drooping crest on the head separates this species from the male ringbill. However, the hens are another matter. In fact, the hen redhead, because of her faintly ringed bill, is easily confused with both the hen ringbill and the hen tufted duck. Even when specimens are in hand, the color differences described in field guides are often ignored by the birds themselves.

Identification, as with birding generally, is a matter of circumstance as well as plumage. Ring-billed ducks are rarely shot over salt or brackish waters. On the other hand, once redheads reach their wintering grounds, they rarely stray far from salt-tainted water, except for that exasperating five percent of the population which winters between the Great Lakes and California. The tufted duck looks more like the ringbill, but prefers a coastal environment with, perhaps, even more salt in it than redheads prefer. If you kill a tufted duck of either sex (lots of luck in verifying the hen), notify the U.S. Fish and Wildlife Service's Office of Migratory Bird Management, Laurel, Maryland 20811. Send a wing, photograph, or both. If you want to keep the wing and mount the bird, I'm sure the biologists won't mind. They merely need confirmation that an individual of this exotic species has once again strayed to North American shores.

Compared to the redhead, the hen ringbill is the very embodiment of maternal enthusiasm. Although little or no nest may be evident when she starts to lay her eggs, by the time the job is complete, the hen ringbill has created a nest, added down, built a ramp or runway leading to it from the water, and woven overhead vegetation into a thatch roof to screen the eggs from the elements and the eyes of avian predators. Once the eggs hatch, contrary to the behavior of most other species of waterfowl the ringbill will bring her young back to the nest for brooding purposes for several days after hatching. She seems almost reluctant to abandon her well-made structure.

The number of ringbills shot every autumn by Canadian and American hunters is steadily increasing and presently averages over half a million. Indeed, the ringbill harvest may soon exceed that of the black duck, whose preference for breeding near forested ponds or bogs and making dusk foraging flights is closely approximated by the ringbill. Biologists are not sure what the gradual rise in ringbill harvest portends. Is the species extending its range, as some authorities contend, or was the ringbill for many decades confused with the lesser scaup and reported as such by hunters—thus invalidating earlier records? Both these considerations are possible. Yet there is another, perhaps more significant reason for the increased kill. Up until greater affluence and mobility altered the economy and recreational interests of people living in the southeastern United States, duck hunting was not such a popular sport in that region as it is today. Back in the late forties and early fifties, for example, we had Lake Okeechobee pretty much to ourselves. Local small-game hunters concentrated on quail, dove, and rabbit, and some thought we were plumb crazy to risk our lives on the big lake just to shoot ducks. Many of the ringbills we used to see by the countless thousands at Okeechobee are now being "short stopped" by the dozens of large, new freshwater impoundments scattered across Alabama, Georgia, Tennessee, the Carolinas, and Virginia—and being hunted by countless thousands of new waterfowlers in those states. When the wood duck passed the black duck in harvest totals for the Atlantic Flyway, that fact told us as much about how the new South was discovering its waterfowling opportunities as it did about the success of the wood duck

Since scaup of both species have gradually replaced canvasback and redheads as the most heavily harvested pochards, considerable research has been carried out to ensure sufficient production of these valuable birds. Here at Delta Waterfowl Research Station in Manitoba, hand-woven Dutch baskets are used by nesting scaup. *(Photograph by Rex Gary Schmidt)*

nesting box effort and the decline of the black duck. After all, more than half the woodies harvested in the entire Atlantic Flyway are shot in the Carolinas, Georgia, and Florida, just as more than 90 percent of all the ringbills killed in the flyway are taken in those four states, with nearly 75,000 ringbills killed in Florida alone.

Scaup

The greater scaup *(A. marila)* is found throughout the subarctic and temperate zones of the Northern Hemisphere. Various subspecies exist, but only an expert with calipers and classification keys can tell them apart. The specific name, *marila,* means "charcoal" in Greek and refers to the vermiculated gray back of the male—an unfortunate reference, since this marking is identical on the lesser scaup *(A. affinis)* and cannot be used to distinguish the species.

Along the Atlantic and Pacific coasts, where the wintering ranges of the greater and lesser scaup overlap, gunners call the greater scaup (which reaches a maximum weight of 3 pounds) the *broadbill;* the lesser scaup (which weighs a maximum of 2½ pounds) is the *bluebill.* Unfortunately, elsewhere in the nation, either scaup may be called "bluebill" or "broadbill," for, in fact, the bills of both scaups are grayish-blue as well as broad. However, the lesser scaup's bill is almost narrow at the base of the bill when compared to the greater scaup's. Yet unless you have representatives of both species in hand, about the only way to tell them apart—aside from the not-always-present purplish gloss of the male lesser scaup's head, contrasted with the not-always-evident greenish gloss of the male greater scaup's head—is by your hunting location.

Just as it is a safe bet that any ring-billed pochard you kill over salt or brackish water is a redhead, any scaup you kill on or near the sea is probably a broadbill. Then just as any ring-billed pochard killed over fresh water is likely to be a ringbill, any scaup you kill over fresh water is likely to be a bluebill.

Having come up with that brilliant scheme for distinguishing species, I now have to confess there are several outstanding exceptions—such as the excellent greater scaup shooting available on the Great Lakes and the equally fine lesser scaup shooting along the Gulf Coast. However, once it is appreciated that greater scaup rarely wander south of the coastal Carolinas in the East or San Francisco Bay in the West, while lesser scaup regularly migrate all the way to Colombia, South America, this helps refine the context of identification according to area.

Contrary to many an old-timer's claim that the word *scaup* refers to the duck's rasping call, the name is an ancient one of Teutonic origin and related to the Old Dutch and French words for scallops, *schelpe* and *escalope* respectively. The Holarctic greater scaup is more largely dependent on shellfish than the lesser scaup—hence, the reason the lesser scaup is generally preferred as table fare—and blue mussels and dwarf surf clams, but few scallops, may make up more than 90 percent of the diet of broadbill wintering in the mid-Atlantic.

Scaup, like teal, have an undeserved reputation for stupidity. Scaup hunters as often make this accusation because the birds didn't come to their decoys as because they did! A scaup hunter may spend thousands of dollars on a large stool of decoys, a gunning rig complete with outboard motor and trailer, then travel a considerable distance to put himself smack in the middle of prime scaup waters. But because the birds do not always cooperate when the hunter is ready for them, the hunter insists the birds are stupid!

In reality, scaup are neither very crafty nor credulous. They, like all wintering waterfowl, are preoccupied by food and sex. (In the spring the birds are preoccupied by sex and food.) Since food and company make the wintering scaup's world complete, unless a hunter is stooled out very near a mussel bed or anchored under a flyway between the birds' rafting and feeding areas, he might as well be on the moon for all the good his decoys and floating blind will do him. Furthermore, even when the hunter has set out one hundred decoys, if a flying scaup sees a distant flock of 1,000 or 10,000 birds (a not uncommon concentration for these species), the hunter will be lucky to draw that singleton to his decoys.

Back in 1939, Clarence Cottam, in a Bureau of Biological Survey study called *Food Habits of North American Diving Ducks,* noted that when greater scaup are hard-pressed by hunters, they develop nocturnal feeding habits not unlike harried black ducks. That is, the scaup fly far to sea just before dawn, raft up and rest during the day, and then return at night, particularly moonlit nights, to forage over mussel and clam beds long after water-fowlers have gone home.

There is probably no place the broadbill is more assiduously hunted in its entire range than the mid-Atlantic region between northern New Jersey and southern New England. For literally tens of thousands of hunters living in that stretch of megalopolis, the greater scaup is their most important game bird. Such enormous hunting pressure has only reinforced the value of Cottam's observations 40 years ago. Unless you own an island in Long Island Sound or are able to pick your time off so as to hunt on windy days following overcast nights, greater scaup can be as frustrating a quarry as black ducks.

My brothers and I learned that our only way to "guarantee" shooting (which means a shot or two at least every other trip) was to hunt during January freezes in the inlets along the south shore of Long Island as the

The vision of artist and photographer merge into one dream of a young man's first hunt for the wings of dawn. *(Photograph by David W. Corson)*

The blue-winged teal is one of North America's most abundant waterfowl, but because it migrates south as early as August, major segments of this species's population are already in Cuba and Mexico when hunting seasons begin in the United States. *(Photograph by O. T. Fears)*

The cinnamon teal is the crown jewel of our western flyways. Although closely related to the blue-winged teal and although their nesting ranges overlap in the Pacific Northwest, the two species rarely hybridize. *(Photograph by Glen Smart)*

The common goldeneye is one of the wariest of waterfowl. Although occasionally shot by hunters after other ducks, best hunting results are obtained by using well constructed and skillfully painted goldeneye facsimiles. *(Photo by Glen Smart)*

One of the soul-stirring sights of waterfowling is a flight of pintail at dawn. Their whistling calls and wings create chills that have nothing to do with the frosty air. *(Photograph by George Reiger)*

Even when teal are on the water, they rarely seem to rest. Their small bodies need constant fueling, and from dawn to dusk they hustle from one potential feeding ground to another. *(Photograph by George Reiger)*

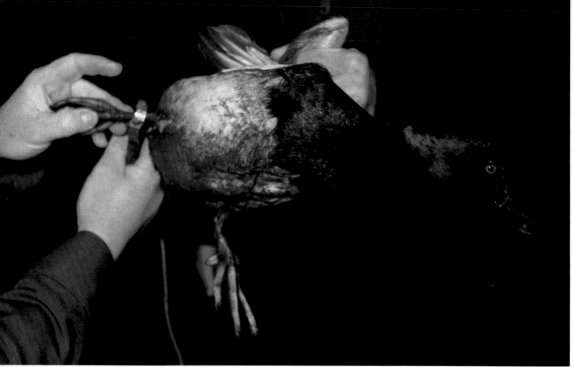

Waterfowl are remarkably hardy birds. This redhead drake was found by the author's dog after a falcon, or utility wire strung across the marsh had torn its scalp so it hung down over the bird's eyes and he couldn't fly. The author sewed back the scalp and within a week the redhead was bullying a pen full of mallards. Here he is being banded prior to release. *(Photograph by George Reiger)*

Not all black ducks behave with supernatural savvy. Some birds, like the one being retrieved by Rod Hennessey on the Virginia coast, glide out of nowhere on a sun-lit afternoon to a spread of paper-mache decoys. However, such individuals invariably turn out to be juveniles. You won't get experienced redlegs hunting like this! *(Photograph by George Reiger)*

The drake hooded merganser is a phantasmagoric bird. In flight, he is streamlined and swift and frequently mistaken for other, non-merganser waterfowl. On the water, a courting male pumps and shakes and throws up his crest almost to appear ridiculous, if he weren't also beautiful. *(Photograph by Glen Smart)*

Thanks to modern farming methods, Canada geese have become a major component of the wings of dawn in all four flyways. *(Photograph by Clark G. Webster)*

Right (facing page): Mallards will make their home in most any environment, but there is something special about flooded timber—as well as the pleasure of hunting them there. *(Photograph by Clark G. Webster)*

A golden retriever "walking on water" toward a fallen green-winged teal. Returning with the bird is not so important, so he decided to swim back. *(Photographs by George Reiger)*

American widgeon (alias, baldpate) can be one of the most frustrating birds to decoy as they will circle and circle and circle before making up their minds—if then—to come in. But when they do, oh, my, how the hunter's heart beats faster! *(Photograph by George Reiger)*

Left (facing page): When jump shooters describe mallards as "exploding" off the water, they aren't exaggerating. A hand grenade might throw less water than these birds are doing! *(Photograph by Clark G. Webster)*

The color of John Gottschalk's clothing is more suitable for a late season cattail marsh than an early season cedar blind. However, he has done what he could to disguise himself and stayed at the back of the blind until the Canadas were within range. *(Photograph by George Reiger)*

Success! A proud moment for a dog and his hunter is when their combined skills and opportunity result in a goose for Christmas dinner. *(Photograph by George Reiger)*

Greater snow geese have increased to the point they will uproot the backsides of fragile barrier islands. Thus, a hunting season was begun in the Atlantic Flyway after more than half a century of total protection. Note the black "grinning patch" on the bill of the bird lying on the ice. This, and not their calling, was the reason colonial hunters called them "laughing geese." *(Photograph by George Reiger)*

The fulvous whistling duck is more closely related to the swans than ducks, and is found increasingly in hunter's bags from southern Florida along the Gulf Coast to Mexico. *(Photograph by Glen Smart)*

While brant declined, the greater snow goose increased, thanks
largely to the abundance of *Spartina alterniflora,* or salt marsh
grass, which composes the bulk of this species' winter diet. Note
the bird in the upper center calling; a flock sounds like a distant
pack of dogs. *(Photograph by Mel M. Baughman)*

The heyday of the Atlantic brant seems
to be gone, along with the lush beds of
eelgrass that once flourished from New
England to North Carolina. Today this
species survives by picking *Ulva* and
other algae from the mud. *(Photograph by
George Reiger)*

Above: Flocks of Canada geese in fields of winter wheat or rye are not nearly so satisfying a sight to the farmer as to the friends he invites over to help him "move the birds out." *(Photograph by George Reiger)*

Left: Most hunters find time to do the neighborly thing when they hear a farmer is in trouble. Here a group waits for legal shooting time–and for the birds to fly a little lower. Michael J. O'Neill, publisher of *Field & Stream,* watches at far left. *(Photograph by George Reiger)*

The most perfect Canada goose habitat, as far as the goose is concerned, is a flooded farmfield in October. *(Photograph by Clark G. Webster)*

Even after the snow starts flying, Canada geese will linger up north as long as they can find open water (sometimes provided by the cooling-water discharge pipes of power plants) and sufficient food beneath the snow. *(Photograph by Clark G. Webster)*

The old expression about "looking beautiful when you're mad" applies to this drake wood duck. At the same time, his white fringed crest and fierce eyes do give the bird a slightly Satanic expression, and we can understand why the hen mallard seems taken aback. *Below:* Once the interloper has been driven away, the drake flails and stretches in triumph. *(Photographs by Clark G. Webster)*

Much of modern waterfowling is done within sight of man's "improvements," including this home along Virginia's intracoastal waterway. Jack Samson, editor of *Field & Stream,* swings on a fast-flying goldeneye. One of the dogs is paying attention; the other is busy mugging for the camera. *(Photograph by George Reiger)*

Northern Alberta provides some of the best waterfowl nesting habitat in North America. More than 30 breeding pairs of ducks and geese can be found here per square mile. The good news is that this area lies far north of most drainage schemes. The bad news is that the area lies close to one of the continent's major tar-sands development sites. *(Photograph by George Reiger)*

broadbill poured out from the bays behind the barrier islands at first light in undulating lines that sometimes stretched from horizon to horizon. Occasional pieces of line—mere punctuation marks—would peel off and descend toward our decoys where the commas and dashes turned into ensembles of 60 or 80 birds that swirled around us and were often gone before we could fire twice. Once when the birds bunched, five ducks were killed with two simultaneous shots. More often we were lucky to stop one apiece.

Since the birds' speed was sometimes greater than our reflexes, we crippled scaup that bounced or cartwheeled along the water and disappeared in a dive even before getting their bearings at the surface. Haunted by this loss of wounded birds, we sometimes hunted our limits around the rocky groins and jetties where cripples would retreat to feed on whatever mussels or other food items they could scrape from the stony surfaces. The melancholy of this activity was increased when we found the remains of birds to which the rats had beaten us.

Since scaup are to mid-Atlantic waterfowling what peanut-butter-and-jelly sandwiches are to school lunch boxes, and since the Reiger boys once spent a good many dawns to dusks in Long Island marshes, these birds taught us some fundamentals of the sport that we have transferred successfully to other areas of waterfowling. One of the most important of these lessons is the use of monofilament fishing line for anchoring decoys and painting decoy weights to match the natural color of the bottom or an oyster or mussel cluster. In any event, we learned to avoid hunting with shiny, new decoy weights and colored lines that can be seen easily from the air against a lighter (or darker) bottom background. If you forget to paint or weather your weights before season opens, at least stomp them as far down in the mud as your booted heel will drive them. If you're in water too deep for that, count your blessings and trust to luck.

The monofilament trick was learned many years ago while Tony, John, and I were hunting over the sand bottom and winter-clear waters of Fire Island Inlet. Despite several flights of birds, we hadn't gotten a shot. The incoming ducks all flared well out of range. A few circled for another look, confirmed their suspicions, and flew on. We were baffled. We were, even then, meticulous hunters, and despite a thorough inspection of ourselves, the blind, and the immediate vicinity, we couldn't see what was wrong. The birds continued to flare out of range. Tony, my older brother, sought out a vantage point behind and slightly above the stool and discovered that in the bright sun and clear water, our tarred cotton decoy lines were harsh black lines against the pale bottom.

John and I weren't convinced that was the problem, but since we had nothing to lose but more potential shooting, Tony went back to the car and returned with a spool of 20-pound-test monofilament fishing line. Meanwhile John and I had pulled in the decoys and cut off the cod line. Within an hour of rerigging the decoys, each of us had his limit. More important, we had our evidence: Not a single incoming flight had flared away.

Today we use 30- to 50-pound-test monofilament (anything heavier gets stiff and unwieldy on cold days) with weather-dulled brass swivels at both the decoy and sinker ends to keep the line from twisting. If we plan to shoot over a rock or oyster-shell bottom, we'll tie in a short length of heavy braided line between the weight and the monofilament to reduce losses due to line abrasion.[4] If you do all your gunning over mud bottoms, a brown or dark green nylon line may suffice. However, since I travel a good deal and use my decoys in a variety of waters, I'd just as soon be rigged for any contingency. Our days afield are all too few, and I'm sure you'd rather have some other excuse for not getting shots than something as easily controlled as the visibility of your decoy lines.

Mergini

"Sea Ducks" include eiders, harlequin ducks, oldsquaws, scoters, buf-flehead, goldeneyes, and mergansers. Like the term "freshwater diving ducks," the expression "sea ducks" is far from adequate. Although all species of Mergini (which simply means "diver" in Latin) may be found along sea coasts, not all individuals of a given species will migrate to the coast. Hooded and common mergansers frequently spend their winters on inland lakes and rivers, and the bufflehead and goldeneyes may offer excellent hunting many hundreds of miles from the nearest sea. "Sea ducks" are regularly shot by waterfowlers in Vermont, Ohio, Nebraska, and Nevada.

---

4 Du Pont Stren has just developed an abrasion-resistant monofilament that may obviate this precaution.

Few people outside Alaska have ever seen wild steller eiders. Any sighted in the lower 48 states should be reported immediately to the nearest chapter of the National Audubon Society. If the bird has been shot, any natural history museum would be happy to acquire the skin for its collection. *(Photograph by Glen Smart)*

Eiders

Having said all that, the first group of birds belonging to this tribe are almost exclusively coastal birds. Your chances of killing a common eider *(Somateria mollissima)* in the Midwest are pretty remote—but not impossible. After all, there are a few hearty souls who annually hunt the "wolf's nose" of Lake Superior and harvest an average of 30 birds per season off St. Louis County, Minnesota, and 15 birds per year off Bayfield County, Wisconsin. Not many, perhaps, but indicative of what else might be done in the way of "sea duck" shooting in the Great Lakes.

Along the Atlantic coast, the king eider *(S. spectabilis)* shares a wintering range from Labrador to southern New England with the common eider, while the latter species strays as far south as North Carolina. Every winter, one or more common eiders (sometimes a dozen) can be found diving for mollusks around the artificial islands of the Chesapeake Bay Bridge-Tunnel. The other eiders—the spectacled *(S. fischeri)* and the steller *(Polysticta stelleri)*—winter in Alaskan waters and rarely stray south of Kodiak Island.[5]

Elsewhere in the United States, eider hunting is principally a tradition of coastal Maine and Massachusetts. Such hunting is bitterly cold and often dangerous sport and has been immortalized in Lawrence Sargent Hall's

[5] In 1977, an aberrant steller eider showed up off Scituate, Massachusetts, and stayed many weeks just off the beach. Even more extraordinary, a smew *(Mergus albellus)*—a rare and strikingly beautiful Eurasian merganser—straggled into a pond near Newport, Rhode Island in the winter of 1976-77—and then reappeared the following winter!

O. Henry Award-winning short story, "The Ledge," a tale about a skilled hunter who takes his son and his son's friend eider shooting one December day, but in making one tiny error, the man costs all three of them (and a dog) their lives.

Because eider hunting is rigorous sport, younger men do not seem to be taking it up with the same enthusiasm once shown by their grandfathers. The Christmas custom of running the family lobster boat to an offshore islet, anchoring the boat, and using a dory or dinghy to row to the island, put out decoys, and retrieve the downed birds, is disappearing Down East. Certainly, the popularity of "coot stew," which features diced portions of eider and scoter, is waning, for a love of such table fare is an acquired taste, and fewer youngsters today have the opportunity to acquire such a taste.[6]

Old eider decoys are turning up in antique shops and decoy shows as old gunners clear out the attic, barn, or boat shed. Since you need to make eider decoys from large pieces of reasonably dense wood so they will ride white-crested swells in a natural manner, and since such wood is not as readily available as it once was, decoys sold to collectors are not easily replaced. Certainly no mass production manufacturer of foam or plastic birds is making eider decoys. Although eiders will stool to white plastic bleach bottles, it is common sense that realistic replicas will draw the most birds.

Although the common eiders which nest in Maine are not tended as nesting birds are in Iceland (the word *eider* comes from the Icelandic *ejdar),* where down is an important export item, the Maine eider population has been growing at an impressive rate. Around Muscongus Bay, nesting eiders have increased from an estimated 800 birds in 1949 to more than 8,000 today. This ten-fold increase has been in the face of severe predation of eider eggs and young by gulls, crows, ravens, and foxes.

Eiders are probably the deepest divers of all waterfowl. Although mergansers, due to their fish diet, are doubtless more agile and swift underwater, a king eider was recorded diving in 180 feet of water and returning with mollusks in its gullet. Earlier in this century, oldsquaw were taken in the Great Lakes from gill-nets set for lake trout at similarly great depths. However, whether the oldsquaw were taken at the top of the net or near

[6] For sea duck recipes, see Appendix.

the bottom was never certain. Rather than argue over which species can actually do the deeper diving trick, suffice, to say that both king eiders and oldsquaw can dive to great depths, possibly exceeding 200 feet if the need arises. For the waterfowler, such impressive diving skills only hint at the difficulty of trying to recover a crippled sea duck.

Harlequin Duck

Histrionicus histrionicus means "the actor" or "clown," repeated. Yet the harlequin duck is neither an actor nor a clown; the male only looks that way. While less pretty than the wood duck, the drake harlequin's swatches of white and autumn red on a slate blue body make him one of the most decorative of all waterfowl.

I feel a little like George Washington confessing to having cut down the cherry tree when I talk about the harlequin duck. One sunny winter morning at Jones Beach Inlet, Long Island, many long years ago, while I sat on a jetty photographing my younger brother in his cartop boat picking up two broadbill he had just shot, John began to wave and point at a pair of birds flying toward the decoys. I thought John was merely indicating two more scaup were on the wing, in case I wanted to try for one with the shotgun lying across my lap.

The birds were good photographic subjects as they swept along the jetty and swung toward the decoys. I took one picture as they passed between John and the shore, another as they swung upwind toward me, and then—quicker than I can describe it—I dropped the camera (fortunately on a strap around my neck), picked up my shotgun, and killed the drake as the birds began to flare back toward the inlet. They were harlequin ducks, and in that instant when I had a choice between another shot with the camera or a shot with the gun—between recording on film the presence of harlequin ducks far south of their normal wintering range along the Canadian and northern New England coasts, and collecting more tangible proof of their visit—I opted for the tangible proof.

John rowed over, picked up the dead bird, and, when he pulled ashore, we admired its stunning plumage. About an hour later, with the bird safely wrapped in burlap with my handkerchief between its mandibles to blot up any blood that might otherwise stain the feathers, John saw what he first thought was a group of surveyors coming down the beach. As they got closer, we could see binoculars and spotting scopes atop the tripods they carried, and we realized it was a party of birders.

The group stopped opposite us to discuss something. Then a contingent of three marched to our shelter in the rocks and asked whether we knew what a harlequin duck was. Yes, we replied. Had we seen a pair that morning? John and I looked at one another, and after a moment's pause, pride and curiosity overcame discretion. I opened the burlap and carefully took out the dead bird.

The delegation of three got very excited and called over their friends, and there followed a memorable scene in which half the birders were so shocked by the sight of the dead harlequin they would have nothing to do with us, and the other birders were so thrilled to have an opportunity to hold a harlequin and examine its amazing plumage, heavy feet, and surprisingly delicate bill, they didn't notice that their erstwhile colleagues and friends had moved off a little distance to disassociate themselves from the scene. Unfortunately for the purists, who had apparently come in cars driven by people admiring the harlequin, there was no escape until the enthusiasts were ready to go. All the satellite contingent could do was fume amongst themselves and give us killing looks.

As it turns out, the purists were revenged. I saved the bird for a renowned taxidermist who had done an excellent job on a widgeon I had given him the previous year. Tragically, this man was a better taxidermist than a naturalist, and I found out too late that all his waterfowl ended up looking like dabbling ducks—stretched neck, fanned tail, et cetera.

Not long ago, I was in Alaska fishing a remote and narrow tributary of the Yukon. The water was high and swift, the hour late (though still well lighted by the midnight sun), and the blackflies and mosquitoes were active, even if the trout and grayling were not. However, I wanted to work one last pool before calling it quits and had just made a cast upstream when winging around the bend came the unmistakable form of a harlequin drake. The bird passed within inches of my extended rod tip, and the wind from his wings caused the slender shaft of bamboo to nod gently in my hand. As quickly as the duck appeared, he was gone.

I retrieved the nymph I had been drifting, clipped it off, and started downstream. To hook even a grayling at that point would have been anticlimactic, for this time I had let my mind's eye do the collecting. No mounting, no diorama, could ever fix that vision of wilderness to satisfy my mortal memory.

Oldsquaw

Clangula hyemalis means a "wintry noise," but only infrequently does a sea duck hunter hear the strange "ughs" and "ows" and winnowing wings of these circumpolar birds. Our best recreation comes on those days when the slap of water against an anchored skiff and the wind soughing over the gunwales masks the mysterious mutterings of the drake oldsquaw.

Because oldsquaw regularly winter as far south as Oregon, the Great Lakes, and the Carolinas, they make up a significant part of the sea duck harvest generally aimed at their cousin, the scoters. Oldsquaw are frequently shot so their arctic beauty can be transformed into a flying mount, and competition between hunters who have such specimens is over whose bird has the most perfect markings (the plumage of the males seems to be in continual flux between winter whites and summer browns), and whose drake has the longer tail.

Sea duck hunting has never caught on in the West the way it has in the Atlantic and even Mississippi Flyways. This may be because Pacific Flyway hunters have so many more desirable options in waterfowling than their eastern colleagues. However, it is also possible that the formidable Northwest Pacific coast, with few natural harbors or suitable access points, offers conditions so much more hostile than those known to eastern hunters that some winters they must verge on the impossible.

From Alaska through California, fewer than 1,000 oldsquaw are shot annually, while in the Mississippi Flyway, mostly along the shores of Lake Michigan, over 1,500 are taken every year. This harvest exceeds the Great Lakes' yield for both black and surf scoters, although some winters nearly 5,000 white-winged scoters are taken off such towns as Chicago, Milwaukee, and Sheboygan.

In the Atlantic Flyway, up to 17,000 oldsquaw are killed annually with a surprising number of these taken in the Chesapeake Bay region by hunters stooled out for river ducks and Canada geese. This phenomenon, plus the great abundance of this species on Lake Michigan, suggests the oldsquaw is less of a sea duck than eiders or scoters. There is a mild paradox in

Although some winters more than 20,000 old-squaw are shot throughout North America, the annual worldwide toll from oil pollution is several times higher. In 1976, a relatively minor spill in the Chesapeake killed over 30,000. Many birds sink before coming ashore; others crawl into the beach grass to escape the chilling wind. Pets and wild predators find the stricken birds, eat them, and in turn succumb to the oil. *(Photograph by George Reiger)*

the thought that oldsquaw commonly breed on tundra close to the sea but may prefer a freshwater lake or river for their wintering habitat, while the harlequin duck nests far up subarctic streams, but prefers to forage in heavy surf during the winter months.

Although the oldsquaw is a pert and loquacious fellow, he does not have many friends in the waterfowl world. The species is most commonly shot by scoter and eider hunters, but very rarely will such waterfowlers actually see oldsquaws flying with those other species. In Lake Michigan and the Chesapeake, oldsquaws avoid or are avoided by such other common wintering ducks as scaup and goldeneye. Male oldsquaw are so competitive, even their hens will sometimes not nest in the territories dominated by the aggressive males, some of which seize the same territory year after year even though they will take different mates each year. Although great concentrations of oldsquaw do occur in some areas, such as the half-million birds which annually winter around St. Lawrence Island, Alaska, individuals do not usually "raft up" to the degree that pochards do.

Oldsquaw are superb divers, but their normal foraging depth is under 25 feet. Even at that depth, they don't stay down long. Half a minute becomes a long dive, and fifteen seconds is more like the average. This compares with a ringbill drake I watched one November morning feeding on bottom weeds in a Virginia pond approximately five feet deep. The ringbill would go under for fifteen seconds, then be up for fifteen seconds, then under again for the same amount of time. In one three-minute period, he was off by only twelve seconds in a nearly perfect up-and-down pattern.

The most impressive aspect of the oldsquaw's adaptation to water is not its dives from the surface, but its dives from the air. When fired at, oldsquaw will sometimes fall to the water as though hit, immediately disappear and then come up *flying* some yards away exactly as though they had been launched from below the surface.

The first time this happened to me was off Montauk Point, Long Island, where I shot at one bird in a flock of twenty or so. The entire formation fell to the water and disappeared. Astonished, I stared at the spot where they'd gone in. I imagined my oldsquaw "kill" was some kind of world record for an ounce and a quarter of number 4 shot. Then all the birds popped from the surface about 70 yards from the anchored dory and sped away. It was more than a letdown; those birds had contrived the perfect waterfowler's put-down!

Scoters

There are three scoter species in the world, all of which are found in North America, and one of which, the surf scoter *(Melanitta perspicillata),* breeds only on this continent. The origin of the word *scoter* is something of a mystery, and those hunters in the mid-Atlantic who call the bird "scooter" are not to be mocked for their mispronunciation. That variant, along with "scout" [7] and "scouter," are used in the British Isles and probably date back before the discovery of the New World.

"Coot" and "sea coot" (to distinguish scoters from the freshwater coot or "blue peter") are used by coastal people in Canada and New England, and the English word may be derived from the Dutch *koet.* Certainly it wouldn't take much to get "coot" and "scoot" confused. Science adds its modest increment to the semantic confusion by calling the black scoter *Melanitta nigra* which means "the black duck which is black." Wonderful.

The black scoter *is* the blacest of all North American waterfowl, and the only noticeable color on the drake as he "scoots" close over the foam-flecked surface of the sea is the golden-hued knob at the base of his bill. All scoters have enlarged mandibles, and the grotesque upper bill and head plumage of scoter drakes provide each species with its distinctive trademark. The white-winged scoter *(M. fusca)* has a reversed, horizontal comma around its white eye, and the bill is darkly feathered laterally to a

---

[7] The word *scooter* is, also, applied to a punt fitted with skids or runners for hunting on ice, and *scout* is locally used by the Scots to describe guillemots and razorbill auks as well as scoters. By the way, black, more commonly than white-winged, scoters breed in Great Britain.

point near the rear edge of the nostrils. The tip of the white-winged scoter's bill is amber with pink overtones. Incidentally, the eyes of white-winged and surf scoter males start out brown, like the females', turn yellow during the first year, and then white during the second year when the drake approaches sexual maturity.

The surf scoter appears to be a clown with two white-plumaged skull-caps, one looking as though it is about to slide off the back of the drake's head, the other as though it is about to fall over his pale eyes. The feathered contrast of white on black is responsible for this species's popular name, "skunkhead." The drake's bill is structured like a Roman nose, sloping from the anterior skullcap in a bizarre blend of black, white, and pinkish-orange. Verily, the surf scoter deserves the specific name *perspicullata* a Latin word combining "conspicuous" and "spectacular."

No one is quite certain of the use of the scoters' unusual bill enlargements. Twenty years ago, I collected scoter skulls for Charles H. Rogers, Princeton University's Curator of Ornithology. Rogers was working on a comparative study of the three scoter species, in part concerned with the function of the enlarged area at the base of the bills. While a gland in tube-nosed sea birds such as albatrosses, shearwaters, and petrels helps excrete salt from ocean water so such birds will not dehydrate, it isn't clear whether the scoters' enlargements are for that purpose (if so, why are not oldsquaw and eiders so endowed?) or whether it is principally a breeding symbol.

In February 1976, an oil spill occurred in the Chesapeake Bay which tarred and drowned tens of thousands of sea ducks. During the attempted rehabilitation process, we were forced to put many of the birds in the same, overcrowded cages. We quickly learned to keep male scoters of the same species apart as much as possible, for despite the gravity of their illness (which in almost every case led to death), the drakes would grab and stab at one another, with most blows aimed at their opponents' bills. Obviously this baroque biological feature has some sexual significance. Since the hens of all three species are so similar in appearance, perhaps pair bonds occur when the peculiar shape and color pattern of each drake's head, bill, and eye transmit a signal of compatibility to females of the corresponding species. (There have been worse ornithological theories.)

The black scoter is also known as the common scoter, which intrigued us as youngsters gunning the eastern end of Long Island, where this species was the least common of the three. We assumed black scoters were a hardy breed and, like the eiders, wintered as far north as they could find open water and food. Only after moving to Virginia and spending many hours off the beaches during September and October did I become aware of the great migration of scoters of all species (particularly juveniles) during those months, flowing down the coast each autumn to winter as far south as the Carolinas and Georgia. Sometimes the flocks appear segregated according to species and sex, and I have occasionally seen large flocks of mostly adult male black scoters followed within half a mile by flocks of adult female and/or immature birds. The U.S. Fish and Wildlife Service discovered vast concentrations of wintering scoters off the Georgia coast several years ago, almost by accident, when a pilot wandered many miles offshore instead of confining his waterfowl survey to the Georgia marshes. These deepwater grounds have now become a regular part of the federal government's annual winter survey.

Because scoters are not important species for most waterfowlers, they are a relatively unstudied group of birds. What little we do know about their breeding habits (for example, unlike dabbling ducks, scoters probably start breeding at the end of their second, not first, year), pair-bonding behavior (apparently short-lived), nest locations (under shrubs, always shrubs), clutch size (somewhere between 6 and 12 eggs), and mortality rates (from 5 percent to 95 percent, depending on weather, predation, and estimator) comes from Europe, where researchers are less burdened than their Canadian and American counterparts by the need to justify the utility of their studies. As a result, while what we know about the Holarctic black and white-winged scoters may be termed "fair" (thanks to European research), what we know about the exclusively North American-breeding surf scoter can be termed "zilch."

Some years more than 55,000 scoters are harvested in the Atlantic Flyway. This should come as no surprise to any waterfowler versed in the traditions of sea duck hunting from Maine to Montauk, where the bulk of this kill occurs. What is surprising is that the Mississippi Flyway yields up to 9,000 scoters annually. While much of the hunting is done by a small, but fervent, band of sea duck aficionados living along the Great Lakes, in one recent season, scoters were killed in every state of the flyway but Arkansas.

The states of the Central Flyway are less well endowed with large bodies of water than the other flyways, and this explains why usually fewer than

1,000 scoters each season turn up there in hunters' bags. Likewise, the very long coastline stretching from Alaska to Mexico explains why, with absolutely no sea duck hunting traditions or particular interest in the species, up to 7,000 scoters are killed each year in the Pacific Flyway. In all four flyways, the white-winged scoter leads the harvest totals. Roughly one-third as many black scoters, and three-fourths as many surf scoters, as white-winged scoters make up the continental bag of nearly 75,000 scoters of all three species. (How's that for statistical confusion!)

Harvesting the scoter clan is approximately as important to North American wildfowlers as hunting hooded mergansers and ruddy ducks. However, the specialty of "sea coot" shooting is a ritual and mystery unto itself, whose adherents compose a special niche in the realm of waterfowling. Hooded mergansers and ruddy ducks are almost always shot incidentally—as a substitute for some other target species. Scoters *are* target species.

Although scoter-hunting traditions bring to mind wooden dories and silhouette decoys anchored off a barren cost, the realities of modern-day scoter shooting often include aluminum outboards, blackened bleach bottles, and beach houses, and high-rises along the busy shore. Scoters are diurnal feeders, for they need daylight to find the shellfish that make up between 80 to 100 percent of their winter diets. After a long night of sleeping on deep, open water, the birds fly inshore to feed over mussel and clam banks, and the best shooting is to be had under the flyway between their resting and feeding grounds.

A string or two of black-painted plastic milk or bleach bottles tied off the stern of a trailerable boat will often be sufficient to swing the flying birds close enough for a shot. I've even killed scoters while sitting in plain view in a 17-foot center-console fishing boat after attracting the birds' attention to my bleach-bottle decoys by standing, shouting, and swinging my shotgun back and forth over my head. (You had to be there to believe it!) I think such an unlikely shooting platform and hunter behavior may actually lull the vague suspicions of scoters. The birds frequently pass fishermen in boats while migrating down the coast, and an occupied fishing boat anchored on or near a shellbed is rarely a threat to scoters. On the other hand, you doubtless miss the more wary birds which might be lured to a disguised craft with no one in view and with a few genuine scoter decoys or silhouettes to spice several strings of blackened bleach bottles.

Dress warmly, and as far as feet and hands go, wool is better than down or any synthetic combination. The old-timers knew what they were talking about when they observed that "even when wool gets cold and damp, it's somehow warm and dry." In the frigid, windswept waterscapes where scoters are found, a novice may be forgiven if he feels the sport is better suited to test the stamina of a polar bear than classified as "recreation."

Shotgun Gauges, Chokes, and Shot

Up until now, I've said nothing about shotgun gauges, chokes, and loads because I find most hunters have developed rather fixed opinions on these subjects by the time they are twenty years of age, and because my friend Bob Brister has written the presently definitive word on the matter in his *Shotgunning—The Art and The Science* (Winchester Press, 1976) for those hunters with sufficiently open minds to absorb some well-reasoned and thoroughly documented information.

However, I do have a few fixed opinions of my own, such as that no responsible waterfowler should ever use a .410 or 28-gauge shotgun. Furthermore, unless a 20-gauge shotgun is equipped with 3-inch chambers, it is, also, too light. Sure, I've killed ducks with such feeble artillery, but even when I carefully picked my shots, I was begging for cripples. There is nothing "sporting" about using shotguns which physically cannot pack the punch to kill cleanly and consistently at 40 yards.

My second bias concerns chokes, which are greatly overrated for making a significant difference in how well and how often you kill ducks. Yes, it is better to use an improved cylinder barrel with number 6, 7½, or even 8 shot for teal over decoys, and, sure, you will kill more scoters pass shooting with a full-choke barrel firing number 4 or even 2 shot. However, as Bob Brister demonstrates, the size of the shot, its hardness, and the way it is packed make a far greater difference in your ability to kill ducks than choke size. I stick with a modified choke in all my single-barreled waterfowling guns, because its margin of error is more kind to an ordinary, frequently uneven, shooter like myself than a full-choked gun. At the same time, because it is the rare shooter who can center his target every time, a modified choke is often more kind (because more killing) to the duck than a full choke.

As for the overwhelming importance of the kind of shell you put in the

As artist A. B. Frost knew, the best ducking guns are those that work in all kinds of weather. Back in 1903, that meant single-shot 8- and 10-gauge goose guns and 12-gauge double barrels. Today it takes an exceptional dose of mud, sand, or seawater to keep modern pump guns or semi-automatics from working. The important thing to keep in mind is not to take a finely engraved heirloom into the marsh. You want killing power and reliability in about equal portions. As for good looks, leave those in the closet with your Sunday suit. *(Courtesy Elman Pictorial Collection)*

chamber of your shotgun, read Brister if you want to find out the facts, or be like my friend Fred, if you merely want to be *au courant* of the most fashionable thinking about shotguns and shotgunning. Fred (not his real name) is a prominent outdoor writer who prides himself on his expensive collection of European double-barreled shotguns. His admiration for European craftsmanship extends to clothing, women, automobiles, and shotgun shells. One weekend he arrived at our farm for goose and duck hunting with a case of shotgun shells packed five to a box and loaded with number 6, nickel-plated lead shot.

"These were made especially for the King of Sweden," he announced. "The king uses them to kill everything from swans to swallows."

"The shot size seems a mite small for swans," I suggested, "and a bit large for swallows."

"Not at all," insisted Fred. "It's the nickel plating that makes the difference."

The first morning we hunted greater snow geese. After firing a dozen times at the large birds with little effect, Fred cursed his shells as being inferior export items, stomped the remaining three from one of his Cigarillo-type boxes into the mud, borrowed several 3-inch magnums loaded with number 4 shot from me, and promptly killed his two-bird limit. Meanwhile I discreetly recovered the three mud-stomped shells.

The next afternoon, after a fruitless morning of goose hunting, we went to one of my sea duck blinds where we were kept busy by small flocks of goldeneye and other divers. Again Fred relied on my 3-inch shells of number 4 shot to bring down birds—until we ran out of shells. When he called for more rounds, I slipped him two of the three shells I had recovered the day before. He didn't even look at them as he loaded; a strange duck was fast approaching. The bird circled, went out of sight behind the blind, then suddenly reappeared with set wings not 25 yards away. What that mallard was doing over that diving duck terrain, I'll never know, but I do know Fred bowled him over with the first barrel. Impressed by this kill which finished his limit, Fred looked at the spent shell casing to discover his erstwhile favorite shotgun shell.

"I told you so!" he exclaimed. "These shells are fantastic! Did you see how that mallard folded? You really should import a case of these, George. It's the nickel plating that makes the difference."

Even nickel-plated shot won't help you kill scoters unless the shot is suitably large to begin with. The amount of lead these birds can carry, particularly the large (4-pound) white-winged drakes, is astonishing. Much of the shot that actually strikes the body may be absorbed by the scoter's especially heavy dressing of feathers and fat. However, on some occasions, the ability of scoters to endure is downright supernatural.

One afternoon three of us were shooting from a flooding sandbar in Long Island Sound. Scoters were flying low over the sandspit, and we thought it would be no time at all before each of us had his seven-bird limit. Other than the fact that we had to retreat from the tide every ten minutes or so, we had almost continuous shooting. Yet only one of us got his limit. Our problem wasn't in hitting the birds; it was in killing them.

Some of those big scoters reacted to the lead we fired as though we were throwing rice at a wedding. One companion swears a white-winged scoter circled and came back to take a charge of ballast under his right wing to balance the load he'd already taken under his left! The range averaged between 20 to 40 yards, so our failure to stop more birds didn't result from sky-busting. However, we were shooting an odd assortment of shells that probably included too many express 6s and 7½s, and not enough magnum 4s.

One of my skunkheads was a particular nightmare. I first hit him about 35 yards out. He shuddered with the impact, but kept coming. I hit him again and completely bowled him over so he tumbled with a mighty splash into the shallows at the edge of the bar. He came up swimming. My final shot patterned a perfect 30-inch circle around the bird. He didn't even bother to dive—merely shook himself and kept swimming! Finally, I had to chase him around the shallows and fire three more shots to finish him. On the way home, I shook that scoter, and shot fell out and went rattling all over the aluminum boat seats and gunwales. That was shot that never even made it to the skin! Believe me, experiences like that give you strange dreams.

Duflecker, the Duck-Eating Dog

Before we move on to bufflehead and the goldeneyes, now may be a good time to talk about dogs. Retrievers are more than an accoutrement of duck hunting. They are indispensable. Any man who loves the sport admires waterfowl, and if he admires the resource, every bird crippled and lost is a bleeding sore to his satisfaction. A dog reduces painful memories to a minimum, and if you are fortunate, you may find such a remarkable animal, as to give yourself a full season of gunning pleasure without a single lost duck or goose.

On the other hand, a poorly trained or spiritless animal is worse than useless, and while bonds of affection inevitably grow between a master and even the sorriest excuse for a retriever, be kind to waterfowl and your own psyche: Leave the bummer at home and hunt with another dog.

The only rebate from a disastrous dog is the tales you can tell when the season is done. You will have become more philosophical about the missed opportunities and lost birds, and you can contemplate with belated humor the conspiracy perpetrated by a truly terrible canine.

Let me tell you about a Chesapeake retriever named Duflecker. Since this indestructible animal is still extant and I am still a good friend of his owner, whom I'll call Linwood, I'll not use the dog's real name—even though it is worse than his alias.

There are good Chesapeake retrievers. I have seen two in my lifetime that were absolutely magnificent—one in appearance, the other in deed. With the latter, I hunted the Lower Potomac, and in weather and water that would have left you or me dead within minutes, that dog sat like a statue. Ice formed on his curly coat, but the dog barely trembled. You would have thought the animal a product of good taxidermy, except when the one scaup that tried to fly by that afternoon hit the water, the retriever had that duck in his mouth before its reflexes stopped working. Turning and coming in through the decoys, that enormous dog looked like a Bengal tiger with a songbird in his mouth.

Duflecker is not of the same genetic stock. He is a small but wiry Chesapeake, and somewhere along the line, as his ancestors' proportions shrank, so did their brains. Some Chessies make up in heart what they lack in smarts; but Duflecker is the only conscienceless canine I've ever known.

Duflecker is not entirely his own fault. His early training consisted largely of being left to roam over the countryside, where he early developed a taste for quail, pheasant, and box turtles. He doesn't eat box turtles, but he does chew them rather ferociously and brings in the shards for show-and-tell. Since the dog's nominal owner was away at school during the critical formative years, the raising of this creature was left to the boy's kindhearted mother, who took all turtle remains from Duflecker, told him he was not a nice doggie, and then threw the remains as far as she could. Of course, Duflecker promptly retrieved the mutilated turtle to have the scene repeated—and repeated. After several days, he would roll on what was left and go off looking for fresh turtles.

Within three years, Duflecker managed to reduce the common box turtle population within a 50-square-mile area to endangered species status. However, he was not so dumb he didn't learn that by keeping a turtle alive when he brought it home, he could use the same turtle for many weeks before brain damage and shell shock finally killed the reptile.

Imagine the horrible fate of being a sentient turtle discovered by Duflecker: First, you are scratched and pawed by the slobbering beast and then carried miles before being turned over to a sweet lady with gentle hands. Then just as you begin to regard her as your savior, she hurls you end over end, high and far back into the underbrush—Aaeeii!—where the yellow-eyed fiend finds you and chews on you before taking you back to the sweet lady with the gentle hands.

One spring several years ago, Duflecker met his match in a 35-pound snapping turtle he attempted to drag back to the house as a substitute for scarce box turtles. The snapper bit off part of Duflecker's nose. The yelping of the dog brought help, and when the turtle was killed, Duflecker's nose was recovered and stuck back on his face. Miraculously, the amputated part fused with the living cartilage, and the only regret is that the sheared fragment grew back slightly off center to its original position. Some people say Duflecker now looks like a gigantic star-nosed mole, which suits his bitchlike compulsion to dig holes in neighboring lawns. I think the deformity gives the dog a gangsterlike air which suits his temperament even better.

Duflecker believes in democracy. He feels he is an equal partner in any outing, and he wants his fair share of the birds—feathers and all. If the shooting is a little slow, Duflecker will sometimes swim out to pick up a decoy and chew it on the way in while at the same time tangling a dozen other decoy lines.

Once I caught the brute behind the blind eating an L. L. Bean magnum mallard. Such decoys cost $17.25 each, and I decided to kill the dog then and there. However, I was the guest that outing, so I merely asked Linwood if it would be all right to "discipline" his decoy-eating dog. "Be my guest," he replied. I smashed the dog with a fearful karate chop behind the ear, but sprained my wrist and broke the fifth metacarpal bone in my hand. Duflecker never stopped chewing.

On another occasion Linwood broke a push pole across Duflecker's shoulders as he towed ashore a string of decoys we had just put out. The dog dropped one of the two decoys in his mouth and looked at us with malevolent eyes that plainly said, "I'll get you for that."

He did. In fact, he did repeatedly. Once Linwood announced he would kill Duflecker if he didn't return with the goldeneye he was swimming toward. Perhaps Duflecker heard him. The dog made an absolutely stunning retrieve, dropped the bird at Linwood's feet and shot me a guileful glance. The next bird down was mine and fell beyond effective shotgun range. Duflecker ate everything but the wings by the time we got the boat, went across to the opposite shore, and ran him down. Linwood was still so impressed by the earlier retrieve, he said he wanted to give the dog "one more chance."

As you have guessed by now, we were the idiots and Duflecker was the genius. Yet so strong is my devotion to the principle of waterfowling with a dog, and so foolish are people about the idea that any one-armed bandit will eventually pay off if only they keep shoving time and money into it, I made too many outings with old Turtle Eyes before finally getting a dog of my own.

One day Linwood pledged to train Duflecker to retrieve properly or kill him in the attempt. In any event, Linwood swore he would make a different dog of Duflecker. He did. I'll never forget my first—and last—outing with the reformed dog. Convinced that nothing could be done to alter the disposition of the crazed Chesapeake, I elected to jump shoot with my dog while Linwood and Duflecker stayed in a layout boat overlooking a small pond in the marsh.

When I got back an hour later, Linwood was beaming and Duflecker looked satisfied about something. It was a most unusual combination.

"How'd you do?" I asked.

"Got a limit of black ducks."

"Outstanding! How did Duflecker do?"

Pause. "Duflecker is a water dog."

"What do you mean?"

Pause. "Well, both birds fell on the high marsh, and while Duflecker didn't retrieve them for me, he marked them down."

"He marked them down? How?"

Pause. "Oh, you know how a dog marks things. I could see him, and when he stopped to lift his leg, I knew he had found the bird."

All dog owners find positive values for even the meanest of their canine friends. However, Linwood represents a new level of tolerance to brute faults. I now know I should have done Linwood, all retrievers, and the tradition of waterfowling a favor, not by asking whether I could strike Duflecker, but whether I could drive a wooden stake through his evil heart!

The Right Dog

Fortunately, few retrievers are as malevolent as Duflecker. Any prospective dog owner can enhance his odds of finding a good puppy by doing a little shopping before buying one, especially from the first seller you see in the classifieds. If you know of no one in your state producing good retrievers, don't be cheap: travel. I stress *buying* the dog because gift animals are usually trouble. It does not take much reflection to realize that unless there is an emergency or disruption of routine in the donor household, a dog being given away is *canis non grata* for probably very good reasons. We have been offered dogs with such "minor" flaws as the habit of chasing small children on bicycles, attacking mailmen, and piddling on rugs at two years of age.

No thanks!

Your choice of breed hardly matters so long as the animal is willing to work hard to please you. Thirty years ago Frank Weed ran the Housatonic Game Farm in Connecticut and used a dachshund to retrieve the dead and crippled ducks on the preserve's assembly pond. The dog worked as well as any pedigreed retriever I have seen since. However, Frank invested a good deal of time during the first year of the dog's life in training the animal. So must you. A retriever has retrieving instincts, but he could end up being more fond of turtles than ducks without proper guidance. The dog you acquire will share ten or more years of your life, and, since you'll probably end up as attached to the dog as Linwood is to Duflecker, you may as well make sure the dog is truly worth such devotion.

Unfortunately, the dilemma of which breed to choose, the question of training, and the cost of feeding and kenneling puts off many a prospective dog buyer, and we have all heard what amounts to the credo of the uncommitted waterfowler: "I don't need a dog; I usually hunt with Joe who has one."

Fine. That is better than hunting with Joe who doesn't have one. Yet how much—how very, very much— of the spirit of the sport is missed.

Shortly after acquiring our present golden retriever, I hunted with a gentleman who approaches recreation as he approaches the rest of life: Hohum. He hit a high-flying mallard that came down almost to the ground before leveling off and laboring across the marsh a few feet off the grass. The new dog was off and after the bid as though his life depended on catching it. There were two small creeks between him and the fluttering duck, and he easily leaped what would have been two sticky crossings for a man. When the bird was more than 300 yards from us and fast approaching a major channel, Rocky put on a burst of speed, leapt into the air, and caught the mallard.

I felt like dancing, doing cartwheels, giving that dog a double ration of steak bone and the key to the nearest city! I ran out to greet him trotting back, wet, his tail wagging happily, proudly with his triumph. I crouched down and hugged the muddy dog and kneaded the cartilage in one ear. He dropped the bird, grinned, and put up one paw for approval.

When I had dispatched the cripple and put it behind the blind and ordered Rocky to his wooden pallet pedestal near the entrance, I turned to my companion and asked the obvious:

"What do you think?"

"About what?"

"The dog's retrieve."

"I guess he saved us some walking."

A good dog will do more than that. He will make you laugh and curse and cry when he dies. Sure, dogs are a lot of trouble. So is painting decoys, building blinds, and most everything else associated with waterfowling. Anything you love is trouble.

Bufflehead and the Goldeneyes

These three species belong to the same genus, *Bucephala*. Besides having "broad foreheads," the three birds share several characteristics: nesting

For a duck hunter looking for a lovely mount, a mature drake bufflehead is a prize—that is, if the dog hasn't "hard-mouthed" the bird on the way back to the blind. Increasing pressure is being put on species like bufflehead and goldeneye as the traditionally more desirable diving species, canvasback and redheads, have diminished in numbers and range. *(Photograph by David W. Corson)*

in cavities, especially trees; first breeding at two or more years of age; and the tendency of brooding hens sometimes to allow another hen with young, or an immature hen, to share brooding responsibilities. On the other hand, some significant behavioral differences exist. Mature drake bufflehead *(B. albeola)* tend to defend hens, rather than territories, and are so aggressive about this, they rarely gather in sizable resting or feeding flocks, as is common with most other species of diving ducks. By contrast, mature drake Barrow goldeneyes *(B. islandica)* defend a rather small territory, rather than hens, and sometimes sizable nesting concentrations of as many as 1,000 pairs per square mile may result. Unfortunately, the temperate nature of the drake is offset by the violent temperament of his hen,

Size really has little to do with what constitutes a hunting trophy. A wingshot green-winged teal is *always* a trophy. Its meat is delicious and the drake's plumage makes a fine gift for a fly-tying friend. And if you have a handsome dog to share the fun, life couldn't be much sweeter. *(Photograph by George Reiger)*

A good retriever is indispensable for a marsh like this in Washington State's Ridgefield National Wildlife Refuge. It is important to have the Lab out where he can see the bird fall. There is no way he can follow hand signals in a cattail swamp! *(Photograph by David B. Marshall)*

Some dog experts will tell you that golden retrievers won't break ice, can't take cold water, have no staying power. Uh-huh. *(Photograph by George Reiger)*

which may attack and kill the young of her own species as well as other small ducks.

Wildlife biologists know that short-lived game species such as rabbits and quail are impossible to "stockpile"—that is, to save up from year to year to provide improved hunting opportunities in the future. Even intense hunting pressure represents only a tiny percentage of the overall mortality of quail and rabbits.

Ducks and geese are a different matter. Band returns for *wild* (captive records are generally longer) waterfowl include a twenty-three-year-old Canada goose, a sixteen-year-old mallard, and a seventeen-year-old common goldeneye *(B. clangula)*. The advantage of longevity in birds is that it permits a hen which loses her brood one year in a prolonged drought, or to predators, to survive to try again the following spring, or the spring after that. In such cases, hunting pressure can become a significant influence on the population of a species during those falls following an unsuccessful nesting season.

That is why the Canadian Wildlife Service and the U.S. Fish and Wildlife Service try to assess nesting results each summer and adjust seasons and limits accordingly. And that is why not being able to make adequate surveys of tree- and cavity-nesting species like bufflehead and goldeneyes bothers thoughtful sportsmen and scientists. When you then learn that such birds must be two years of age or older before they start reproducing, and that bufflehead, at least, display a strong homing instinct for both their nesting and wintering areas, it is more than their "cuteness" which keeps me from shooting many bufflehead.

Biologist Anthony J. Erskine discovered that bufflehead hens return to the same local area, if not the same nesting tree, spring after spring; bufflehead of both sexes return to the same wintering grounds. Of sixty-four bufflehead banded in Oregon, New York, and Maryland and shot in subsequent winters, forty-five were recovered less than 10 miles away, nine were recovered between 9 and 33 miles away, and ten between 32 and 50 miles away from their banding sites.

When we first moved to Virginia, there were large numbers of bufflehead on a tidal creek that meanders toward a favorite duck blind. As many as 400 birds used to be sighted in the little-over-two-mile run between the public launch ramp and the blind—and such concentrations were notable for a species that normally does not like much of its own company.

Over the years considerable hammering of this local population of bufflehead has been done by the many new duck hunters who have come into
the area. Bufflehead are still to be found in that two-mile stretch of tidal
creek, but these winter days, you are lucky to see 100 birds (more often a
couple dozen) where once you saw several times that number. Whether
overshooting has driven the birds to less hazardous areas along the coast, or
whether it has removed a significant proportion of the immature birds
which without such hunting pressure might have lived twelve or more
years,[8] I don't often shoot bufflehead anymore.

We forget the bufflehead was once so reduced by overshooting that in
the eastern half of the continent in the 1920s and 1930s, it was considered
an uncommon sight for birders. Throughout the Dust Bowl years, it was
one of several species (including the goldeneyes) completely protected by
federal law and since then has made a more or less steady recovery. Now
with our swelling human population disturbing its once remote nesting
grounds as well as putting increasing hunting pressure on the species—
especially from novice hunters for whom the pretty drake bufflehead is a
special prize—the recovery trend may be reversing itself.

Anthony Erskine suggests in his lengthy monograph, "Buffleheads"
(published in 1971), that complete protection "would occasion little hardship for most hunters [since fewer than one percent of all the ducks killed
in North America are buffleheads]. Conversely, increased hunting of buffleheads in the forms of larger bag limits or longer seasons could apprecia-
bly influence their populations without giving real satisfaction to hunters."
Yet, surely, there is a middle path between complete protection and larger
limits, particularly since no sportsmen's group is pushing for the latter, and
there is no scientific data yet indicating the bufflehead is in danger of
becoming, once again, a threatened species.

Although harvest figures may not always give satisfactory warning of
the imminent collapse of a species, the number of bufflehead killed every
year in the United States has averaged between 100,000 and 150,000 birds
for over a decade, which certainly indicates the species is being hunted on a
sustained yield basis. Approximately nine-tenths of the annual harvest is

[8] The oldest bufflehead known was a drake banded on February 18, 1956, at Kent Island, Maryland, as an adult at
least twenty months old. It was shot west of Port Huron, Michigan, on November 10, 1967, at an age of at least
thirteen years, five months.

distributed about evenly between the Atlantic, Mississippi and Pacific fly-ways, with roughly one-tenth killed every season in the Central Flyway.

Like the bufflehead, the population dynamics of goldeneyes is affected by hunting pressure. However, adult male goldeneyes are among the war-iest of waterfowl, and a mature drake in breeding plumage is an uncommon hunting trophy. Although goldeneyes will visit a stool composed of non-goldeneye decoys, the birds will most often fly by outside effective shotgun range. If you intend to hunt goldeneye, you need goldeneye facsimiles to draw the birds, and the best available by mail are sold by L. L. Bean in Freeport, Maine 04032.

Setting Decoys

Since I usually put out diving duck decoys from a boat where crowd-ing, not weight, is the only limiting factor to the number of birds I use, I prefer solid wooden or pressed cork stool. There is an esthetic satisfaction in shooting over well-made and well-maintained wooden blocks (perhaps, ones you've made yourself), but there is also the practical benefit in that western red cedar, white pine, or pressed cork decoys hold up better than most synthetics under the icy conditions prevalent where the best diving duck hunting is found. Equally important, pine and cedar blocks (and to a lesser extent, pressed cork) have ideal weight and riding characteristics for the choppy waters most often associated with diving duck shooting. Prop-erly balanced, a solid wooden decoy will bounce and bob far less than any synthetic yet devised. Further, it will be less inclined to turn over in a crosswind and more likely to carry a load of ice without sinking than hollow or lightweight plastic birds. And if you can remember to stick a tube of petroleum jelly in your hunting kit, a thin rubbing of the grease across the backs and heads of the decoys as you put them out will help prevent icing. Although you will have glossier decoys than is natural, this is better than having your decoys sink under rapidly accumulating ice.

Never throw out decoys helter-skelter, relying on their keels to right the birds. For one thing, you'll invariably end up with a few bunched decoys or with a line draped across the back or around the neck of one of the birds. As previously noted, goldeneyes are wary waterfowl, and little mistakes can add up to a slow morning in the blind.

Whistlers, alias goldeneye, are among the swiftest and wariest of waterfowl. A clean-kill double is in every respect a "trophy experience." Just as drake whistlers have white cheeks and otherwise dark heads, the hunter has darkened his pale cheeks to break up the outline of his face. *(Photograph by John S. Gottschalk)*

Since goldeneyes do not travel in big flocks, not more than a dozen decoys are needed to bring them in. On Lake Champlain, where goldeneye shooting is a specialty, some hunters put out two or three dozen decoys, but this is mostly to make sure that a passing bird sees the rig spread near rocky headlands or at the back of shingle coves. In the coastal mid-Atlantic region, where goldeneyes are unpredictably, but not uncommonly, shot, one or two pairs of goldeneye decoys set to one side of a spread of scaup, or even in the deeper water beyond a spread of puddle ducks, is enough to encourage visitors. And juvenile goldeneyes, like the juveniles of any species of waterfowl, will happily pitch to anything that looks older and wiser than they are.

Mergansers

Three seems to be a magic number when dealing with the more highly evolved sea duck genera, for just as there are three scoters and three members of *Bucephala,* there are three mergansers. Additionally, there are curious correspondences between the *Bucephala* and *Mergus* clans. First, all goldeneyes (and we now include bufflehead) and mergansers are tree-hole or cavity nesters. The smallest and the largest mergansers (the hooded,

Mergus cucullatus; and the common, *M. merganser)* prefer tree sites, but the red-breasted merganser *(M. serrator)* prefers cavities near or on the ground. Likewise, the small bufflehead and the large common goldeneye prefer tree sites, while the Barrow goldeneye commonly nests on the ground. The small bufflehead and hooded merganser [9] hens usually expropriate old woodpecker nests, while the larger common goldeneye and common merganser hens frequently nest in stump depressions in the tops of dead trees. Barrow goldeneye and red-breasted merganser hens prefer to nest in depressions under brush or in rocky caverns and cavities near swift streams or rivers.

Next, since it is characteristic of smaller ducks to winter further south than larger ducks of the same type, we are not surprised to find that bufflehead, with a maximum drake weight of 1.3 pounds, commonly winter in central Mexico, while Barrow goldeneyes, whose drakes may weigh 2.9 pounds, rarely stray south of Puget Sound in the West and the St. Lawrence River in the East. The even larger common goldeneyes, whose drakes may weigh 3.1 pounds, frequently winter in the Aleutian Islands in the West and around Newfoundland in the East.

Similarly, hooded mergansers, with a maximum drake weight of 2 pounds, winter in central Mexico and along the Gulf Coast to the Yucatán Peninsula; red-breasted mergansers, whose drakes average 2½ pounds, commonly winter in San Francisco Bay in the West and the Chesapeake Bay in the East; and common mergansers, whose drakes frequently exceed 4 pounds, are abundant in British Columbia in the West and the Maritime Provinces in the East.

On their wintering grounds, the little bufflehead and hooded merganser are more frequently found in tidal creeks and streams than their larger cousins, which prefer more open waters. The two larger mergansers manage to stay out of each other's way because the red-breasted merganser fishes in tidal waters from the ocean to large estuaries, while the common merganser prefers lakes and large freshwater rivers.

Thus, in comparing three closely related mollusk-eating ducks with three closely related fish-eating ducks, we see how similar all six species are

---

[9] Contrary to fears expressed by a few ornithologists, there should be little conflict between hooded merganser and wood duck hens for the same nesting sites in those areas where their breeding ranges overlap (i.e., the Pacific Northwest and throughout the upper tier of the eastern United States). Wood ducks prefer trees standing in or near quiet, murky backwaters, while hooded mergansers prefer their tree nests located near clear, running streams.

in those behavioral characteristics which involve no ecological conflict, but how different the three ducks within each genus are in those behavioral characteristics where nature offers but one niche for each species.

The thoughtful hunter perceives the complexity of this design with respect and wonder. It is part of the reason no person should be licensed to hunt until he or she is educated to understand his or her potentially disruptive impact as a predator. God or Evolution (call it what you will) has spent an eternity weaving an intricate living system from which mankind can derive both esthetic and physical sustenance. However, this is possible only so long as we restrict the growth of our own numbers and restrain those who seek to exploit waterfowling's capital as well as its interest.

The hooded and red-breasted mergansers are extraordinarily different in their mating behavior. Hooded mergansers begin to pair on their wintering grounds at least as early as the second week of December. Once paired, the two birds are exceptionally loyal to one another, and twice I have seen one of a pair circle its shot companion until, in one case, the other bird was shot as well. On another occasion, while I was jump shooting black ducks on a tidal creek in Virginia, a pair of "hairyhead" (as hooded mergansers are locally called) started to pitch below the densely reeded sodbank on which I was standing. The hen saw me, but the drake did not. He landed within ten yards of me and immediately began to display his head crest, I suppose, imagining the hen was still with him. Meanwhile the hen had flown upstream, uttering the guttural alarm cry peculiar to the species, but because of the gusting wind and the location of the drake in the creek bottom, he could not hear her. The hen circled upwind in a wide figure eight and continued to call. On one swing she came within 30 yards of me. By this time the drake noticed he was alone and began to swim down the creek looking for his mate. The hen—I suppose, despairing that the male would ever get the message—turned, came down the creek, and passed not 5 feet above my head. As soon as the drake heard and saw the hen, he took off and joined her.

By contrast, red-breasted mergansers form pair bonds late in the winter, and they are never very firm. Polygamy is common in the species, and if one of a pair is shot, the other red-breasted merganser doesn't even slow up to look back. However, both red-breasted and common mergansers will occasionally cooperate when fishing. One late winter day on Fisherman's Island, a small national wildlife refuge at the mouth of the Chesapeake Bay, I watched a flock of about 30 red-breasted mergansers form a line partway across a sizeable salt pond and drive small fish, probably mummichogs *(Fundulus sp.)*, ahead of them with much lunging and wing-splashing. Perhaps, because there were not enough birds to span the pond, the fish started escaping around and between the birds. The apparently organized drive broke up before reaching the opposite shore, and it was then every merganser for him- or herself. Similar behavior has been observed in common mergansers, but not in hooded mergansers, possibly because concentrations of hooded mergansers are not needed to fish the narrow creeks and streams frequented by these birds.

The origin of the word *merganser* offers a small controversy. According to Paul A. Johnsgard, it is derived from the Latin *mergus,* meaning "diver," and *anser,* meaning "goose." Yet the vernacular *goosander* (applied to the common merganser in Europe and parts of North America) comes from the Old Norse *gas,* meaning "goose," and *ønd,* meaning "duck." Some other authorities believe that *merganser* is Germanic in origin, combining the words for "sea" *(meer),* and "goose" *(ganser).*

When the Swedish naturalist Carolus Linnaeus gave the common merganser its scientific name, *Mergus merganser,* in 1758, he might have derived the specific name from the popular *meer-ganser* or created a Latinized word from the concept of a "diving goose," or, as its full name is translated, a "diving diving-goose." Since Linnaeus Latinized everything he ever saw—including his own name, which was originally Carl von Linne—the odds are Johnsgard is right. Still it's nice to know we Americans have invented our own word for the species: *sheldrake.*

Wildlife romanticists would have you believe that mergansers eat only slower, so-called coarse fishes, and not the swifter game species. Unfortunately, when swift game species are small, they are no faster than the coarsest of bullheads and sculpins and are a lot less prickly. Salmon parr as well as small trout and grayling are chateaubriand to mergansers. However, that fact should not be used as an excuse for a pogrom against "fish ducks." If a local merganser population is taking more suckers than salmon, that may be to the salmon's overall advantage. But if a salmon nursery stream is being worked over by a family of mergansers, then the less valuable of the two resources will have to go. Man is always making choices and taking sides. That is what wildlife management is all about. We call such management "scientific" when we don't allow sentimental assumptions or fashionable thinking to stand in the way of the logical choice.

Although I have read and heard a good many opinions regarding the "inedibility" of mergansers, in every case when I had the opportunity to cross-examine the talker, he allowed as how he had never eaten a merganser himself, but cousin so-and-so had, and his cousin says, blah, blah, blah. Well, I have eaten probably half a hundred red-breasted mergansers and possibly a dozen hooded mergansers. (I have not tried common merganser, but only because they are uncommon where I do most of my shooting.) I cannot recall an "inedible" red-breasted merganser, and some of the hairy-head were better than black ducks taken from the same marsh. Respectable outdoor writers do not often admit to something as uncouth as "I've eaten and enjoyed fish ducks," but I will, partly because I operate under the sportsman's rule, "You eat 'em if you shoot 'em," and partly because I have learned that there is very little life associated with water that either swims, flies, crawls, or merely grows in one spot that man cannot eat with satisfaction.

Of the two mergansers with which I am familiar, the hooded is generally superior because its smaller size makes it more tender and because in our outlaw-inhabited region of the nation, the hooded frequently has the opportunity to feed on whole corn. A fundamental practice of Virginia poachers is to put corn in the brackish water ponds (called "salt ponds") that occur on the upland tidal marshes. The corn is scattered close around the edges of the pond so the bait can't be spotted by aerial surveillance. (Experienced wardens can still tell whether a pond has been baited by the way its edges are eaten out.) When the hooded mergansers arrive to feed on the small fishes trapped in the ponds by receding tides, they are attracted to the bright yellow kernels and may consume quite a few. The first time I killed a hooded merganser in Virginia, I rapped the wounded bird's head on a corner of my blind, whereupon the concussion dislodged half a dozen corn kernels from the bird's gullet and scattered them over the ground. As soon as I recovered from my astonishment at finding corn in a merganser, you can bet I was down on my hands and knees picking up every grain!

Whether or not red-breasted mergansers eat corn, their flavor is sometimes excellent. A friend, who is highly regarded as a gourmet in Washington, D.C. social circles, went hunting with me one morning and shot a black duck, a bufflehead, and a red-breasted merganser. When he returned home, he held a dinner party for some friends and colleagues and supplemented the three Virginia ducks with a corn-fed mallard shot at a game farm. Every guest tried each one of the four birds without knowing what it was, and an informal survey of their favorites was made. The bufflehead (alias, butterball) took top honors for both flavor and texture; the merganser and the black duck were tied for second place. The mallard came in last, with the general complaint that it was tough and flavorless. So much for traditional rankings of waterfowl as food.

Mergansers are strong and swift flyers, and their inability to flare like a puddle duck makes them a pass shooter's dream-come-true. However, the number of places where this expensive (what with today's cost of magnum shells) hobby of pass shooting can be exercised is limited, because mergansers, unlike scoters, do not congregate by the thousands to trade back and forth between a sedentary food resource and a more or less permanent resting area.

Although mergansers will stool to decoys of other species, they usually offer passing shots at extreme range as they trade by just beyond the furthest decoy. To get such birds to stool, you should have at least one or two merganser decoys, depending on which mergansers you will most likely encounter in your area of the country. In coastal Virginia, where mergansers have long been important food and game birds, decoy carvers of olden days like Ira Hudson and Doug Jester made many hooded and red-breasted merganser facsimiles. Since such birds are more often today found in museums than marshes, you will have to make your own since none are commercially available.

Unfortunately, a majority of mergansers are shot by dominionist hunters who have had an uneventful dawn and want action, any kind of action. Since mergansers never trade around until after the sun comes up (they need to see the agile fish they pursue for breakfast), and since most moonlit nights are not bright enough for successful fishing, mergansers fly by the decoys on those bluebird mornings just about the time the hunter is yearning to have his gun go off. Bang! And the bird is down. The shooter feels he has received a little compensation for the license he bought and his early rising. In some instances, he lets the wind or current take the "target" out of sight, and if his dog brings in the "smelly fish duck," the poor mutt is reprimanded before the shooter flings the merganser far back into the reeds.

Generous limits are attracting increasing numbers of hunters to sea duck shooting. These red-breasted mergansers can be prepared so their flesh is not the abomination most people, who have never eaten "fish ducks," imagine them to be. *(Photograph by George Reiger)*

There appears to be no way to prevent such purposeless killing. However, I would like to persuade the kind of hunter who shoots first and asks questions later to try cooking a merganser, at least once. My formula for subduing the sometimes strong (which is not to say, rank) flavor of sea ducks in general and mergansers in particular is to skin the birds and to wrap their bodies in bacon in order to keep the ducks from drying out during cooking. Some purists object that this means you're merely eating meat saturated with bacon fat, and not wild duck. However, while bacon fat will flavor the meat, it never saturates or overwhelms the natural flavor of the duck unless you cook the bird too long at too low a heat. As for the occult business of stuffing diving ducks with apples, oranges, or onions to drive away the heebie-jeebies or whatever such stuffings are supposed to do, this curious ritual is entirely unnecessary. Perfectly good fruits and vegetables are too costly these days to be wasted and should be saved for legitimate bread stuffings with a plucked goose or puddle duck.

Mergansers are not easy birds to flay, and the skin particularly likes to stick around the keel of the breast bone. However, skinning is still quicker than plucking, and, besides improving the flavor, skinning will reduce the potential ingestion of pesticides and other chemical compounds which concentrate in the fatty layers of the body, including skin. All waterfowl are haunted by the specter of agricultural and industrial residues, but none more so than mergansers, which eat fish and thereby concentrate the PCBs and kepone absorbed by the fish. Since nonnatural chemical compounds are found mostly in the skin and internal organs, I discard both (a shame when it comes to the giblets) to lessen the impact such poisons may have on the highest predator in the food chain, me.

For recipes in which mergansers can be substituted by scoters or eiders, see Appendix.

Stiff-Tailed Ducks

Our last group of diving ducks is also the most specialized. These birds demonstrate that specialization is not always to wildlife's advantage, especially when confronting the works of man. One of the features of all eight species of stiff-tailed ducks found worldwide is that their large feet are placed so far back on the body, these birds are practically helpless on land and can only get airborne from the water. Thus, twice within the past six years, I have heard of ruddy ducks *(Oxyrua jamaicensis)* becoming stranded on local roadways during evenings when misty rains caused the pavement to shine like a river. This problem must be fairly common, because the seaside Delmarva peninsula does not represent prime ruddy duck wintering habitat, and because these birds migrate mostly at night when it is both more difficult for the ducks to distinguish roads from rivers and for drivers to find the birds after the ducks have laboriously pushed themselves onto the grassy shoulders where cats, foxes, and owls undoubtedly account for most grounded ruddies.

The only other stiff-tailed species found in North America is the masked duck *(O. dominica)*. This duck is uncommon to rare north of the equator, and, in its South American breeding range, it has the doubtful distinction of having the piranha as the principal predator of its ducklings. In this country, the masked duck may be establishing a breeding population in the extreme southern corner of the Texas coast. Any specimen of a striped- or black-faced, stiff-tailed duck with white wing speculums should be reported to the Office of Migratory Bird Management, U.S. Fish and Wildlife Service, Laurel, Maryland 20811.

The ruddy duck has the misfortune to share the same diminishing breeding range with the canvasback and redhead. Furthermore, the redhead

A distinctive white cheek marks this bird as a male ruddy duck. Also called "butter duck," its largely vegetarian diet makes the ruddy duck an important secondary game bird throughout its range, but most notably California where up to 70 percent of the North American population winters. *(Photograph by George Reiger)*

adds insult to injury by parasitizing ruddy duck nests, notwithstanding the fact that such nests are usually well concealed and tucked beneath a reed bower. The ruddy duck sometimes revenges itself on the redhead by parasitizing its nests, but this is hardly constructive behavior for two species with enough trouble trying to find suitable breeding habitat in the first place.

Because the ruddy is one of our smallest ducks (a goliath wouldn't weigh 2 pounds); because it is a diver associated with at least a partial diet of shellfish on its wintering grounds; and because the brownish drake doesn't assume his blue bill and reddish body plumage until several weeks after the last legal hunting ends in January, the ruddy duck is not popular as food or as a trophy for mounting. Still, some seasons more than 80,000 are shot, with nearly half of these taken in the Pacific Flyway where between 60 and 70 percent of the entire North American population winters.

In the Atlantic Flyway, roughly half the wintering ruddies are distributed over the many brackish water estuaries of the Chesapeake Bay. Years ago, while teaching at the U.S. Naval Academy and often out at the mouth of the Severn River on December mornings before classes, I used to row my boat through a local raft of several hundred ruddy ducks on my way to and from a blind where I shot mostly redheads and widgeon. One bluebird morning with no shooting at the blind and with a promise made the evening before to a young lady for a "wild duck dinner," I wondered whether Rock Cornish game hen would be an acceptable substitute. I rowed back through the ruddy raft, which divided to let me pass, and it suddenly dawned on me that a ruddy was both legal and a "wild duck."

My sporting principles insisted the bird be killed in the air and not on the water. Accordingly, I cut out a segment of the raft and tried to move it toward shore where I was confident the birds would turn, get airborne, and pass over my head. At the time I didn't realize I was breaking the law against "rallying waterfowl." The birds were reluctant to fly, and I must have rowed backwards (to keep my eyes on the birds) more than a mile as I worked from one side of the cove to the other, trying to force my "trapped" birds into the air.

Just as I was ready to quit, 20 birds got up, flew to the back of the cove and then turned to me. I fired as they went by and was astonished to see *five* ruddy ducks fall, four of them stone dead, plus a swimming cripple which I promptly killed. When I picked that fifth duck from the water, I inadvertently broke my second federal law by taking into possession one more bird than the daily limit allowed. Still, my young lady friend and I eventually ate all five of those ducks, and we found their texture (that is, tenderness) to be superior to a redhead and their flavor about the same. They were delicious!

By the way, so pleased was I by my lady friend's fondness for wild duck and her interest in the way I prepared the birds, I married her. But since that day I have never shot another ruddy. I now live in a part of the country where ruddy ducks are scarce. Maybe that's just as well. I know I'll never top my personal record of five ducks downed with a single shot!

SEVEN: THE CRAFT OF THE DECOY

When a visiting sportsman suggested that Miles Hancock's decoys were less than perfect imitations of live birds, the Virginia carver retorted, "When they get close 'nuff to tell they ain't real ducks, it's too danged late!"

LIKE THE BUILDING of log cabins, the aging of bourbon, and the playing of jazz, decoy carving is a peculiarly American craft. Hunters have probably known for tens of thousands of years that imitation birds will lure live ones, but only with the arrival of the red man in North America was the making of facsimile birds on its way to becoming an art.

As the Asiatic wanderers moved south and east across the continent, they discovered ducks wherever they discovered water. Although the Indians found birds vulnerable during the spring nesting season and the summer moult, the birds were scattered or hidden and not always easy to locate. During the fall, however, ducks gathered into great flocks and stray birds would readily come to assemblies of decoys fashioned from mud, reeds, or even a stone set atop a larger rock. The heads and skins of ducks and geese that were killed with bow or sling were converted into decoys to lure still more of their wild brethren.

The hunters were mostly nomadic. Even those tribes which planted crops sometimes trekked considerable distances from their fields to hunt and fish, then returned in time for the harvest of corn, squash, or beans. With the exception of the muscovy in Mexico, no waterfowl were domesticated by North America's Indians. However, captured and crippled ducks and geese were sometimes kept for short periods of time as a ready source of fresh food, and some of these may have served as live decoys before joining the fowl they lured into the pot.

The Indian attitude toward decoys was equally practical. Improvised stools were not saved, because new decoys could be quickly fashioned from available materials, and because a hunter already had too many essential items to carry to tote things which could be rapidly replaced when the need arose—which, for no reason at all, reminds me of the old joke about the fellow who gave up elephant hunting because he got weary of lugging around the decoys.

When a choice waterfowling area was discovered, or when a craftsman took a little more time to make his artificial birds, decoys were sometimes hidden after the hunt to be recovered and used again the next day or the next season. Such a cache comprises the treasure of eleven decoys found in Lovelock Cave, Nevada, in 1924. These birds, clearly identifiable as canvasbacks, are made of tule reeds covered by duck skins or painted and stained to resemble live birds. The decoys are still in useable condition and are at least twelve hundred years old.

When the Europeans arrived in North America, the Indians taught them how to hunt birds native to a continent to which both races of men were originally strangers. Sturdy decoys became essential to the systematic slaughter indulged in by white men, for while Indians hunted primarily for their tribes out of pride, not profit, Caucasians soon began hunting to provide food and feathers to total strangers living in distant towns and cities. The reed and stuffed-skin birds used by the Indians were too fragile for the daily labor some colonists made of waterfowling. Thus, eighteenth-century correspondence reveals that wooden decoys were in use even before the Revolutionary War.

White cedar was probably the most popular wood, for its malleableness, buoyancy, and durability. But in areas where such wood was scarce or quckly eliminated, any driftwood would do. Heads of holly or oak roots were set on pine or cottonwood bodies, while in Florida as well as Cuba, blue-winged teal may have been killed over decoys fashioned from coconuts. Today, the tradition of local artisans working with local woods is mostly gone by the board, and many of the wooden working decoys still commercially available are made from such alien trees as balsa and cork.

Rubber decoys were introduced in 1867, followed by canvas, metal, papier mâché, and waxed cardboard used in full-bodied and silhouette models. In the past quarter century, plastic and styrofoam birds have become most popular. Low cost and light weight are the virtues of such

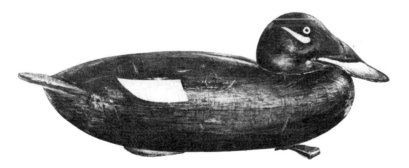

Since black-painted jugs will often do just as well as finely carved decoys for scoter shooting, this century-old Connecticut bird is extremely rare—and the market reflects that fact. The owner of this white-winged scoter carved by Albert Laing (and illustrated by Milton Weiler) could easily get $10,000 for the bird, but it is not for sale. *(Reproduction courtesy Winchester Press)*

decoys. However, factory birds are usually life-size or smaller, and this was considered to be a drawback by open-water hunters more than three-quarters of a century ago when diminutive Dodge or Mason broadbill were laughed off the Lower Chesapeake or Currituck Sound. The old-timers knew that one had to use big decoys for big water, and that is why so many of them made their own oversized wooden birds until very recent times.

Furthermore, while foam and plastic decoys perform well enough, there is something about their standardized shapes, the seams down their backs and heads, even about their "automatic tipright molded-in keels," that minimizes the pleasure of their company. A man's decoys, like his shotgun, dog, and duck call, should reflect his personality and be part of the diversified tradition that makes up waterfowling. For that reason, when I shoot over factory-made birds, I prefer L. L. Bean decoys. They are larger than life-size; they can be obtained with resting, feeding, or preening heads; and any wood, even pressed cork, has character.

Just as the production of cupronickel coins, commencing in 1965, quickly drove silver coinage out of circulation, the prevalence of synthetic decoys has taken most wooden birds out of the marshes and put them on mantels. When I was a boy, "blocks" were often just that. Yet the same kind of crude and anonymous shapes we hunted over now appear in antique shops with $100 price tags.

In 1970, I wrote a piece on decoys for *Rod & Gun* magazine, an elegant *Life*-sized publication selling for the then-unheard-of price of $1 a copy. Decoy collector William J. Mackey, Jr., supplied an 800-word insert for the article on contemporary decoy prices. He mentioned that a pair of Mason factory premier-grade mallards in original paint might bring as much as $200 and a premier Mason wood duck alone would go for $500. Then he pulled out the stops "to stimulate" (as he put it) the reader and noted that a Charles "Shang" Wheeler decoy had recently been auctioned for the unbelievable price of $975.

The world turns. Today Bill Mackey is dead, and his fabulous decoy collection is scattered to the four winds. A pair of premier-grade mallards is worth at least $1,000, and three times that figure *might* bring you a premier Mason wood duck—so long as not too many other people find out about it. If so, expect to see the Mason wood duck sell for as much as $4,000. The "Shang" Wheeler goose pictured in Mackey's *American Bird Decoys* was auctioned off for $4,500, and the anonymous Susquehanna River goose

Believe it or not, the asking price for one of these Barnegat Bay sneakboxes, complete with cockpit hatch, cork decoys, and trailer to tow the outfit home was $200. Only one of the rigs was sold; most people thought that was too much money to tie up in duck hunting paraphernalia a decade ago! *(Photograph by George Reiger)*

pictured on page 8 of Adele Earnest's *The Art of the Decoy* sold recently for $12,000.

Death has a curious way of enhancing values. When Chincoteague carver Miles Hancock died a few years ago, the prices for even his crudely wrought birds began to soar. Today a pair of Hancock buffleheads sell for $300, and a single brant will go for $250. Even *Rod & Gun* is dead, and old copies of any of the three issues of this briefly lived magazine sell for $10— when you can find them.

Inflation has helped change the complexion of decoy collecting from a hobby indulged in by sentimental waterfowlers to one favored by investors and antique dealers—some of whom do not know the difference between a mallard and a muscovy. They merely want to put their eroding dollars into something that is "as good as gold." Still, the thoughtful investor knows that what he buys at the retail level can only be resold at wholesale prices.

These hollow wooden bufflehead waiting to be painted have many advantages over the fiber birds on the shelf above them—not the least of which is that the bufflehead bills will last longer! *(Photograph by Nick Karas)*

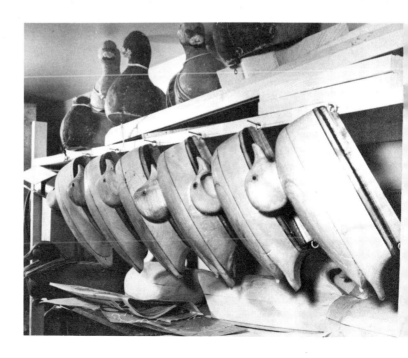

Steve Ward at a Barnegat Bay decoy show a decade ago. He has since passed away, and his brother Lem now does very little carving. Consequently, the value of Ward brothers' decoys has soared in the past several years. *(Photograph by George Reiger)*

Thus, unless the price of rare birds continues to escalate, there is simply no way the collector is going to recover the full value of his investment.

A decade ago, Mackey thought $1,000 was the sky-top limit of duck decoy prices. (Quality shorebirds would have sold for more.) Today most dealers think that $12,500 is the limit, but they, of course, are hoping they are wrong. The value of birds is based on demand, but demand is sometimes a product of efficient publicity, dealer hyperbole, and buyer gullibility. For example, while there is no doubt the Ward brothers of Crisfield, Maryland, have been superb craftsmen who produced some of the most persuasive decoys ever to swim on the Chesapeake Bay, the value of a Ward bird is based partly on the melancholy fact that Steve is dead and Lem no longer carves birds. No more Ward Bros.-brand decoys will be forthcoming.

Furthermore, since a foundation was established in their name in Salisbury, Maryland, to enshrine the noble pastime of decoy collecting, even the most casual collector is familiar with the name of Ward. Thus, a single Ward brothers' decoy sells for between $1,500 and $5,000, with the upper end of the spectrum reserved for pre-1950 birds in original paint. Singer Andy Williams paid $7,500 several years ago for a pair of Ward widgeon out of the Mackey collection that are now worth at least $10,000. Henry Fleckenstein, one of the most knowledgeable collectors and dealers in the mid-Atlantic, sums up the prevailing attitude: "Everybody wants a Ward."

Meanwhile at the head of the Chesapeake, R. Madison Mitchell has been producing functional decoys for over half a century. His birds are characteristic of the Susquehanna Flats near where he lives, and his diving ducks are especially well crafted. His cans are as handsome as this species ever comes.

For close to half a century, Mitchell has run something like a European artist's atelier where numerous carvers and painters have been employed turning out tens of thousands of birds using Mitchell patterns, while Mitchell himself may not actually put his hand on every decoy with his imprimatur. Furthermore, Mitchell is still alive, and if you would like to buy a Mitchell, although there is a fearsome waiting list, and so long as you

This turn-of-the-century postcard-photograph shows Jesse Poplar in action, one of the Susquehanna Flats' best known wing shots and market hunters. A *Baltimore Sun* story dated November 1, 1893, describes how 5,000 ducks were killed that day on the Flats with Jesse Poplar taking the most birds from a sinkbox and using a matched pair of double-barreled guns to bring down 235 redhead, scaup, and widgeon. He and his partner in the pickup boat split nearly $150—a princely sum for those days. *(Reproduction courtesy Chesapeake Bay Maritime Museum)*

promise to use the birds for hunting, not mantelpiece purposes, you can still visit Madison in Havre de Grace and place an order.

Such fecundity and availability naturally depresses the value of a Mitchell decoy. A collector pays only about $120 for a pair of canvasbacks, because a hunter can still buy cans directly from Mitchell for $15 apiece. If you can find a Mitchell decoy certifiably carved and painted before 1950, its individual price may climb to $200. However, dating Madison's stuff is difficult because his work has not gone through the several noticeable style changes familiar to fanciers of Ward decoys, and responsible dealers are leery about assigning positive pre-this or post-that dates to any Susquehanna Flats material they see. Furthermore, since so many carvers at the head of the bay all use the same patterns, you can never be absolutely certain that the "Mitchell" bird you have in hand was in fact turned out by the Mitchell workshop.

However, all such nuances only tend to obscure the fact that Mitchell's birds are superbly crafted working decoys. If what you want is a reminder of the Susquehanna's days of glories, a Madison Mitchell canvasback is collectible in the best sense of that word. Thus, with the knowledge that the following account of a visit I made to Mitchell's shop over a decade ago, will help publicize his decoys and consequently enhance their value, I beg the forgiveness of the dozens of good carvers, past and present, who have immortalized "the Flats" and ask the reader to see how a typical relict carver worked and still works. I have not changed the 1968 prices in order to give you an additional feeling for how rapidly the world turns.

As you drive north from Baltimore, you can't overlook the turnoff from Route 40 to the town of Havre de Grace. In fact, at this point in the trip, it's Route 40 that seems to turn off while the momentum of the highway continues straight ahead, crossing a bridge over railway lines once critical to the life of this waterfront community, and then running quickly into a sometimes forgotten town at the headwaters of the Chesapeake.

Though the outskirts of Havre de Grace have many modern buildings reflecting contemporary prosperity, as you continue toward the bay, the older homes stir memories about this town when it was once the center of the most compelling of Maryland's early industries—the slaughter of waterfowl for the big city markets of the mid-Atlantic. A century ago, trains and wagons moved south to Baltimore and north to Philadelphia bearing the fall and winter harvest of the Susquehanna Flats.

Primitive cameras and slow films were useless for attempting to capture the panorama of canvasback shooting on the Susquehanna Flats in the 1870s. So James T. Holly of the Havre de Grace Holly family of decoy carvers and market hunters turned his decoy painting talents to canvas to bequeath this wonderful primitive of nineteenth-century Maryland duck shooting. *(Reproduction courtesy the Chesapeake Bay Maritime Museum)*

"The market had stopped before I actually ever took up gunning," recalls Madison Mitchell, "but we had men here—my father, for example, who farmed on Spesutie Island. He got $14 a month salary and five acres of ground to do with as he pleased, as well as the fishing and hunting rights to the lower farm. If he hadn't gunned for the market, we would have been hard pressed to make ends meet. In those days, the gunners got five dollars for a pair of canvasbacks, $3 a pair for redheads, and a dollar for blackheads [greater and lesser scaup and infrequent ring-necked ducks]. Wildfowl were one of my father's biggest forms of income."

Such high prices tell us more about the U.S. dollar's steady value before 1900 than about how scarce ducks had become by the turn of the century, for even in 1800, canvasbacks were worth $3 a pair. The stories about labor contracts stipulating a limit on the number of days workmen could be fed wild duck are pure myth. Still, sink-boxes, floating and point blinds, bushwhacking, body booting, punt and swivel guns, and traps of every possible design were used to thin the ranks of ducks, geese, and swans. The birds funneled out of Canada to find open water and clasping leaf pondweed and widgeon grass in the rivers and along the shores of the upper Chesapeake and a wealth of wild celery and eel grass covering the more than one hundred square miles of silt-laden flats. The waterfowl poured south by the millions. They returned north by the tens of thousands.

Pollution today and severe hurricanes in 1954 and 1972 have done much to reduce the attractiveness of this area for wildfowl. The hurricanes rooted out much of the remaining wild celery, which had already been thinned by the industrialization of Baltimore and the suburbanization of the surrounding areas. Though the celery is making some comeback in the face of competition from milfoil (a plant much adored by coots, but not much sought by ducks), one still finds pods and small rafts of canvasbacks, where once entire islands of waterfowl rode the choppy winter waters at the mouth of the Susquehanna.

The gunners who manned the market rigs were like Madison Mitchell's father, mostly hard-working farmers or watermen who for nearly six months a year drew all or part of their incomes from this convenient resource. In the spring, after the birds had gone north, these men made what money they could from the seining and selling of herring, shad, and striped bass. (The latter are locally called "rockfish.")

The names of some of these early baymen are well known to the youngsters hunting the Flats and neighboring shorelines today. One of these legendary figures would, in a single month of gunning, kill more birds than today's youngsters can legally shoot in a lifetime. Opportunity and practice made superb shots out of ordinary men, and two missed birds in a row were the cause of considerable ribbing by other members of the gunning fraternity. The Barneses and the Morgans, Ben Dye, Dick Howlett, Jesse Poplar, Bob McGaw, and the fabulous "Daddy" Holly were all excellent shots, but their lingering fame has nothing to do with anything as transitory as shooting skills. These men all carved birds with hatchet, spoke shave, and whittling knife for service in their gunning rigs. Realistic, practical, hard-working and now, we belatedly realize, irreplaceable—these decoys reflect the nature of the men who carved them.

In the spring great timbers of white pine would flood down the Susquehanna, and the off-season wildfowlers would go out in boats to snare the drifting logs and haul them ashore for use in their workshops. This was in the days before the Susquehanna was dammed and when white pine was still sufficiently plentiful so that a piece of knotted wood ended in the fireplace rather than on the carver's workbench.

Decoy carver R. Madison Mitchell with part of his woodpile of western red cedar logs. Eastern red cedar is too dense and heavy to make good decoys, and white cedar and white pine are now too scarce and expensive to form the basis of affordable working decoys. Hence, Mitchell has much of his raw material shipped to Maryland from Michigan. *(Photograph by George Reiger)*

Although Madison Mitchell still prefers to hand carve decoy heads, he has been using a lathe to fashion the bodies and a belt sander "to smooth out the wrinkles" since the 1920s. *(Photograph by George Reiger)*

In a week of time off from his funeral business, Madison Mitchell may finish a dozen birds like these geese waiting to be painted. *(Photograph by George Reiger)*

"Almost all the good white pine is gone now," observes Madison Mitchell. "I get most of my stock by listening around so that when I hear of an old building that's being torn down or one that's been partially destroyed in a fire, me and my apprentice go over in a truck to see if we can recover any of the big timbers that may be left. Even then more than half my wood stock is western red cedar railed in from Upper Michigan or Idaho. Eastern cedar is just too hard and too heavy to make good decoys."

R. Madison Mitchell is a contemporary legend of the mid-Atlantic. Born in Havre de Grace on March 11, 1901 (the "R." stands for Robert), Mitchell went to work for carver and guide Samuel T. Barnes in 1924. Two years later Barnes died of pneumonia, and Mitchell, already occupied with a funeral business, took up Barnes's craft as a sideline. At an age when most other men are retired, Madison Mitchell is still carving and painting decoys to get out about "ten years of backlog."

Known for the quality of his painting and the sturdiness of his birds, Mitchell did not come easily by his skills. When one watches him at work today, swiftly applying the coats of paint that dry into the marvelously alive rippling patterns of a drake canvasback or redhead, it's difficult to believe

Most decoy makers agree that the most difficult bird to paint is the drake pintail. This one is by Jim Pierce, a younger member of the Susquehanna Flats School who has been carving decoys for only little more than a quarter-century. *(Photograph by George Reiger)*

Madison Mitchell when he tells you that painting was the hardest part of his job to learn. When asked what is the most difficult decoy to paint, without hesitation he tells you the drake pintail, for it requires considerable concentration and skill to control the brush as one works around the areas of white color.[1]

Madison Mitchell doesn't make so many diving ducks as he once did. When redheads and canvasbacks were still plentiful and limits high, Mitchell and his assistants would turn out between two and three thousand diving duck decoys per season. In the recent past, two and three hundred have been more like his annual production of these birds.

Though the upper Chesapeake is known primarily for the quality and numbers of its diving ducks, many other species of decoy have been produced in the vicinity, and some of these are especially sought after by collectors. Joel Barber, the dean of decoy fanciers, in his classic *Wildfowl Decoys,* first published in 1934, describes his discovery and ultimate purchase of a beautiful swan decoy carved by Samuel T. Barnes about 1890. Barber found the bird sitting in front of a grape arbor in a side yard of a house on Washington Street, where Madison Mitchell still lives and works today. After considerable negotiation, Barber acquired the swan decoy for his collection where it, thereafter, occupied a place of honor, appearing around the country at a number of national decoy exhibits.

Even after the shooting of wild swans was outlawed in 1913 and while the use of live puddlers and Canada geese for decoys was still legal, Madison Mitchell made wooden swans to act as confidence birds in a large rig of ducks and geese. A black duck is particularly susceptible to a few swan decoys gliding near a group of his brethren. In recent years, however, the very few swans Mitchell has turned out have been immediately bought by collectors.

Mitchell also made and still makes geese decoys, as well as large numbers of baldpate, mallard, and black duck. For a number of seasons he even made coot decoys with a variety of head positions. The artful shading of black on slate grey lends these birds a delicate quality somewhat offset by their curious ducklike bills. Mitchell purposely designed a broad coot bill to give his bird a stronger chip-resistant head for rough handling, and

[1] For this reason, and the fact that pintail have never been abundant in the Atlantic Flyway where so many of the best carvers worked, turn-of-the-century pintail are among the rarest of decoys.

Fifteen years ago, a waterfowler still had a good chance of finding old decoys in the marsh. This group was collected during two seasons of occasional gunning on Maryland's Choptank River. It includes a Mason teal *(in hand)*, a Madison Mitchell canvasback *(center profile)*, a Susquehanna Flats scaup of unknown vintage *(center facing)*, and a derelict body of unknown species. Although few people hunt with fine old wooden birds today, every waterfowler harbors the hope that one day he will discover a rare relic tucked in the reeds like this Ira Hudson pintail. *(Photographs by George Reiger)*

because he feels that the correct color pattern, not anatomical perfection, is what counts with working decoys. The bone-white bill of the coot is one of its most noticeable features, and emphasizing the bill helps, rather than hurts, the drawing power of the wooden facsimile.

A very few old blue-winged teal decoys have been found in the vicinity of the Flats and were probably produced by baymen fond of these small and agile ducks, which provided them with so much early season sport and small change before the major flights of more substantial waterfowl got underway. By the time a gunner had sharpened his eye on the twisting, darting flight of a teal, the steady, driving flight of a fat drake canvasback mut have made, quite literally, for "duck soup" shooting. One of my favorite mantelpiece birds is a blue-winged teal drake, the ancient body of which I found floating in the Severn River off the Naval Academy and for which Madison Mitchell made a pert head and added his distinctive finishing touches of design and color—touches indicating a not unpracticed hand in the production of teal.

Green-winged teal, of course, migrate later and often stay in the vicinity of the Flats until well into the coldest winter. Many green-winged teal decoys were found in Chesapeake stools, and earlier in the century a number of these birds came from the Dodge and Mason decoy factories in

Detroit, Michigan. However, quite a few of today's green-winged teal decoys are of local manufacture.

One of the pleasures of talking with old baymen is to share fragments of their early experiences from a world somehow less cluttered than ours today. Unlike conversations with retired bureaucrats or corporate business-men, who so often enlarge in retrospect the importance of their essentially administrative lives, listening to old baymen is hearing men with remark-able confidence and integrity who all seem to share the awe and even humility for having seen and participated in the passing of that most essential ingredient of the American pioneer experience—the wilderness.

When once asked if there were any distinctive characteristics that easily identified a Mitchell decoy, Madison Mitchell laughed and replied with words that would be vain if they were not also true: "Ninety percent of the gunners from Columbia, Pennsylvania, to Richmond, Virginia, can tell you whether what they hold in their hands is a Mitchell decoy or not—unless 'Speed' Joiner [2] made it. If 'Speed' made it, even he can't tell whether it's a Mitchell decoy or not. He uses my patterns and he paints almost the same as I do. He learned right here in this shop, working five years, and most of the time he put in was in painting."

For thirty years Madison Mitchell has been warned by a variety of sources that the demand for handcrafted decoys was nearly over. Synthetics would replace his heavy wooden products. For thirty years Mitchell's orders and a backlog of orders have been growing.

It's not just the quality of design and color that makes Mitchell, Joiner, and other upper-baymen's decoys distinctive. It's little details such as the fact that Mitchell never paints during the hot days of July and August, when the paint dries on the outside but stays damp on the inside in a way that eventually leads to blistering, splitting, and peeling. Therefore, Mitchell decoys have to be repainted less often than less conscientiously created products.

It's also the fact that Mitchell and Charles Joiner have experimented extensively and discovered that a blend of 60 percent Japan and 40 percent oil paint gives the best finish and holds up longest under the rugged,

[2] Charles "Speed" Joiner worked for several years in Mitchell's atelier, where he developed most of his skill as a carver and painter. Joiner then moved to Kent County, Maryland—he now lives in Chestertown—and some decoy collectors no longer consider him part of the "Susquehanna Flats School" of decoy makers.

knockabout conditions inherent in gunning the brackish and salt waters of the Chesapeake.

Though Madison Mitchell has experimented with hollow decoys, he abides by a solid product in the belief that solid wood rides the choppy surface of the bay more naturally than does hollowed wood, and certainly better than does papier-mâché or plastic.

He employs a special keel on his decoys rather than using a strip of lead or iron to weight the birds, for he has discovered that a keeled block "works" better at the end of an anchor line than does a more casually weighted decoy. Depending on the length of the anchor line, a Mitchell decoy either plunges over the waves like an eager canasback pushing to the head of a feeding flock or courses back and forth across the surface like a fastidious mallard seeming to examine and pick at occasional bits of floating weed.

Rather than attach the decoy heads to the bodies with dowels, Mitchell uses three 30-penny galvanized nails driven through the head, securely anchoring the base of the neck to the body. In addition, two 4-penny nails fix the head in front. While sooner or later, and mostly sooner, heads attached with wooden dowels work loose, this is impossible with a nailed head which, even if it fractures, will remain attached to the body and only need repainting.

In an exceptionally productive day, Mitchell may carve as many as 24 bird heads. Cutting the rough form from a flat piece of wood with a band saw, then using a drawknife and the spokeshave to shape the head into recognizable form, and finally with a whittling knife and by sanding, as many as two dozen heads will end up in the bottom of one of the many bushel baskets which are scattered about the ground floor of his shop.

The next day will see Mitchell and an assistant cutting some of the logs piled outside his shop into suitable lengths and then working at cutting the hearts from the wood, knowing that hearted wood has a tendency to fracture. Then with the assistance of a lathe and sanding belt, two dozen bodies to match the two dozen heads of the day before take shape. While the lathe has proved to be a marvelous labor-saver for Mitchell (he first began to use one in 1929), he recalls that Sam Barnes could hatchet and spokeshave a timber about as fast as a lathe does this job today. "The real advantage of a lathe is that it permits us to work with knotted wood. Sam would just throw all the knotted stuff to one side. White pine and western cedar are just too expensive for us to do that kind of thing today."

Shooting pump-guns from a pair of "coffins." Wouldn't you like to add one of those iron canvasback wing decoys to your collection? Wing decoys were sometimes made of wood and were mostly fashioned by cutting the bottoms off defective floating decoys. *(Photograph courtesy Chesapeake Bay Maritime Museum)*

On the third day, if work in the funeral home still permits a few leisure hours to spend with his decoys, Madison Mitchell attaches the heads, and sands and finishes the surface of the birds. By the end of a week, as many as two dozen canvasbacks or a dozen mallards complemented by a dozen baldpate will be the products of the Mitchell workshop.

I once asked Madison Mitchell if there had ever been a time when he had made decoys his exclusive source of income. He laughed and replied that decoys had cost his funeral business money every year he has made them. "Oh, if I could have stayed in the shop, I might have made some profit. But you can't finish enough decoys to pay for your material and other work as you go along. If you did, your price would be at least thirty percent more than what it is now. Forty years ago I charged $1.50 for a canvasback. Now I've got to charge $4.50, but I still think that's too much money. I hate to make a bill out for a funeral, let alone for a decoy."

Canvasback decoys made and sold by Madison Mitchell within the past decade for less than five dollars are already finding their way to antique display windows with a $25 price tag. [Remember, these are 1968 prices.] Mitchell is both amused and embarrassed by this kind of thing, and though he is justifiably proud of his handicraft, he tends to view such dramatic inflation of his original purchase price as a sure sign that people nowadays don't know what to do with their money.

Joel Barber called decoys "floating sculpture." It's a phrase that suggests an attempt on the part of the original carver to capture something of the spirit of the waterfowl he was shaping as well as its bodily configuration. But for a man to capture the spirit of any creature he must know that creature well. For a man to carve viable decoys, he must learn as much as he can about the birds he carves. In the early days of gunning the Upper Chesapeake, it was experience and observation in the field combined with a keen memory and sense of the esthetic that led to so many of our finest reminders in wood of those wondrous days when America's waterfowl seemed illimitable. Traditions of substance and solidarity, value for one's money, simplicity of design and durability, pride in craftsmanship from "Daddy" Holly to R. Madison Mitchell, the decoys they carved embody the souls of men who made their livings from the bounty of Maryland bordering the Susquehanna Flats.

Need and genius are complementary elements in all the world's best art. The language of Sophocles and Shakespeare is more imaginative than the language of modern playwrights, in part, because ancient and Renaissance stages were unadorned amphitheaters. Sophocles and Shakespeare needed to create a panorama of lavish language to compensate for their lack of elaborate settings and revolving platforms.

Thus, along the shores of the lower Delaware, from just below Trenton to where the river merges with the bay, a highly specialized form of waterfowling required highly realistic decoys. Here originated the custom of carving bas relief wings and grooved back and tail feathers. And although etched nostrils and mandible markings appear elsewhere on decoys in the Atlantic and Mississippi flyways,[3] nowhere are such design features made so precise as on "Bordentown birds" at the turn of the century.

The reason for such stylish flourishes was not esthetics alone, but function. The Delaware River wildfowlers set their decoys in promising eddies and rowed upstream to a hiding place. When a passing pod of mallards, wood duck, black duck, or teal turned and stooled to the perfect facsimiles, the hunter would drift or scull down to the resting ducks. Delaware River decoys not only had to draw birds but to hold them while a suspicious object (the hunter) drew near.

The "dugout" decoys characteristic of coastal New Jersey were not created to astonish people with their light weight. Their light weight was in response to the limited freeboard found on sneakboxes, punties, and

---

[3] More care is everywhere given to decoy heads than decoy bodies, because hunters have long known that distinctive head markings, particularly on drakes, seems to give each duck species its unique character. Generalized body shapes and color patterns are important, but the quality of a decoy's head and eyes is what spells the difference between flybys and wild birds pitching to the decoys.

A nineteenth-century photograph showing Captain John Keen and Bob Vandiver sitting in a pair of sinkboxes probably on the Susquehanna Flats amidst what today would be a fortune in Barnes, Dye, and Holly-made decoys. *(Photograph courtesy Chesapeake Bay Maritime Museum)*

other small boats used by coastal hunters. Reasonably large spreads were necessary for the open waters of Barnegat Bay, and nearly twice as many hollow decoys by Jesse Birdsall or Harry Shourds than solid pine or cedar birds could be stacked on the back of a small boat with room to spare for shooter, shotgun, shells, and the birds with which the hunter hoped to return.

River hunters designed birds with high rounded breasts to ride flowing waters without persistent yawing. Keel weights were shifted aft to counteract the tendency of swift currents to pull under the heads of anchored birds. Some midwestern carvers fashioned their birds with high necks to decrease the possibility of ice forming on the birds' bills and to enhance their visibility on stump-studded and debris-laden waters. Function even dictated a smaller-than-life-size decoy for standard-grade Mason and Dodge factory birds in order to reduce shipping costs.

Need precedes and often inspires artistic forms, and art is usually richer for such constraints. This is why it is hard for me to get excited about the latest trend in bird carving. To design a group of teal swirling over the tops of cattails, and to make every exquisite detail from wood—including the cattails—is undeniably a woodworking achievement. However, lacking function, such sculpture seems akin to making model ships out of matchsticks or constructing homes out of beer cans. These elaborate tours de force, whose value lies largely in the hundreds of creative hours involved, are less works of art than artistic curiosities. All art seems to move from periods when form and function are closely allied to periods when increasingly convoluted additions supplant function. Baroque and rococo eras are evident in theater, music, painting, and landscape gardening. I suppose they were inevitable in decoy carving as well. However, pardon my prejudice if I insist that decoys will always be just that: birds carved by hunters to be used by hunters.

A well-known art critic once told me he was amazed to find that many old carvers have so little sense of the value of their decoys. He complained they only wanted to fix the broken birds and repaint them, thereby destroying their "purity." In reply I told him that years ago, I took some badly beaten blocks to Madison Mitchell who handled the decoys with care and called them "cripples." I've yet to hear the first auctioneer or nonhunting collector refer to split-billed, lead-shot blocks as cripples.

Finally, when the masterpiece mentality invades the world of waterfowling, acquisitiveness, covetousness, and greed corrupt a once uncontaminated part of the sporting experience. Twice our Virginia home has been broken into and old decoys stolen. Although the Accomack County sheriff eventually apprehended the thieves, the largest part of my decoy collection is gone, fenced to dealers in Maryland and Long Island and soon sold to people who, perhaps, yearn for something hand-made in their largely machine-made lives.

This may be just as well. Since form should be based on function, the only proper place for a working decoy is in a marsh, on a river, or a white-capped bay where living waters design the pedestal and overcast skies provide the indirect lighting for flights of wildfowl, which are a wooden bird's most critical and only meaningful audience.

EIGHT: WATERFOWL STAMPS AND PRINTS

A prominent art dealer was asked why, considering the prestige and the possibility of earning over half a million dollars in print sales, not all the nation's best wildlife artists participate in the annual duck stamp contest. "Pride," he replied. "Can you imagine the embarrassment Arthur Singer or Roger Tory Peterson would feel if he only won second place?"

"MY WORLD IS divided into three kinds of people," said the postmaster of Onley, Virginia. "Those who don't like stamps, those who collect them, and those who don't care one way or t'other."

This homey bit of philosophy was shared with me a few years ago when I bought five $5 duck stamps from the postmaster. He clearly thought I wasn't wrapped too tight to spend $20 more than I needed to hunt ducks. However, because I asked for four of the stamps in a plate block, he had me pegged as a stamp collector, all right.

Stamps have been an important part of American history since 1639, when the first postal service began in Boston. Of course, stamps as gummed bits of paper to be stuck on mail were nonexistent in the seventeenth century, or even the eighteenth century when the infamous Stamp Act of 1765 became a prelude to revolution. Up until 1840 in England, and 1845 in the United States, "stamps" were merely the various marks used by postal authorities to indicate that the cost of carrying a newspaper, letter, or parcel a given distance had been paid.

The first federal stamps as we think of them today depicted former deputy postmaster general, Benjamin Franklin (five cents), and former president, George Washington (ten cents), and were issued on thin, bluish woven paper. Gradually, other political figures and, starting in 1869, scenic and commemorative designs were added to the postal pantheon. However, from the earliest issues to the Great Depression, U.S. stamps were exclusively concerned either with the delivery of mail or the taxing of certain transactions or commodities such as tobacco, alcoholic beverages, playing cards—even canned fruit and matches. Then in 1934 appeared the first of a unique series known officially as the Migratory Bird Hunting Stamp, but which most folks simply call "the duck stamp."

The idea of a stamp for waterfowlers which would furnish funds to save some of America's vanishing wetlands was not a new idea. Ray Holland had first suggested the idea in print in the July, 1920 issue of *Field & Stream*. Under the Migratory Bird Treaty of 1916 with Great Britain (on behalf of Canada) and the Migratory Bird Treaty Act of 1918, the federal government had a clear obligation to help manage and protect the waterfowl resources of North America. However, you can't manage or protect any resource without money, and as a federal game warden, Holland was more sensitive to this fact than many of the lawmakers in Washington.

Another nine years passed before the Migratory Bird Conservation Act of 1929 authorized a program of land and water acquisition to provide refuges where waterfowl could rest, feed, and breed. Even this public law would have been just so much rhetoric without the dynamic leadership of Jay N. "Ding" Darling, who served from 1934 to 1936 as chief of the Department of Agriculture's Biological Survey, precursor to the Interior Department's Fish and Wildlife Service today.

Darling was from Iowa and an avid duck hunter. He had seen the prime waterfowl nesting habitat of his home state disappear under the abuses of poor land management, and he feared that unless a national effort of preservation and restoration of wetlands was immediately undertaken, he would not only lose his recreation as a sportsman, the continent would lose its most spectacular renewable resource: ducks, geese, and swans.

Exploiting his talents as a popular political cartoonist for the *Des Moines Register,* Darling kept the pressure on Franklin Roosevelt from the time the new president took office in January, 1933 until an exasperated Roosevelt asked Darling to come to Washington to put up or shut up! At first Darling served as one of three members of an advisory council on wildlife resources that included Aldo Leopold, the father of modern wildlife management, and Tom Beck, a prominent sportsman and managing editor of *Collier's* magazine. This committee stressed that wildlife needed as much financial relief as people, and that draining marshes and attempting to put such marginal lands into grain production did neither ducks nor people any good in the long run. Darling used the almost daily reports of dust storms and land erosion in the Midwest to drive the point home. Finally, on March 16, 1934, the bill authorizing the duck stamp was made law, and every hunter of waterfowl 16 years of age or older–including scientific collectors–had to carry a validated (signed) duck stamp.

A story concerning the first stamp design is that Ding Darling was asked to submit an idea, and the busy artist-administrator rapidly sketched a sample and sent it over to the Bureau of Engraving. When he later asked what the printers thought of his concept, he was told that his "sketch" had been reworked and was already in production. Darling was furious! He was

How Man Does Improve On Nature

Ding Darling knew you could communicate a simple idea more directly and to more people with pictures. This contrast between the Iowa farmlands he knew as a youngster with the farmlands of the thirties really needs no comment at all. *(Courtesy J. N. Ding Darling Foundation, Inc.)*

convinced such an imperfect design would hurt first-year stamp sales. Years later he even asked if he could do an improved version which could be sold to stamp and print collectors.

However, Darling need not have worried about the new $1 stamp. It was an immediate success. First year sales were 635,001. At a time when marshland was selling for as little as 25 cents an acre in some parts of the country, Darling's design of "mallards alighting" helped preserve a good many wetland acres for mallards seeking a place to alight.

In 1935, wildlife artist Frank W. Benson was asked to design a stamp featuring the canvasback. Ding Darling's intention was to give emphasis to prairie pothole nesters directly affected by drought and poor land-use practices. All throughout the thirties and forties, the duck stamp program was aimed at establishing breeding sanctuaries in the upper midwestern United States which, combined with the prairie provinces of Canada, produce more than 70 percent of all the ducks in North America.

Darling hired Missourian, J. Clark Salyer II, to survey the Midwest to find areas which should be saved as waterfowl habitat. Salyer traveled 18,000 miles in six weeks and planned 600,000 acres of refuges. Over the next twenty years as chief of the refuge system, Salyer was in almost constant conflict with vested agricultural interests which saw acquisition efforts by the Fish and Wildlife Service as inimical to their use of Agriculture Department subsidies to drain and cultivate wetlands. In turn, Salyer tried to persuade farmers to accept Interior Department payments *not* to tamper with their marshes.

Even today, when we know wetlands are more productive of life than even the most fertile farm fields, and when a slew of new wetlands protection laws has been passed by the U.S. Congress, various state legislatures continue to make it difficult, if not impossible, for the Fish and Wildlife Service to continue its wetlands acquisition efforts in precisely that region of the country which produces the most waterfowl. In 1977, the North Dakota legislature passed a law giving county commissioners veto authority over federal wetlands purchases which require state approval. In Minnesota, a similar veto power was given to the counties by the governor and the state's natural resources commissioner.[1] Such edicts are probably

---

[1] Northwestern Minnesota used to be one of the most important waterfowl production and staging areas on the continent. As recently as 1947, an estimated one million ducks and geese frequented the region. Today state politicians and the U.S Army Corps of Engineers are pushing through a $30 million project (first conceived in 1914) that will effectively drain the Roseau River Wildlife Area to benefit approximately 80 flax farmers. At last count, only about 25,000 waterfowl were still using the area.

Sepia-tinted, Frances Lee Jaques' pair of black ducks is one of the most beautiful of all the duck stamp designs. With the emphasis on 4-color reproduction today, it may be hard for the black duck to win again, even though its declining numbers warrants the attention. *(Reproduction courtesy U.S. Fish and Wildlife Service)*

While some of the nation's best wildlife artists have not yet won a duck stamp contest, the surge in popular interest in waterfowling paintings and prints, generated in part due to duck stamp prints, has enhanced the value of such work as Bob Kuhn's classic portrayal of a Chesapeake retriever going into action, "First Down." *(Reproduction courtesy Remington Arms Collection of Game Art)*

During the first two decades of the duck stamp series, all the illustrators were wildlife artists, first, and stamp designers, second. Today the situation is reversed. Several of the recent duck stamp winners have been draughtsmen, first, and wildlife artists, second. Furthermore, while Frank W. Benson (1862–1951) might have made a few hundred dollars peddling prints of his duck stamp design, today's winners make up to $1 million selling signed and remarqued prints. These Ross geese, which won the 1977–78 contest, represent the first time amateur illustrator Martin R. Murk ever entered the competition. *(Reproduction courtesy U.S. Fish and Wildlife Service)*

unconstitutional in that they deny the right of an individual to sell his property to whom he pleases. However, they reflect county antagonism to previous federal condemnations and purchases and to the novel, but increasingly necessary, concept of land-use planning. Even after these laws are tested in the courts and rejected, they, and the attitudes they embody, will not make the essential task of wetlands preservation any easier, especially in those areas of the nation where duck-stamp dollars could do the most good. In death, J. Clark Salyer II had his revenge on farmers opposed to wetlands preservation when the Lower Souris National Wildlife Refuge in North Dakota was renamed for him. One marsh in the midst of North America's "duck factories" perpetuates the memory of a man who cared so very much for waterfowl.

During the 1935–1936 waterfowling season, stamp sales declined to 448,204. Up until 1942, all unsold stamps were destroyed at the end of each duck season. Therefore, Benson's "Canvasback Ducks Taking to Flight" is today the rarest and most expensive stamp in the series. Even a canceled (that is, signed by the hunter and without gum on the back) Benson stamp is worth about $40, and one in uncanceled, well-centered condition goes for up to $250.

Until the late 1940s, duck-stamp designs were commissioned by the Interior Department, and such prominent wildlife artists as Roland Clark ("Pintail Drake and Duck Alighting"), Lynn Bogue Hunt ("Greenwinged Teal"), and Francis Lee Jaques ("Black Mallards") contributed to the series. In 1946, Robert W. Hines of the Ohio Division of Conservation and Natural Resources designed "Redhead Ducks," which became the first issue to sell more than two million stamps. Hines was then asked to come to Washington, D.C., as a staff artist for the Fish and Wildlife Service by Frank Dufresne, a former *Field & Stream* field editor who was then director of information of Fish and Wildlife.

"I was told I would be working for someone named Rachel Carson," recalls Hines. "Of course, no one outside the Fish and Wildlife Service had heard of her at the time, and, to be honest, I wasn't too keen on working for a woman. But she was an exceptional person in every respect, and I never worked so hard—and enjoyed work more—in my life."

Bob may soon retire as director of Audio-Visual Services at the Fish and Wildlife Service and thinks he will start submitting entries to the duck stamp contest again. "We've never had a design win with a red-breasted merganser," says Bob. "I've got a couple good ideas I'd like to try for that species."

Until 1959, all duck stamp designs were black and white tinted with a color such as orange or violet. In 1959, a design by Maynard Reece depicting a Labrador retriever carrying a mallard drake won the competition, and two additional colors were used to accent the phragmites reeds and jumping mallards in the background. This design was controversial in that some contestants felt cheated when "a dog, not a duck, won the contest." However, most hunters were pleased with the stamp and appreciated not only its colorful appearance, but the fact that it featured the use of retrievers to reduce the loss of crippled game.

Another controversy cropped up when the 1975 stamp depicting a canvasback *decoy* was selected from a field of more traditional designs. Jealous rumors circulated that the design had been preselected and that the judges had been ordered to choose the canvasback decoy. However, having served as a judge in two recent duck stamp contests, I can attest that, if anything, such heavy-handed tactics by an Interior Department official would only tend to prejudice selection *against* his favored stamp. The simple reason the decoy design won in 1975 was that it was the best entry. In addition, it does reflect the great and growing interest in decoy collecting as an integral part of the tradition of waterfowling in North America. Furthermore, the issue proved to be immensely popular, adding over $12.4 million to Interior's wetlands acquisition fund.

Over the years, the price of each stamp has gone from $1 in 1934, to $2 in 1949, to $3 in 1959, to $5 in 1972, to $7.50 in 1979. As of this year, close to 75 million duck stamps have been sold, providing the federal government with more than $200 million for the purchase of critical wetlands for an average cost well under $100 an acre. In addition, Congress has extended the Interior Department a loan of $93,400,000 for the acquisition of wetlands, and this money will be repaid with duck stamp revenues beginning October 1, 1983.

What has this meant for waterfowl? A total of 2.3 million acres of migratory bird habitat has been saved with duck stamp money. Of the more than 300 national wildlife refuges, some 220 are managed primarily for waterfowl, totaling approximately 800,000 acres. In addition, there are literally thousands of waterfowl production areas totaling approximately 1.5 million acres. Writing as a waterfowler, birder, and stamp collector, and as someone who recognizes that the preservation of wetlands means a great deal more than just the preservation of my recreation, a $10 stamp would still be a bargain. You pay more than that for one box of 3-inch shells!

And now that we're talking dollars and acres, this is a good time to lay to rest some of the myths concerning misappropriation of duck stamp funds. The Migratory Bird Hunting Stamp Act of 1934 originally provided that not less than 90 percent of the total proceeds received from the sale of the stamps would be used to supplement other funds for the purchase, development, administration, and maintenance of waterfowl refuges throughout the country. The remaining 10 percent was to be used for the printing and distribution of the stamps as well as for the enforcement of federal laws affecting migratory bird conservation.

Right from the beginning there was criticism that too much money was being spent on wetlands development and not enough on acquisition. However, as various nongovernmental refuge owners such as the National Wildlife Federation and The Nature Conservancy have discovered in more recent decades, acquisition is only the first step in preservation. During the thirties, many hundreds of thousands of acres of public domain were available for restoration or development as waterfowl refuges. The Civilian Conservation Corps and the Works Progress Administration could provide a large labor pool, but there was no money for lumber, wire, cement, steel piping, fence posts, draglines, bulldozers, trucks, and the other hardware realities of wildlife management. Accordingly, a good many duck stamp dollars went to make waterfowl breeding habitat more effective sooner than would have been the case by merely purchasing more drained and dusty potholes.

On October 20, 1951, President Harry S Truman signed a law which authorized an increase in expenditure of duck stamp funds for enforcement and administration from 10 percent to 15 percent of annual receipts. However, duck hunters were miffed that any part of their duck stamp dollars should go to pay the salaries of federal wardens when prime wetlands were increasingly in short supply. Thus, on August 1, 1958, a law was signed by President Dwight D. Eisenhower increasing the price of the duck stamp to $3 and specifically earmarking *all* proceeds from duck stamp sales, "less the expenses of the Post Office Department in connection with engraving, printing, issuing, selling, and accounting for the stamps and the moneys received from their sale," for the acquisition of wetlands. That is the way the law stands today, except that in February, 1976, an amendment was passed modifying the name of the stamp to include the words "and conservation" to encourage nonhunters to buy the stamp as a means of protecting all species of wildlife dependent on marshes for existence.

Many waterfowlers have saved their duck stamps as souvenirs of seasons past. They are surprised to find their collections are now worth a fair amount of money. A complete set of used (that is, signed) duck stamps from 1934 to the present (45 years) is worth over $300. If the stamps are all unsigned, well-centered, in excellent condition, and without hinge marks on their gummed sides, a complete set may cost $2,500.

Michael E. Berger, assistant conservation director of the National Wildlife Federation, actually prefers signed stamps, for he is putting together a collection of autographs of prominent wildlife artists, scientists, and conservationists on duck stamps. Mike's job is made a little easier by the fact that the U.S. Philatelic Agency sells duck stamps at face value for three years after their hunting season's expiration dates. This special extension generates more funds for the purchase of wetlands since most other U.S. revenue and commemorative stamps are available for only a year after the date they first appear. (More information on how to obtain particularly fine, well-centered duck stamps from previous seasons can be obtained from the Philatelic Sales Agency, U.S. Postal Service, Washington, D.C. 20402.)

The Department of the Interior has revised its publication *Duck Stamp Data* and issued the book in a three-holed, looseleaf form so that new pages can be purchased annually from the Superintendent of Documents, U.S. Government Printing Office, Washington, D.C. 20402, as new stamps are issued. This book provides possibly more information than you care to know about duck stamps, but there is a space on each looseleaf page where the duck stamp fits, and a complete set makes for a stunning volume.

If you are not interested in collecting duck stamps, but would like to use them to make a contribution to conservation above and beyond the original purchase price, send your old stamps (including any other special hunting or fishing stamps) to the Florida Audubon Society, P.O. Drawer 7F, Maitland, Fla. 32751. Your stamps will be sold to collectors, and the money raised will be used to protect the bald eagle in Florida. This work includes the acquisition of eagle habitat, an annual survey of nesting birds, and the maintenance of captives which, for whatever reason, cannot be released to the wild.

Even duck stamp reproductions have served the cause of conservation. In the spring of 1978, the Citizens Committee to Save the Cache River

Basin (515 South Main, Stuttgart, Arkansas 72160) offered sets of reproduction duck stamps (1935 to 1976) in a full color print for $30 each, or $45 framed or laminated. All proceeds were used to fight the U.S. Army Corps of Engineers' proposal to channelize the Cache River, a project which would drain approximately 200,000 acres of prime waterfowl habitat. Since any struggle with the Corps involves years of litigation and tens of thousands of volunteer dollars to offset the Corps's seemingly limitless supply of our tax dollars, you may still want to make a contribution to waterfowl conservation in the Mississippi Flyway and receive a reproduction duck stamp set for less than one-tenth the cost of a canceled set.

The future success of the duck-stamp program was not as clearly perceived 40 years ago as it is today in retrospect. Both the 1935 and 1936 stamp sales were lower than the original issue of 1934. Ding Darling remained hopeful that, in the long run, duck stamp money would protect important breeding areas for waterfowl. However, he gradually came to believe that the most important task of conservation was to educate the citizens who owned the land to manage for wildlife as well as for food and fiber production rather than encourage Uncle Sam to buy out the landowners and do the management himself. Darling was a strong advocate of having "Uncle" do only what the states and private individuals could not do.

Thus, Ding Darling decided to devote his considerable energies to an even larger goal than the federal preservation of wetlands. In February, 1936, he resigned his government post (for which, by the way, he never took a salary) to devote himself to developing an organization whose mission would be the teaching of conservation in every public school in the country: the National Wildlife Federation.

Before he left office, Darling got President Franklin Roosevelt's word that he would make some kind of personal contribution on behalf of the infant organization. While political promises are sometimes forgotten, Darling arranged a meeting on August 12, 1937, between FDR and a group of concerned conservationists to persuade the president to proclaim a National Wildlife Week sometime during the following year. Among those represented were Secretary of Agriculture Henry Wallace, Senator Harry B. Hawes of Missouri, and Carl Shoemaker, conservation director of the National Wildlife Federation. This is how Shoemaker remembers that historic scene:

The president was in a jovial mood as he sat behind his big desk cluttered with ships, anchors, and other naval miniatures. We lined up in a semicircle facing him. The group had selected Senator Hawes to state the purpose of the meeting, but first the senator had to tell a story about a retriever dog he once owned. It was a good yarn and reminded the president of one time when he was out goose hunting.

It was a clear day and shooting was poor. Finally, Roosevelt said, he saw two geese overhead coming ino the decoys. They were pretty high, but he stood up and fired at the lead goose and hit it. He then swung around and fired at the second one, but he didn't know whether or not he hit it because the first goose landed on his head and knocked him down in the blind. He thought it might have killed him!

"Everyone laughed, and Senator Hawes, with a smile, remarked, "I'll bet that John L. Lewis [2] wished it had." That was at the time Lewis was having a row with the president over the coal mines.

Senator Hawes then stated the purpose of our visit, outlined the benefits that would flow from a Wildlife Week and urged the president to issue a proclamation establishing it. The idea appealed to him and out of a clear sky, he asked, "When do you want it? What dates do you suggest?"

That was something that neither Hawes nor any of the rest of us had decided. There were blank stares on all our faces, and everyone looked at me. I reached into the clouds and blurted out, "The first week of spring."

"All right," said the president. "I'll have Mac [Marvin McIntyre, the president's secretary] fix it up." With a thank you and a few more pleasantries, we left the office, and the Wildlife Week proclamation was in the bag.

To commemorate the week, Ding Darling decided to create a sheet of wildlife stamps that would be given to anyone making a donation of a dollar or more to the National Wildlife Federation. While some writers claim the Federation's stamp program was inspired by Darling's "success" with the duck stamp program, it is more likely the nongovernmental National Wildlife Federation stamp effort was patterned after the Christmas Seal program run by the American Red Cross and the National Tuberculosis Association.

---

[2] John Llewellyn Lewis, born in 1880 in Lucas, Iowa, was from 1920, and throughout the Roosevelt Administration, president of the United Mine Workers of America.

The idea of Christmas Seals was born in Denmark in 1904. A postal employee by the name of Einar Holboell decided to "sell" decorative stamps to raise money for charitable purposes, and he persuaded postal authorities in Sweden and Iceland, as well as Denmark, to cooperate with his scheme. By 1907, Christmas Seals had caught on in the United States, and while not an official postal issue, the colorful stamps quickly became popular with collectors and with people using them to decorate letters and packages at Christmas time.

Ding Darling hoped for a similar charitable effort on behalf of wildlife. He designed the first stamps himself and purposely chose sixteen game birds and mammals that had either been saved through conservation or which were particularly well suited to wildlife management. Of all types of hunting, Darling was most passionately a waterfowler. Thus, five—Canada goose, canvasback, mallard, greater scaup, and a shorebird, the Wilson's snipe—of the eight birds depicted are covered by the Migratory Bird Hunting Stamp Act, which Darling helped to create as chief of the Biological Survey. The originals of this first series, half of which Darling created on a train between Des Mines, Iowa, and Cheyenne, Wyoming, are supposed to be stored by the Smithsonian Institution. However, when last asked, Smithsonian officials were unable to locate the Darling art, and it is feared that over the years, various museum employees have taken the paintings home for "temporary display" and never returned them.

The fate of stamps produced from the paintings was equally unfortunate. The campaign began well, for during the week of March 20–26, 1938, pictures of the president sitting at his desk in the White House admiring the first sheet of National Wildlife Week stamps appeared on the front page of newspapers across the country. Roosevelt was well known as a philatelist, and such publicity should have been a great boost for first-year sales.

However, Wildlife Week stamps are not duck stamps. There is no law which requires you to buy them. In the same way that commemorative medals are never as popular with collectors as coins of the realm, voluntary donations for Wildlife Week stamps have never been as generous as mandatory "donations" for duck stamps. Just as in recent years we have seen various volunteer efforts fail in Ohio and Colorado to raise substantial funds for the preservation of nongame species, first-year sales of Wildlife Week stamps among sportsman's groups were disastrous.

For over forty years, the National Wildlife Federation has raised money for conservation with wildlife stamps, many featuring North American waterfowl. So attractive are these issues, and so far superior in subject and design to most U.S. Post Office Department issues, postal clerks regularly handle mail bearing National Wildlife Federation stamps as postage. Depending on how the clerks feel that day, they sometimes let the federation-stamped letters go through without payment; sometimes not. *(Courtesy George Reiger)*

Many nations have produced postage stamps honoring waterfowl and waterfowling. This small sample includes a shoveler from Czechoslovakia, a pair of common eiders from Saint Pierre and Miquelon, a duck hunter from San Marino, a Canada goose from Canada (where else?), a pair of mandarin ducks from Japan, and a mallard from Yugoslavia. *(Courtesy George Reiger)*

The National Wildlife Federation still hears occasionally from someone who has just found a box of 1938 stamps in an attic or garage where a well-intentioned volunteer had stored them—"temporarily." Far worse were instances involving theft or embezzlement. One volunteer bought a new car and paid for it all with $1 bills received from stamp donations. Another did so well, he opened up a huge "regional office," bought new clothes for himself and his family, and finally contributed exactly $31 to the Federation headquarters in Washington, D.C.

The next few years were not much better. Ducks Unlimited had been formed about the same time as the National Wildlife Federation, but instead of staying within the aegis of the Federation, "to present a united conservation front," as Darling hopefully described his futile dream, Ducks Unlimited went its own way, taking a number of major financial contributors. In the dark winter of 1944, Ding Darling wrote a "Coroner's Verdict" for his organization which ended: "Good-bye, Federation. Good-bye to all our high hopes of a vocal and informed conservation popular front. Good-bye to the only conservation mechanism which had promise of uniting 36,000 local conservation organizations which, un-united, are practically helpless in combatting the major exploiters of our natural resources."

This "last will and testament" shamed several well-heeled sportsmen into making sizeable donations to help the Federation survive. After World War II, the organization sought the assistance of professional sales and advertising personnel who quickly scrapped the volunteer program and eventually turned debt into profit. Direct mail campaigns replaced the more personal, but highly unreliable, system of door-to-door appeals. In 1941, the National Wildlife Federation received little more than $16,400 in stamp donations. Today the stamp program earns more than half a million dollars annually for the organization.

The popularity of stamps depicting wildlife has led to something approaching an avalanche of production by other nations eager to provide collectors with attractive educational issues that will also bring in foreign dollars to feed hungry government coffers. In 1951, for example, the former Portuguese colony of Angola issued a bird series that sold at the time for a few dollars. Today the set is worth over $200.

Back when Europeans still had empires, many of the colonial issues (particularly those of the British) were rich and varied in depicting wildlife. Unfortunately, all too often today, the former colonies have abandoned their wildlife heritage in governmental policy as well as postage stamps, and the hard, unattractive faces of politicians and generals decorate the stamps of "liberated nations." Perhaps, they are only imitating the unimaginative track record of the United States.

Retired federal biologist Russell T. "Oz" Norris is one of many stamp collectors who specialize in wildlife. Besides being one of the nation's most active bird banders (over 2,500 birds last year), Oz Norris is a recognized authority on that branch of topical stamp collecting known as "bio-philately."

"When people ask me why I collect so many foreign stamps," says Norris, "I have to tell them honestly that, with the possible exception of Italy, no other nation has done a worse job of publicizing its natural resources than the United States. By contrast, the Soviet Union may issue in a single year nearly as many wildlife stamps as we've put out in our entire history."

The reason for this poor U.S. showing is that our Post Office Department's stamp selection process has traditionally been geared to pay off political debts, not to enlighten the people. Powerful lobby groups like the wool growers, truckers, and poultry breeders have little trouble getting stamps honoring their activities. While more people might prefer wild ducks to chickens on their postage stamps, such interest is generalized and, therefore, politically weak.

However, a breakthrough occurred in 1956 when a direct appeal was made to President Dwight D. Eisenhower by a close friend and fellow sportsman, Samuel E. Neel. The president was shown two paintings by Bob Hines and asked why it was so difficult to get postal authorities to accept wildlife themes for commemorative issues. Eisenhower, too, wanted to know the reason why, and in no time at all, three 3¢ stamps designed by Hines and depicting the wild turkey, pronghorn antelope, and king salmon were rolling off government presses.

More wildlife conservation postage stamps have been issued since 1956, and among my special favorites is the 6¢ wood ducks designed by Stanley W. Galli. Unfortunately, politics again, rather than merit or esthetics, dominated the thinking of the postage stamp committee which selected this design in 1968. Henry Schmidt, chairman of the board of Ducks Unlimited and then president of the Consolidation Coal Company, "suggested" to Congressman Michael Kirwan of Ohio that it would be nice to commemorate the fortieth anniversary of the Migratory Bird Treaty with a waterfowl postage stamp. Furthermore, the stamp should be issued in

Cleveland, where Schmidt's company's headquarters were located. Representative Kirwan was an influential member of the House, and although that year the Congressional postal committee was busy paying off debts to the Army Corps of Engineers and Walt Disney, it still found room, after Kirwan's urging, for Schmidt's wood duck stamp.

Several states require special hunting and fishing stamps. New Jersey's $3 woodcock stamp and Nebraska's more sophisticated $7.50 wildlife habitat acquisition stamp are just two examples. These programs, but principally the federal duck stamp effort, have inspired the envy of a number of influential sportsmen's groups and state wildlife administrators. Without very clear ideas as to what they would do with the money when they started, various states have been climbing aboard a state duck stamp bandwagon.

California began the trend in 1971, followed by Iowa in 1972, Maryland in 1974, Illinois and Massachusetts in 1975, Indiana in 1976, and still others pending or recently approved. The irresponsible approach to the duck stamp concept assumed by a few states is characterized by the fact that Indiana's premier issue was copied by state biologist J. "Sonny" Bashore from a jumping green-winged teal design on the June 1955 cover of the Ohio Conservation Bulletin, originally painted by Edward J. Bierly, three-time national duck stamp contest winner.

When Bashore attempted to market prints of his plagiarism ("$65 unframed; $105 framed with mint stamp"), he was confronted by Bierly, who persuaded Bashore to sign a confession of guilt in exchange for a promise that he would not be prosecuted. However, Ed Bierly did expect the state of Indiana to publicize the shame of its first duck stamp and, moreover, to adopt duck stamp contest regulations similar to those used by the federal government to prevent just such instances of artistic theft. Instead, Indiana has continued on its own stubborn course. In the best tradition of bureaucratic loyalty, the state had Bashore produce another duck stamp for the 1977 season. Furthermore, art dealers continue to sell the "Bashore teal" to unknowing customers.

By law, Maryland is required to use the majority of its duck stamp revenues, not to preserve wetlands, but to release pen-reared mallards into the Atlantic Flyway. The ducks often leave Maryland, providing sport to hunters in surrounding states where duck stamps are not required. In addition to the waste of money such stocking efforts represent, there is always the chance that domestic waterfowl diseases will be spread to wild birds, not to speak—as I have at greater length in chapter five—of the unwarranted competition created through hybridization for the black duck.

Meanwhile other states have begun sharing their considerable duck stamp proceeds with Ducks Unlimited, amounting to over $4 million by 1978. DU is striving to raise $75 million during the next few years in order to begin approximately 1.25 million acres of wetland projects in Canada. Such benefit-sharing by the states is a light-years improvement over the business of stocking mallards. However, writing as someone who has not had enough law schooling to make him a jogger, but just enough legal training to make him ask embarrassing questions, the states participating in this program may be open to challenge in the courts over the issues of whether state-raised revenues can be spent in a foreign nation, and why other nongovernmental waterfowl-interested organizations like the Nature Conservancy and the Wildlife Management Institute do not share in this wealth, particularly since they can spend funds within the states which generated them through research contracts or wetland acquisitions.

Meanwhile the federal duck stamp program continues to pioneer another trend, this one having to do with the remarkable escalation in values associated with prints made from duck stamps. To select each year's design, the Fish and Wildlife Service conducts an annual contest, open to all interested artists for the next year's duck stamp. Details of the contest are announced in midsummer, and all entries must be postmarked no later than October 15. (Rules for the contest are available from the Public Affairs Office, U.S. Fish and Wildlife Service, Washington, D.C. 20240.)

Previous to 1949, outstanding illustrators were invited to submit entries, but that year, the contest was open to give any artist a chance to compete. Several thousand entries are typical today, ranging from superb material by many of the nation's best wildlife illustrators to pictures submitted by grade-scool students. Three of my favorite also-rans have been a pair of mallards bursting through an American flag in honor of the bicentennial; an enormous mallard, which in perspective would have weighed over 500 pounds, about to land on a startled hunter putting out decoys; and a roasted bird about to be carved up for Christmas dinner. Since the rules now stipulate that a live bird must be seen somewhere in the stamp, a vague V, presumably of geese, could be made out through the window behind the hungry family's heads.

The judging is held in the main auditorium of the Interior Depart-

In 1956, Edward J. Bierly won the contest with this Oriental-style pair of common mergansers. Although merganser species have been depicted three times on duck stamps, the red-breasted merganser has yet to appear in the series. *(Reproduction courtesy Edward J. Bierly)*

ment, and up until a few years ago, there was a relatively small audience for the contest. After all, the winner receives no compensation from the government except an album containing a sheet of his stamps. Until 1970, if a winning artist could capitalize on his design by selling autographed prints and earning a few thousand dollars, he was almost viewed with suspicion by Washington bureaucrats earning fixed salaries. In 1970, when Ed Bierly received $55,000 for two years of print production of his winning Ross geese design, he was as astonished as his colleagues were envious, for Bierly was then able to retire early from the National Park Service and concentrate on improving his wildlife art.

Today such sums are bush-league money. The 1976–1977 design was a scratchboard representation of a family of Canada geese done by Alderson "Sandy" Magee of Sharon, Connecticut. I was one of a panel of five judges—ornithologists, conservationists, and editors—who selected that picture from nearly 300 entries. We circled the stage where all entries were anonymously on display and individually made a selection of approximately 30 designs which we then voted on as a group. Except for minor consultation between the judges as to the accuracy of a bird—for example, had the artist painted the hen red-breasted merganser he intended, or was it an immature male common merganser? Questions were asked of technicians from the Bureau of Engraving and Printing as to whether a particular background is too "busy" for reproduction, or whether there is room for the logotype and other information the Fish and Wildlife Service needs to print on the stamp—preliminary selection is a strangely quiet process. Everyone on the stage speaks in whispers, while everyone in the audience strains forward in an attempt to hear what is being said. Art dealers, artists, and journalists dominate the first ten rows, and biologists, bureaucrats, friends of the family, and the merely curious are scattered in seats throughout the rest of the auditorium.

The next step in the contest has the judges taking seats with their backs to the audience and being given a bindery of white cards with numbers printed on both sides: 1 through 10. As the pictures are held up by a Fish and Wildlife Service official at the back of the stage, we held up what score we gave it so both the official and the audience could see the number simultaneously. As in a diving competition, the higher the number, the higher the score.

Preliminary judging reduces the entries to five, and from those five, first, second, and third place winners are chosen. However, the only meaningful winner is number one. It is unheard of in my experience that there is any doubt among the judges regarding which pictures constitute the top three. By the last round of judging, you simply don't see one judge hold up a number 2 while the others hold up number 10 cards. While one or two judges may feel that the second-place winner should have been first, the majority and the logic of mathematics determines that the artist who wins the duck stamp contest usually wins with at least 48 out of a possible 50 points. Alderson Magee won all 50.

There are two amusing anecdotes associated with Magee's triumph.

One is that he won on his first try after barely making the midnight deadline on October 15. Magee had quit his job with Pratt-Whitney Aircraft in 1971 and was struggling to make a living as an artist. When word came that he had won the contest, he had forgotten he ever entered! Furthermore, he relates, "I wasn't aware of the financial implications until well-wishers explained what it could mean."

When the Bureau of Engraving and Printing representative saw Magee's black and white scratchboard, he was upset, for the bureau was eager to prove its versatility and capability with any combination of colors like those found in Daniel Maass's wood ducks of 1974. The representative suggested he would have to tint the Magee scratchboard. We went to get the art critic for *The Washington Post* to have the bureau's representative

This is the scratch-board design with which Alderson Magee won the 1976 duck stamp contest—and made himself a rich man in the process. *(Reproduction courtesy U.S. Fish and Wildlife Service)*

repeat his suggestion for the benefit of the press. After the newspaper reported the idea, the Bureau of Engraving and Printing thought better of it. Thus, Magee's stamp was issued as the black and white design it was intended to be, and the bureau added just the right touch of color with green lettering at the top and bottom of the stamp.

Sandy Magee has signed and sold 3,600 prints at $100 each and "re-marqued" (made a small original drawing on the print) 1,000 additional prints at $250 each. Even with 40 percent deducted for production costs and dealers' commissions, Magee has earned more than $350,000 from his winning duck stamp.

This sum is more than three times the value of the Nobel Prize. Yet the fact that "limited editions" of duck stamp prints now reach 10,000 enabled Albert Gilbert's 1978–1979 hooded merganser design to gross more than $1 million.

When will this dizzy spiral stop? Art dealer Russell Fink believes not for many years. He points out that there are over two million duck hunters in this country owning a current duck stamp, and every hunter is a potential duck stamp print purchaser. Furthermore, since there is no more contagious disease than the collecting fever, thousands of new print buyers may have only the slightest interest in waterfowling.

"The chain letter is just getting started," said one hopeful artist.

"If an entry wins with Donald Duck on it, people will buy it just to complete their collection," comments Ed Bierly.

Longtime investors are having a field day with the prints of early duck stamp artists. Lynn Bogue Hunt's green-winged teal is now worth $5,000 and Frank Benson's rare canvasback of which only 100 were made, is worth nearly $10,000. Ironically, these figures might be even higher if there was more of a chance for more collectors to assemble a full set of duck stamp prints. However, since most collectors begin with a print from the past decade, this is where the greatest inflation in original price has occurred. Maynard Reece's cinnamon teal duck stamp print sold for $75 in 1972, when it first appeared. Today it sells for $3,500. Maass's wood ducks design sold for $100 in 1974 and is now worth $800, even though this print series is unnumbered. Even Magee's Canada geese print, which in 1976 sold for $100, is presently valued at $600.

A complete collection of duck stamp prints which originally cost less than $1,500 over the past forty-five years is today worth well over $50,000.

Envious people have suggested transferring the print profits from the artist to the U.S. Treasury. Since the government takes most of the profits in the form of taxes, the duck stamp contest is one of the few chances an artist has for occupying, albeit briefly, the catbird seat. When you consider all the satisfaction wildlife stamps have given us in the decades since Lynn Bogue Hunt and Roland Clark submitted their etchings, it is good to see their inheritors reaping at least a partial harvest from our pleasure.

Friends of mine are surprised to find, what with my interest in duck stamps, decoys, and old books on waterfowling, that I don't collect duck stamp prints as well. I try to explain that I collect things which blend artistic form with function. Fine old arrowheads are more beautiful for me than most modern cut-stone abstractions, because arrowheads were designed for a particular and necessary purpose. In the same way, I often find the finished duck stamp more attractive than its print.

Some friends say they agree, but misinterpret my point when they add "duck stamp prints aren't really art; they're too heavily influenced by the camera." That is a curious remark. It is like saying Renaissance statuary reflects too much in the classical era. Contemporary duck stamps inevitably show the influence of the camera, because any piece of modern representational drawing and painting does. Duck stamps are not intended to be "artistic." They are waterfowl illustration—anatomically correct, pleasingly designed, and reduced to a 1¼-inch by 1¾-inch format. Furthermore, they must have sufficient "nonbird space" in the stamp for nearly twenty words and numerical groups of governmenal information.

On my home walls, there are several old maps framed and hung. Such things are not art. Certainly the cartographers who created them had no illusions along these lines. But such material gives me, as I trust it gave its creators, satisfaction. This is the same way I view a collection of duck stamps. Although I have made much of rising duck stamp values in this chapter, I groaned aloud when I first learned what was happening to their monetary values from my stamp dealer and birding friend, Charles Vaughn. Instead of having bits of paper that are mementos of seasons past and plate blocks that make me feel virtuous about the contribution I've made toward wetlands preservation, I have an "investment"—which means something I can no longer keep casually around the house but must now insure with a fine arts policy or lock away in a bank vault.

So forgive me if I fantasize about a duck stamp counterfeiter who starts reproducing old Bensons and Hunts at a tremendous rate, flooding the market with precise replicas, and destroying forever anyone's chance to boast about how he is going to pay for a new vacation home with duck stamps. Then, when the brokers, agents, and bankers pack up their money bags and abandon the world of biophilately, I'll be left to contemplate what a lovely pattern of lines and color there is in any grouping of old stamps and recall the secret reason I never traded in my canceled 1958–1959 Canada geese design for a mint—more valuable, but less personal—replacement.

NINE: CANADA
AND DUCKS UNLIMITED

"The operation of the game preserve system, which within a few years has become so extensive, is doing something to protect the birds, yet, in the nature of things, it cannot affect them much. Each year the ducks become less and less."

George Bird Grinnell, in 1901

"DU has been successful over the past four decades because it has steadfastly adhered to its singleness of purpose: habitat restoration."

Dale E. Whitesell, executive vice-president
of Ducks Unlimited

For MORE than one-quarter century I've hunted waterfowl in North America. I've crouched in islands of water hyacinth and watched Okeechobee ringbills sweep into the decoys. I've hacked channels through ice to reach open water where broadbill and brant passed in wavy lines. I've jumped mallards from the crystalline headwaters of the Mississippi and tumbled pintail from the crystalline skies of California. I've watched tens of thousands of geese whiffling toward earth in all four flyways.

I thought I knew something about the waterfowl resources of North America, but I was wrong. You know less than half until you've seen black ducks winging over the boreal forest and lakes of Quebec, goldeneyes nesting in chimneys and treetops in Ontario, ruddy duck drakes displaying in Manitoba sloughs, colonies of eider squatting in the coastal tundra of the Northwest Territories, and clouds of geese staging on the Athabasca River Delta. You can't begin to comprehend waterfowl in North America until you've sampled the breadth of summer Canada.

Canadian biologists take great pride in their waterfowl resources and quite naturally look on them as something Canada loans to the United States, not the other way around.

"Why should there be two standards of wildlife consumption?" asks Doug Stephen, a regional director for the Canadian Wildlife Service. "Americans and Canadians accept the fact that anadromous fishes, such as salmon and shad, belong primarily to the nation in whose rivers such fishes spawn. Neither Canada nor the United States would spend tens of millions of dollars a year nurturing salmon to allow Japanese or Danes to come along and catch them all. Why should it be any different with ducks?"

We were flying over Manitoba's Waterhen Lake when Doug made his remarks. Below was a body of water that had once been famous for its late summer concentrations of diving ducks. In the 1950s, Waterhen Lake commonly contained 200,000 molting redheads and canvasbacks. Today 30,000 is reckoned to be a sizable number.

"Canadian biologists and sportsmen look on most North American ducks and geese as *our* resources. We produce them. They breed in our

The best time to make the summer census of waterfowl in Canada and to acquire birds for banding is during the post-breeding molt. These flightless ducks are being herded by an airboat and wading men toward a banding trap in Saskatchewan. *(Photograph by Rex Gary Schmidt)*

potholes, lakes, and sloughs, and Canadian insects and grain provide them with a start in life. Every fall, we take what we consider to be a fair share of the birds and watch the rest, still in great flocks, fly across the border. Next spring, we see them straggle home, in some instances reduced far below what legal hunting should have allowed and so laced with mercury, lead, and other contaminants picked up in the cesspools into which you've

A soft-mouthed retriever can be a help in locating molting birds hiding in the underbrush. This black Lab is turning over a young mallard to his master for banding. *(Photograph by Fred Glover)*

converted so many marshes and bays, we get to wonder whether we shouldn't encourage all our ducks and geese to short stop in Canada."

Such talk is provocative, of course, and Doug would be the first to acknowledge that even if migratory instincts could be altered and enough open water could be created in Canada for the tens of millions of waterfowl that breed there, there would be no way Canada—or all the nations of the Western Hemisphere, for that matter—could afford to feed artificially so many birds all winter long. Doug Stephen's words were intended to stir Americans into perceiving waterfowl-related problems from a broader perspective than that provided by their local river or marsh where ducks are seen only during the gunning season.

Canada's failures in land-use planning are similar to our own. However, since Canada is the wellspring for most of the waterfowl bred in North America, Canada's mistakes reverberate in every county of the United States. In this nation, for example, when the Conowingo Dam and pollution destroyed the *Vallisneria* beds at the mouth of the Susquehanna River, wintering canvasbacks switched to clams found at the mouths of other Chesapeake tributaries. The birds survived, even if they didn't flourish as well as before. However, once a Canadian canvasback breeding marsh is drained for the production of wheat for export to China or Russia, there can be no more canvasbacks produced there ever again—which, every year, means fewer canvasbacks to survive on Chesapeake shellfish.

While it is true that until very recently the United States had set a relatively poor example in wetlands protection, Canada has learned little from our past errors. A good many people in Canada know what the problems are and what has to be done to alleviate them, but such people have national and international perspectives not shared by the real power-brokers in Canadian affairs: the provincial politicians. High wheat prices have inspired an orgy of land clearing, pond and marsh draining, and shelter-belt destruction all through the prime farming and waterfowl-nesting habitat of southern Manitoba, Saskatchewan, and Alberta. The current agricultural boom is reminiscent of earlier land-clearing operations during World War I. However, nothing then approached the magnitude of abuse of today in this region, which produces up to 60 percent of all the mallards in North America. The birds have traditionally nested on the five to six million potholes formerly found there.

It is an old story: The cash-poor farmer cannot meet his obligations with what he has, so he clears a few more acres and produces a bit more wheat. That adds to national overproduction and causes prices to sag, keeping the farmer at the minimal level where he started. So he drains still more land until he is so strung out he is on the verge of bankruptcy. Then the Chinese or Russians have a rice or wheat failure, and the farmer is suddenly able to make enough to pay off most of his obligations and buy a new tractor or combine. Then the pattern of debt and more land clearing begins all over again.

In Saskatchewan alone, nearly 60,000 acres of wetlands have been drained with governmental funds since 1950; more than 40,000 acres of the total have been drained in the past decade. Presently, over 100 major governmental drainage projects in southern Saskatchewan are underway with approximately 25 new ones coming on the line each year. Furthermore, none of these statistics begin to describe the *thousands* of *private* drainage projects carried out each year without the assistance of government funds and without the meager restraints associated with federal or provincial projects. Tragically, Canadians do not have a Presidential Executive Order or a Section 404 clause within a Federal Water Pollution Control Act to discourage the destruction of wetlands as we do in the United States.

Manitoba's classic prairie pothole region around Minnedosa is increasingly taking on the character of a Waterfowl Disaster Area. From 1930 to present, the amount of land cleared or cultivated has risen from 48 percent to better than 80 percent. In just one accounting of 1,200 potholes made between 1949 and 1964, sixteen percent were drained and plowed, 37 percent were stripped of their shoreline vegetation, and 13 percent "were adversely affected by road construction." More than a decade later, of the remaining 408 unaffected potholes in the original survey, only a couple dozen continue to produce ducks as they did during what old-timers already describe as the "glory years" immediately following World War II. Across all of Canada, more than 30 percent of the most critical nesting ponds have been lost in just the past ten years.

The most disturbing aspect of these enormous man-made changes in the land- and waterscape of western Canada is that some farmers recognize they are destroying ducks by destroying their habitat and delight in such activity. Many prairie farmers regard waterfowl as vermin, and Manitoban biologists describe a veritable pyromania each spring throughout the province as farmers burn off pond and ditch margins after the birds have started nesting.

"Not all the destruction of ducks is incidental," asserts Robert Nero, wetlands development specialist. "Some of the burning is intended to fry hens on their nests."

The reason for such animosity is crop depredations. In the fall, after young mallards and pintail join their parents in swathed fields where the wheat has been cut and left to dry and ripen in windrows, the potential for destruction amounts to more than 5,000 tons of grain consumed or trampled every day until the wheat is combined or the ducks head south. Field-feeding waterfowl destroy several millions of dollars worth of Canadian wheat and other cereals every fall. Even though the Canadian federal government raised its waterfowl depredations compensation fund from $1 million to $2.8 million in March 1978, it is not enough, and prairie farmers are not likely to get additional relief from this quarter for at least another five years. Furthermore, since $25 per acre is the maximum allowable reimbursement for crop losses due to waterfowl—a payment far below the 1979 value of the grain yield per acre, which the farmer receives only after considerable paperwork and delay—Canadian farmers understandably see little beauty in the clouds of ducks and geese that settle into their fields each fall before harvest.

Although losses in prairie pothole country average $1,000 per farm,

The Minnedosa farm at left has been drained with the hope of producing a few more acres of grain. The Minnedosa field with potholes at right yields both wheat and ducks. Unfortunately, Manitoba's present farm policy seems to favor drainers. *(Photographs by George Reiger)*

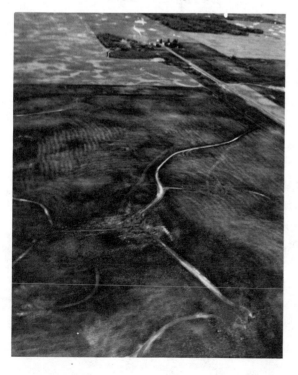
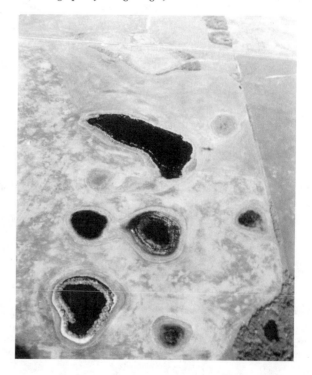

For every pintail earning an honest living by tipping for his food, there are dozens which find it easier to rip off Canadian farmers of their unharvested wheat. American sportsmen, through Ducks Unlimited, can established much good will in Canada if they begin to de-emphasize production of such field-feeding species as pintail and mallards and do more to restore threatened divers like canvasback and redheads. *(Photograph by George Reiger)*

with a few fortunate farmers escaping depredations completely, such distributed statistics are misleading in that they give no indication of the locustlike damage created by field-feeding waterfowl in a prime concentration area such as Oak Hammock Marsh, just north of Winnipeg. This area was set aside and developed in 1973 by Ducks Unlimited, the Canadian Wildlife Service, and the Manitoba Department of Mines, Resources and Environment. Many geese are produced on the marsh, and every fall, some 80,000 Canadas, snow, and blue geese gather here before moving further south. The hunting is reported to be superb.

However, crop depredations are even more spectacular, and some farmers have had to accept governmental charity to avoid bankruptcy, even though they had excellent harvest and profit prospects before the birds arrived. Regulated hunting alone offers insufficient control for the damage, and as the protests of farmers grow louder each year, provincial officials are wondering whether the refuge at Oak Hammock Marsh was such a good idea in the first place.

Some American sportsmen have suggested that Ducks Unlimited or the U.S. government contribute to the compensation fund administered by the Canadian government. However, aside from the Congressional approval needed for federal assistance to other nations and the strict prohibition against U.S. citizens giving money directly to a foreign government, there is the awesome fact that not all the money Ducks Unlimited or the federal duck stamp program raises annually could make adequate restitution to all the Canadian farmers adversely affected by waterfowl.

On the other hand, because American biologists and conservation administrators working for the state and federal governments are already absorbed by the task of protecting and managing the remaining wetlands in the United States, if there is hope that Americans can do something to help work out a compromise to the terrible paradox that Canada's best grain-producing lands are, also, the continent's best duck-producing lands, it lies with the nongovernmental, nonprofit, and Chicago-based organization known as Ducks Unlimited, or simply DU.

Chicago lies near the geographical center of the continent. However, this is not the only reason this city hosts the headquarters of DU. The Chicago-to-St.-Louis-to-southwest-Texas diagonal across the Mississippi and Central Flyways has been a popular recreational pathway for some of waterfowling's most enthusiastic and influential participants for over one hundred years. Just as George Bird Grinnell and Joseph W. Long documented waterfowling activities in the Atlantic Flyway before the turn of the century, William Bruce Leffingwell and William Chester Hazelton described the great days of "ducking" in the Mississippi and Central Flyways from the 1880s through World War I.

Born in 1870, Hazelton and other wealthy men of his generation followed waterfowl from the Great Lakes—the shooting along the south shore of Lake Michigan once ranked with the best found anywhere in the continent—to Missouri and Arkansas. When the birds, mainly redheads and pintail, retired to Texas [1] to wait out the late winter storms, Hazelton, Clark McAdams, Joseph Pulitzer, Jr., and other waterfowling zealots would pursue the ducks aboard yachts or take trains to the coast where they would stay at one of several fashionable Texas spas such as Port Aransas' Tarpon Inn.

---

[1] In his *Book on Duck Shooting* (published in 1939), Van Campen Heilner reports that in all his wanderings across Europe and North America, he "never saw duck shooting like they have down in Texas. It is something which must be seen to be believed. There are probably more pintails and red heads there than in any other part of the country."

However, S. Kip Farrington, Jr., also hunted in nearly every state of the union, and in *The Ducks Came Back* (published in 1945), when he listed his favorite seven from the standpoint of waterfowl diversity as well as numbers, Texas ranked third. Farrington's order of preference was California, Utah, Texas, Illinois, North Dakota, Louisiana, and Arkansas.

On a 1919 hunt, Clark McAdams used Pulitzer's yacht, the *Granada II*, for his base camp and summed up his Texas experience in these terms: "We could not use more than we could eat, so we shot only part of every day. The rest of the time we cruised about, or enjoyed our ease upon the yacht. It was on the last day that we really saw ducks. . . . The Captain said the bunch we had before us was two and a half miles long and in some places half a mile wide."

In one memorable line of waterfowling prose, McAdams recalls that "the darkness of thirty thousand ducks came upon us, and we lit up the feathered dusk with the flash of our guns."

When this fabulous abundance started its nose dive about 1910,[2] a few of the Midwest's peripatetic hunting corps wanted to know the reason why and, if possible, to do something about it. They were not content to assume, as many less well-traveled people were saying, "the birds have all gone elsewhere." Hazelton and McAdams had been "elsewhere" and found the birds missing there, too.

St. Louis attorney Dwight C. Huntington decided continental waterfowl populations could be saved by using the same techniques developed by British gamekeepers to enhance hunting in England and Scotland—only in America, the techniques would be applied on a colossal scale. By artificially propagating and releasing young mallards, and then destroying any and all possible predators—cats, coyotes, crows, foxes, hawks, mink, northern pike, owls, raccoons, skunks, snakes, snapping turtles, weasels, you name it: if it could eat a mallard duckling, it had to die—first, the Mississippi Flyway could be "restored," then all of North America could have mallards galore!

With modern hindsight, we realize Huntington's plan was both fantastic and hopeless. he major problem confronting waterfowl seventy years ago is the same problem confronting the birds today: diminishing habitat. What Huntington and so many of his contemporaries failed to appreciate was that unless they could persuade road builders, industrial and suburban developers, and especially farmers and ranchers, to accept new constraints on traditional ways of using land and water resources, releasing artificially reared birds would be (and was) an exercise in futility.

Another drawback to Huntington's mallard release and predator-con-

---

[2] For obvious demographic reasons, waterfowl declines were felt first and most severely in the East, a decade or so later in the Midwest, while certain shortages—notably canvasbacks and redheads—only began to show up in the Pacific Flyway after World War II.

trol scheme is that predators, including man, are rarely a threat to the well-being of any species in an undisturbed environment. Indeed, predators play an essential role in most wildlife habitats where the vigor of all species is enhanced by their successful dealings with a broad spectrum of predators and parasites.

The problem is that man has severely disrupted nature over most of the lower two-thirds of this continent. Certain predators have been given an unfair advantage over waterfowl. Raccoons, for example, which were once kept in check by wolves and mountain lions, now flourish in city suburbs and eastern rural areas. They have also been provided with travel lanes (complete with road kills and fast-food trash barrels) to parts of the upper Midwest where they were not even found 30 years ago. Still, until we modify the causes of a given predator's advantage, we are only acting out a variation on the myth of Sisyphus in trying to eliminate such animals one at a time.[3]

Despite the futility of most predator-control programs, enormous sums were paid out during the early decades of this century and even into comparatively recent years by federal, state, provincial, and county governments to rid the world of such pests as crows and magpies. In its early years, Ducks Unlimited paid several thousands of dollars for crows' feet and magpie eggs, and one campaign in 1937, in conjunction with the Manitoban provincial government, resulted in some rather awkward publicity to the effect that DU was "stocking crows"! What happened was 137 rows were banded with "reward" rings and released. Only four were returned. The survivors were presumed to be off raising broods of wiser crows which would learn how to steal duck eggs without being shot!

Huntington compounded his misapprehension of the role of predators by favoring one species of waterfowl above all others. This was because the mallard is the easiest of waterfowl for amateur breeders to raise. However,

---

[3] Under certain circumstances we have no choice but to play Sisyphus, who was condemned to the never-ending task of rolling a rock to the top of a hill, whence it always rolled down again. Raccoons prevent waterfowl production at many national wildlife refuges in the Atlantic Flyway. They have also stopped all research and banding efforts, because these prolific and highly adaptable predators, who make a mockery of the phrase "predator proof," eat not only duck eggs, ducklings, and brooding hens, but turn banding traps into banquet tables set for them and their friends.

Wildlife sentimentalists have successfully lobbied to prevent the use of leghold traps—one of wildlife management's most effective tools—at many refuges. It is time that concerned sportsmen lobbied back to restore the original purpose of the refuge system. National wildlife refuges were never intended to be Holiday Inns for raccoons ony.

because of its adaptability, aggressive sexuality, and fecundity, the mallard may jeopardize the evolution and existence of such closely related dabblers as the black duck and southern mallards. If our firearms and ammunition taxes, duck stamps, license fees, and donations make sportsmen the treasurers of the nation's wetlands, we should accept our responsibility to ensure wildfowl diversity and acknowledge that never knowing what duck species may suddenly appear over the decoys is one of the principal pleasures of our recreation. If every duck was a mallard, and all we wanted from hunting were targets, waterfowling could be made simpler and cheaper by all of us going to the nearest game farm and pass shooting pen-raised birds.

Still, credit must be given Huntington for his concern about the future of waterfowling. He may not have had the understanding of modern wildlife managers, but as early as 1912, when many of his wealthy and thoughtless friends were shooting ducks as if there was no tomorrow, Dwight C. Huntington was trying to find ways to ensure that there would, in fact, be a tomorrow. This concern was inherited by his son, John, who eventually helped develop his father's Game Conservation Society and its magazine, *The Game Breeder,* into the focused program of wetlands restoration in Canada known as Ducks Unlimited.

First, however, Huntington's original concept had to go through one more evolutionary step, and the catalytic agent for the metamorphosis was Joseph P. Knapp. This astute businessman inherited the American Lithographic Company from his father, and, in 1906, purchased the Crowell Publishing Company, and gained control of *Collier's Weekly* in 1919. Knapp eventually blended his two acquisitons into the Crowell-Collier Publishing Company and served as it's chairman of the board until his retirement in 1946. More significant, in 1929 Knapp sold the American Lithographic Company just before the stock market crash and spent the rest of his life spending the profits of his shrewd good fortune on a broad range of conservation and public service ventures.

In 1930, Knapp founded the More Game Birds in America Foundation. Its original board of directors included John C. Huntington and Thomas Hambly Beck, the editor of *Collier's Weekly* and, in 1934, the chairman [4] of

[4] Thomas Beck did more than chair this committee. In an article written in 1953 for the *National Parks Magazine,* Ding Darling recalled that Beck "had the resonant voice of a sideshow barker; [he] could outshout both Aldo Leopold and me. He held the floor against all attempts to get a word in edgeways, and insisted on stating in the report to the President that the Biological Survey was incompetent and unscientific and should get the ax, and he wanted to be present to see the heads roll."

These are a few of the informational items published by Knapp's More Game Birds in America, Inc. By far the most important was the 107-page book *More Waterfowl by Assisting Nature*—remarkable in 1931 for demanding stronger anti-pollution laws and research for a lead-shot substitute that would reduce serious annual losses of waterfowl due to lead shot ingestion. *(Courtesy Ducks Unlimited)*

President Franklin Roosevelt's Wildlife Restoration Committee. Beck was not merely Knapp's employee, he was his alter ego as well. Whereas Joseph P. Knapp preferred to exercise his power through huge, but anonymous, donations of money to whatever cause took his fancy, he also derived great satisfaction from watching the *Collier's* flag (that is, Knapp's personal pennant) carried into conservation battles by such a flamboyant and outspoken critic of bureaucratic procedures as Thomas H. Beck.

More Game Birds was barely incorporated when it attacked the Biological Survey's recommendation that the waterfowling season be reduced from three months to one. This emergency measure was promulgated by the federal government with little consultation with the states, where many of the fish and wildlife directors still smarted at the iea that local waterfowling regulations were developed in distant Washington, D.C. When Knapp found only deaf ears at the Biological Survey, he took his protest directly to President Herbert Hoover, who then called a special meeting of the Waterfowl Advisory Board on October 7, 1931 to discuss alternate plans for the fall hunting season.

Knapp and the president of More Game Birds in America, Colonel Arthur Foran,[5] argued that an abrupt reduction of the season might create economic hardship in many duck hunting areas where farmers and watermen traditionally counted on guiding fees to carry them through the winter. The two men acknowledged that the number of shooting days should be reduced, but they requested that the reduction in actual shootng days be leavened with nonshooting or "rest days" two or three times a week so that the season could be extended over a two- or three-month period. The government's representatives insisted that such regulations would be impossible to enforce and too much temptation for the ordinary hunter to ignore.

There was no meeting of the minds. Sportsmen knew that rest days worked. After all, they were currently in force on the Susquehanna Flats where you could shoot only on Mondays, Wednesdays, and Fridays. Furthermore, rest days were used on half a hundred clubs across the country, and woe to anyone caught violating them or the club sanctuary!

---

[5] There were many reasons for the bitter feelings between federal biologists and "Knapp's gang," as the bureaucrats called the board of directors of More Game Birds in America. For one thing, at a time when the chief of the Biological Survey earned less than $8,000 a year, Colonel Foran earned $25,000, plus expenses.

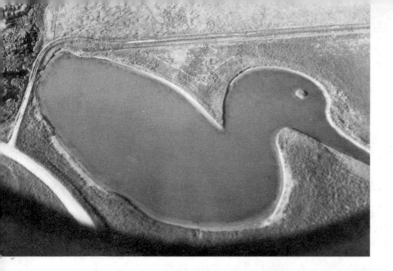

This duck-shaped lake is one of Ducks Unlimited's more whimsical projects. (DU has a goose-shaped lake as well.) The lake's edges are barren and uninviting to waterfowl, and only the "eye" would appeal to a bird looking for an island site on which to nest. However, this lake is part of a larger water project which produces its share of real ducks. *(Photograph by George Reiger)*

Federal wardens saw a different side of waterfowling. They had arrested farmers and watermen who hunted ducks when the birds were available, not when legal days said the birds could be shot. And while gentlemen–sportsmen stood by the fireplace with drinks in their hands, wardens had caught the sportsmen's guides wringing the necks of ducks taken from traps. Sportsmen were accustomed to privilege and courtesy; wardens were accustomed to assault and battery. The federal representatives on the Advisory Board refused to modify their position.

This meeting was, in some respects, an epoch-making confrontation between what had become the established power of the sportsman following his victory over the market hunter two decades earlier and the new power of the professional biologist and bureaucrat. Patrician hunters had forgotten that to break the political backs of game marketeers, they had enlisted the support of the middle class, asserting that waterfowl should belong to everyone, not just those who could afford roast canvasback at the Savoy. Now, with the Depression, the people's politicians and bureaucrats were coming forward to claim their due. Many of the best duck clubs in the country were on their way to becoming national wildlife refuges.

Joseph P. Knapp still had the political clout to restore the locks on the Albermarle and Chesapeake Canal so salt water could be kept out of Back Bay and Currituck Sound where it was ruining the canvasback and redhead shooting for Knapp and his friends. But Knapp's property was marked by a fate at least as conclusive as death and taxes: eminent domain. Where Knapp and his cronies once cartwheeled ducks from the skies, sons and daughters of the middle class now photograph protected birds.

The rift that began in 1931 reached its peak in 1935, when More Game Birds in America decided to organize and carry out an international wildfowl survey. The area involved was nearly one million square miles and included the Canadian provinces of Alberta, Saskatchewan, and Manitoba, as well as North Dakota, South Dakota, and Minnesota. The director of waterfowl activities for More Game Birds in America was Alexander C. Camerle, a transplanted Hungarian, and it is assumed that Camerle was the inspirator of the aerial survey concept, a technique that had already been tested successfully in Europe in censusing a variety of wildlife.

The most important fruit of the More Game Birds in America survey was that it confirmed how essential Canada is to the well-being of water-fowl populations throughout the continent. All three surveyed states combined didn't show one-third the number of ducks found in Manitoba alone, which, in turn, revealed about half as many ducks as each of the other two censused provinces.

Unfortunately, the survey gave the impression that the drought had broken, that the Dust Bowl had reverted to potholes, and that once again, North Americans had more than enough ducks for a long season and generous limits. More Game Birds in America projected an estimate of 65 million ducks in North America during August 1935.

The ground surveys and agricultural reports used by the Bureau of Biological Survey to determine bag limits and season length indicated no such healing of the land and waterfowl resources. If anything, drought seemed to be extending itself into new areas of the country. The new director of the Biological Survey, Ding Darling, acknowledged the usefulness of aerial surveys and promised that if and when the federal government could afford to fly them, it would do its own. Howevr, federal biologists in the future would not make the same mistakes made by the inexperienced and overly enthusiastic counters for More Game Birds in America. Not only must the Biological Survey reject that organization's inflated statistics, it must once again impose a 30-day hunting season for waterfowl and eliminate baiting and the use of live decoys.

The gauntlet was down. Those states which agreed with the Biologcal Survey's assessment accepted the new federal regulations. Those which disagreed (a significant minority) preferred the optimistic waterfowl population estimates of More Game Birds in America and actively resisted the new federal regulations. Illinois even brought suit against the Biological Survey under the direction of Colonel Foran.

Ding Darling was stung hard and responded with a sarcastic personal attack on Joseph P. Knapp in the November 2, 1935, issue of *Today* magazine. Knapp, in turn, responded with an equally sarcastic letter to Darling, implying that since his job called for "executive and administrative ability of a high degree which you do not possess," Darling should resign. Soon afterward, he did—but three months later Darling was elected president of the General Wildlife Federation (soon to be renamed the National Wildlife Federation) and the former cartoonist from Iowa devoted his considerable energies to making sure the Federation didn't go the way his career in government had. However, not only was Darling unable to tap the enormous financial reservoir embodied in the board and membership of More Game Birds in America, the residual bitterness of his conflict with Knapp created a schism in the ranks of sportsmen everywhere, many of whom did not even know why they were supposed to oppose a perfectly good idea like the National Wildlife Federation.

When Knapp began to turn More Game Birds in America into Ducks Unlimited in 1936,[6] Darling tried to persuade the directors of the new organization to bury the hatchet and come under the umbrella of the more generalized conservation efforts of the National Wildlife Federation. They laughed in his face. Thus began in earnest the political arm wrestling between these two organizations for the sportsman's allegiance and his tax-deductible dollars that continues to the present day.

There is symbolism in the fact that Ducks Unlimited (DU) headquarters are in Illinois—the state that supported the More Game Birds in America law suit against the Biological Survey—especially when one learns that the National Wildlife Federation is headquartered in Washington, DC.—home of the old Biological Survey, now the Fish and Wildlife Service, and the site of all the alleged federal interference in state wildlife affairs from restrictive waterfowling regulations to endangered species legislation to the introduction of steel shot.

For all the turmoil of personalities and politics in its formative years, what has saved and guided Ducks Unlimited from the outset was its clear-cut and easily comprehended objective of restoring Canadian wetlands for waterfowl. No conservationist—whether he works for the federal govern-

---

[6] Joseph P. Knapp wanted his new charity to be called "Ducks." His friend and future DU director, Arthur M. Bartley, pointed out that corporations in Canada have the word "limited" after their names. "Limited, hell; I want Ducks *Un*limited!"—and so it stuck.

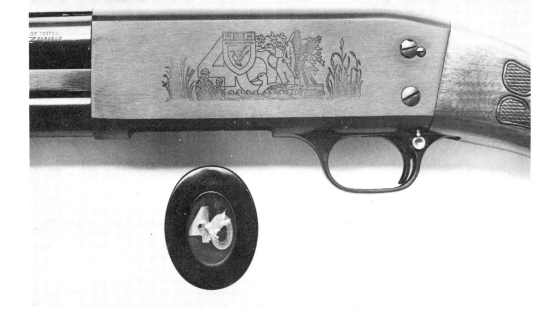

In 1973, Remington Arms issued a special model of its, 1100 semi-automatic shotgun to commemorate DU's 1,100th wetland restoration project in Canada. Each year since then a different firearms company has contributed a limited edition of a popular model shotgun to DU committees across the country for fund-raising events. The 40th anniversary (1977) edition of 1,125 shotguns was donated by Ithaca. *(Photograph courtesy Ithaca Firearms)*

Field & Stream's enthusiastic support for the concept and efforts of Ducks Unlimited is symbolized by a water project named for the magazine and donated by publisher Eltinge F. Warner in 1946. *(Courtesy Ducks Unlimited)*

ment, a state wildlife agency, or any other nongovernmental conservation organization—can contest the merit of this plan. In one of his first acts as Darling's replacement as chief of the Biological Survey, Ira N. Gabrielson wrote John C. Huntington to tell him, "We will be glad to give any information and help that we possibly can to secure the success of this program."

With the help of tens of thousands of people, both in and out of government, and the financial contributions of millions more, Ducks Unlimited has flourished over the past forty-two years spending more than $80 million on over 1,600 water control projects in Canada. The organization now has plans to raise an additional $75 million before 1984 in order to initiate still more projects, many of these in largely neglected areas of Canada such as British Columbia and the Maritime Provinces.

As a result of its success, DU has some of the same problems experienced by the rich man who retires to the country: Local bankers want to mind his money, while his neighbors want to mind his business. Each contributor to DU has his own, sometimes very positive, ideas on how to get more ducks for the dollar, or how to get more dollars for ducks. The competition between regional fund raisers has occasionally caused embarrassment to folk working in the Chicago headquarters. One example involved a map at a Maryland Waterfowl Festival some years ago in which an arrow was drawn from a nonexistent water project in Newfoundland directly to the vicinity of the festival. An earnest young man with a pointer in his hand described how each $5 donation to Ducks Unlimited would send another black duck directly down the pipeline to the area where Maryland hunters would have a chance to bag it.

In addition to the absurdity of the proposition that Ducks Unlimited can control the migratory movements of waterfowl, this little sideshow dramatized what too many DU donors feel about their sport: Dollars in equals Ducks out. We have all heard variations on the theme: "I contributed $500 this year, and I expect to get $500 worth of shooting." People like this presumably give money to churches with the understanding they will be guaranteed a place in heaven. However, charitable donations are not investments from which you expect to draw personal interest. While DU regional directors can do little to improve the personality of such egotists, they should do more than smile, say "Yes, sir!" and take the man's money.

Another milder disappointment is that because the function of fund-

Half a century ago when Charles Dana Gibson of Gibson Girl fame drew a pair of duck hunters, he was not doing anything daring to suggest that women could and should hunt with men. Many of the early members of Ducks Unlimited were women, and DU historian Kip Farrington described his pleasure in attending DU functions in the thirties and forties where so many beautiful wives, daughters, and lady friend hunters were present. *(Reproduction courtesy Elman Pictorial Collection)*

raising has become a tail, wagging the dog of waterfowl conservation, women are excluded from most DU dinners. This is not national policy, and executives in the Chicago office are trying to alter the parochial view that girlfriends, wives, and daughters inhibit men from spending large sums of money on drinks, raffle tickets, and auction items. (At those comparatively few dinners where women have been present, they have sometimes bought such expensive items as the commemorative shotguns for themselves!)

How different the present "Drakes Only" situation is from the one Kip Farrington described in *The Ducks Came Back,* in which he suggested that because of the large number of attractive female members in Ducks Un-

Duck Unlimited's executive vice president, Dale E. Whitesell, discusses a film script with Bing Crosby during the shooting of one of the many movies produced by DU explaining the purpose and value of wetlands projects in Canada. *(Courtesy Ducks Unlimited)*

limited—avid waterfowlers all—the name of the organization should be changed to "Good-Looking Women Unlimited." Corny, of course, but Kip believed that the more often women hunt with men, the more often men will be able to get out hunting. Furthermore, men tend to hold to higher standards of conservation and behavior when women are present, and the definitions of what constitutes "sportsmen" and "sportsmanship" take on more refined meanings. While it may be naive to hope that a majority of waterfowlers—many of whom hunt to get away from women—will one day be happy to share their blinds with the ladies, at least those men who do enjoy sharing experiences with their wives should be allowed the option of bringing women with them to the annual DU dinner.

On a deeper level, the most important question DU contributors and administrators can ask themselves today is whether DU is responding to the devastating trends in land and water use by Canada's ever-expanding population. Should, for example, Ducks Unlimited reconsider its forty-year-old, self-imposed prohibition against buying land in Canada in order to permanently protect threatened wetlands? Although the Canadian government frowns on Canadian property being owned by U.S. citizens or U.S. corporations, this problem is easily solved by turning over land titles to Ducks unlimited (Canada) or the Canadian Wildlife Service.

Another question is what role education—call it public information for U.S. and Mexican hunters as well as Canadian farmers—should play in the future distribution of DU funds. Executive vice-president Dale Whitesell parries all thrusts suggesting alternate uses of DU money by insisting that a conservation organization is most effective when it sticks to one objective, and a single program for accomplishing that objective. Since DU's objective is the restoration and enhancement of waterfowl breeding grounds in Canada, every dollar should be directed toward that end.

Excellent. No one disputes the value of this "singleness of purpose," but a single purpose does not preclude more than one method to accomplish that purpose. We are reminded of the distinction between most U.S. wildlife refuges which constitute "duck hotels" and comparable wetlands in Canada which are veritable "duck factories." When you then realize that the vast majority [7] of waterfowl bred in Canada are produced on private, non-DU wetlands—many currently threatened by the dragline or plow—there must be other, more conclusive, ways to ensure the perpetuation of waterfowl in North America than managing water levels in an array of showcase marshes scattered across Canada. When we discuss the perpetuation of species, we must plan for viable populations of such creatures, not mere remnants confined to a chain of sanctuaries.

This is not to belittle Ducks Unlimited's many remarkable achievements. One project alone, Cumberland Marsh in east-central Saskatchewan,

---

[7] Since DU has rarely released figures on the numbers and species of waterfowl produced on its leased wetlands, there is no way to make a precise comparison between DU's production and what happens elsewhere in Canada. However, it would be safe to estimate that less than two percent of all the waterfowl bred in Canada are produced on DU projects. Remember, too, that many far northern nesters, including brant and snow geese, are completely weather dependent for their nesting success, and it is doubtful DU or any man-directed agency will ever manage anything other than staging or wintering areas for such birds.

represents the largest wetlands maintenance and restoration effort in North America. The Hudson Bay Company had formerly leased this 332,000 acre area for the production of such furbearers as mink and muskrat. However, controlling water levels proved too tricky and expensive for the fur company, so in 1960, DU took over its lease. During the past twenty years, 180,000 additional acres (the Sitanok Marshes) have been merged into the same water control system, and the vast wetlands now produce about 76,000 ducklings a year, mostly ringbills and scaup. DU's marsh managers intend to produce more dabbling ducks by regulating the area's water levels.

However, by striving to increase the production of mallards and pintail—the two primary field feeders in prairie Canada—for the benefit of DU contributors south of the border and not doing anything to alleviate crop depredations north of the border, DU is inadvertently compounding the mistrust between Canadian duck producers and American duck hunters. In addition, DU has no focused program for troubled species like the canvasback, which never invades farmers' fields to feed, but which suffers along with the mallards and pintail during spring burnings and pothole drainings. The Delta Waterfowl Research Station has made a dramatic breakthrough in the captive propagation of canvasbacks. With DU funds and encouragement, artificially bred birds could be used to repopulate still viable wetlands that have not seen a fertile hen canvasback in many years. Not all waterfowl restoration is done with dikes and pipes and pumping stations.

Thus, this writer is a kind of hybrid between the rich man's nosey neighbors and his local banker. As a compulsive DU contributor, as the scriptwriter for the 1978 Ducks Unlimited film "Ours to Bequeath," and as a staunch advocate of the important role the American hunter has to play in the preservation of North America's nonrenewable wetlands so their renewable wildlife resources will, indeed, be "ours to bequeath," I also believe a good organization can always be made better.

One of my farming neighbors in Virginia strained his budget last year to give Ducks Unlimited $150. I know a man in Pittsburgh who strained nothing to give $50,000. The magnitude of such gifts to conservation may differ, but since each donor expects his money to make a difference, the real challenge of Ducks Unlimited is to see that it does.

TEN: THE FUTURE OF WATERFOWLING

"As population increases, and as the fowl become fewer, the number of men who must go without shooting will increase. It is one of the conditions under which we live, and there is no escaping it."

George Bird Grinnell, in 1901

"The real concern is for us, the people. We who wish to keep marshes and their waterfowl must study ourselves and our human society."

H. Albert Hochbaum, in 1955

THE SPORTSMAN'S tomorrow is haunted by that same swelling spectre that shadows every kind of human endeavor. All our problems and most of our confrontations between legislators, biologists, and resource managers, between law enforcement agents and hunters, hinge on the complex question of how many people can this continent support and at what standard of living?

If you think this an exaggeration, ask yourself whether the streams, rivers, and marshes you hunted as a youngster are still as healthy as they once were. Is the diversity of wildlife as great? How much closer has the city or suburbs moved to the wetlands? Is hunting still permitted? Or are the marshes still there?

In most parts of North America, the prognosis is glum. Yet, strangely, we keep adding new waterfowlers to an already overloaded system. In the most recent U.S. Fish and Wildlife Service "National Survey of Hunting, Fishing and Wildlife-Associated Recreation," the contracted analysts (Booz-Allen & Hamilton of Philadelphia) estimated that in 1975, there were 4,831,000 duck hunters in the nation who spent over 36 million days afield. Yet that same season, only 2,218,589 federal duck stamps were sold. When you discount the significant number of stamps purchased by non-hunting stamp dealers and collectors and the more significant number of stamps *not* purchased by people who should have had them to hunt, and after cranking in the probability of survey error, you are still left with the amazing thought that possibly half of all the duck hunters in the United States are 15 years of age or younger—namely, those not required by law to carry a signed federal duck stamp in addition to their state licenses.

Although more than half of all the states now require boys and girls to take hunter-education courses before they are issued their first state licenses, the emphasis of these courses is on safe gun handling, not wildlife biology, woodcraft, nor shooting skills. As a result, most young hunters are sadly unfamiliar with such essential elements of waterfowling as bird identification and when a duck (according to species and, therefore, size) is within effective killing range of a shotgun. While hunting safety is an important

Classroom instruction for young hunters is not enough. Their knowledge and proficiency with firearms should be tested on the skeet range and afield. Incidentally, the shotgun sling is an idea whose time is overdue. Slings provide the safest possible position for carrying firearms, yet in no way do the leather straps interfere with shooting. Additionally, both hands are free for carrying equipment when moving back and forth to the blind. *(Photograph by David W. Corson)*

subject, it can become deadly dull for bright students after it is hashed and rehashed by an uncreative instructor for six, ten, or however-many hours of mandatory classroom attendance. Some states offering voluntary hunter-safety courses acknowledge a high dropout rate after the first hour or two of instruction, but few state administrators bother to analyze the reasons why.

Young people are almost universally interested in wildlife, and that is what they want to see and touch when they go afield. However, encouraging the young to become sportsmen by sparking their interest in natural history may be less difficult than persuading unimaginative wildlife administrators to change their tedious approach to hunter education. Yet not to introduce youngsters to the wonders of migration, the mysteries of evolution, or even the fundamental differences between species is to deny them much of the satisfaction of waterfowling and, perhaps, to rob their children of its possibility.

Sixty years ago, many of the states and the federal government began to democratize all forms of hunting as part of the campaign to outlaw commercial gunning. The theory was that since wildlife belongs to all the people, it should not be exploited by the few for their exclusive benefit. Even a landowner who wants to kill a mallard in his backyard for dinner must possess a valid state hunting license and, since 1934, a migratory bird hunting stamp as well.

Members of duck and goose clubs in every part of the country supported—in fact, helped create—this policy, never imagining it might mean the death of many of their customs as well as those of the market hunter. Yet as Winston Churchill once noted, democracy tends to homogenize all levels of society into an egalitarian frappé, and the reflexive prescription for any real or imagined social ill is to call for still more democracy.

Thus, the elitist traditions of sportsmanship, along with the duck clubs that both sponsored and institutionalized such traditions, have all but died out. Some clubs have been converted into National Wildlife Refuges, others into Audubon or Nature Conservancy sanctuaries. Many others, less fortunate, have been turned into towns or "industrial parks." (This latter phrase is one of our language's examples of a contradiction of terms.)

Those clubs which still survive are likely to be eliminated by the Revenue Bill of 1978. Formerly, the Internal Revenue Service permitted the cost of running a hunting lodge to be tax deductible if such expenses were (1) "ordinary and necessary," (2) the facility was used for the furtherance of business more than 50 percent of the time, and (3) the costs were directly related to the active conduct of a business. Today the nation's lawmakers insist that hunting is too much fun ever to be business-related and, therefore, hunting lodges are personal or family assets. They cannot be regarded as useful to a trade, business, or any other profit-seeking venture. The land-use consequences of this law are enormous, and we can certainly expect to see many more fields and timber bottoms where pintail and wood ducks now whiffle down to feed on acorns and soybeans converted to shopping plazas where people congregate to feed on pizzas and soybean milkshakes.

The passing of the duck clubs has meant the passing of what was once a typical way for young men and women to learn the skills and obligations of waterfowling. No longer do teenagers spend weekends with their fathers or uncles learning that it doesn't matter whether you are left- or right-handed, you shoot off the shoulder on the same side as your master eye; that a sportsman always stays at least 500 yards from another hunter and never puts out decoys downwind—that is, under the flight path—of birds approaching another hunter's rig; and that no matter how slow the morning's activity, sportsmen do not shoot grebes, herons, hawks, muskrats, or whatever else happens along "to liven things up."

The old duck clubs provided the very best proving grounds for retrievers. The Labrador would not be the high-caliber breed it is today without the millions of man-hours in training and field work provided by the guides and dog handlers at half a hundred of this continent's once great hunting clubs. *(Photographs by Clark G. Webster)*

No longer are the majority of young waterfowlers taught by their elders that binoculars are as satisfying an accoutrement as a shotgun for a successful day afield; that so long as a hit bird has his head up, you shoot and shoot again until the duck is dead; and that it is improper, as well as foolish, to fire at birds out of range.

Some clubs' rules dictated that any hit bird, whether recovered or not, was part of a member's limit. It was wonderful how this code cut down on sky-busting and spurred a hunter in his pursuit of a cripple! At Bellport, Long Island, you had to pay a fine for every bird you shot at beyond reasonable range, and, in some cases, club members put "shame money" in the kitty even when they had killed the long-distance bird. In other clubs, you were penalized for killing a hen mallard, hen pintail, or hen canvasback.

Bands

Perhaps, the most telling signal in the breakdown of tradition is that some young waterfowlers today have no idea what to do with a banded duck. Still others know they should report its number and the date and location where they killed the bird to the address stamped on the band, but they are either indifferent or frankly hostile to cooperating with government-sponsored research. One "retired" outlaw keeps a crock full of bands by his front door and tells the young people who visit him that anyone who reports a band is helping the "feds" make still more restrictions on duck hunters. For lack of any other cultural model or wiser point of view, few of the young hunters who know this man are inclined to report banded ducks—or help biologists or wardens in any other respect for that matter.

Half a century ago, many duck clubs banded birds, and E. A. "Ned" McIlhenny at Avery Island, Louisiana, personally banded thousands of ducks every season—so many, in fact, he would have to cease banding by the end of December because so many "repeats" were in his traps; he spent too much time checking hundreds of banded ducks in order to find one that was still unbanded!

For all hunters in those days, reporting a banded duck or goose was considered to be a contribution to science as well as a great adventure. Shooting a banded bird was a bonus thrill to waterfowling. Where had the bird come from? Where may it have been going? How old was it?

On January 19, 1970, I killed a male greater scaup in South Oyster Bay, Long Island, less than ten miles from where it had been banded seven years earlier. Altogether, the drake was nearly nine years old. For the better part of a decade, that bird had navigated between a tundra lake, possibly as far west as Alaska, to a relatively small area on the other side of the continent. That he had done it once was wondrous; that he had done it nine times enthralls the human imagination!

The scaup swept over the decoys with a dozen of his kind and from the evidence of the three others my companion and I killed, many of the flock were birds of the year, birds the drake was leading over a route which their descendants are still following and will, hopefully, follow for centuries to come. The fact the bird was banded made the day memorable. The information provided by the band has enlarged my understanding and love of waterfowl. Anyone who rejects the awe inherent in a banded bird is rejecting a large part of the meaning—and the responsibility—of our sport.

Realities

If we hope to plan for the future and see both waterfowl and waterfowling perpetuated, we must be realistic about a present that is stronger on form than substance. Recently, the U.S. Department of the Interior revised and reissued Bob Hines's useful *Ducks at a Distance, A Waterfowl Identification Guide.* (This booklet is available for $1.80 a copy from the Superintendent of Documents, U.S. Government Printing Office, Washington, D.C. 20240.) The South Carolina Wildlife and Marine Resources Department (Building D, Dutch Plaza, Box 167, Columbia 29202) has produced a movie showing what ducks look like as they pass a blind. The film employs stop-motion sequences to help the viewer identify flying waterfowl. Both efforts are commendable aids to educating novice hunters, but we cannot pretend they do the whole job.

Ducks Unlimited has a "Greenwing" program for hunters eighteen years of age and under. Many regional sportsmen's groups sponsor father-and-son and father-and-daughter activities, and some non-club-affiliated fathers and uncles still try to teach the rudiments of sportsmanship to their youngsters. However, the awful truth is that many—far too many—teenagers teach themselves to hunt through trial and error, mostly the latter.

The realities of waterfowling today include a carload of kids shooting ducks from a California freeway, kids bringing guns into a midwestern zoo to kill birds in the waterfowl exhibit, and kids sneaking into a Long Island duck farm to try their luck with bow and arrow. "That's not waterfowling!" you exclaim. "That's vandalism or youthful high jinks." Maybe. But in each case, the kids told the arresting officer they were "hunting."

A few years ago in Wisconsin, college students were trained to watch waterfowl hunters and record their behavior. The hunters did not know they were being watched, and many violated the law. After the hunters came out of the marsh, they were interviewed. With this information the state was able to develop a profile of the typical violator: He is under thirty years of age. (Many were in their teens.) He hunts within 25 miles of his home. (The stereotype of the nonresident violator is false. People are more inclined to break laws on their own turf, where they feel "safe," than in a strange area.) The typical violator hunts the first week to ten days of the season,[1] and once he breaks the law, he will probably break it again. Many

---

[1] This characteristic probably has less to do with the implied lack of dedication of violators—that is, their unwillingness to stick the season out to its bitter cold end—than with the fact that hunting pressure helps move birds down the flyway so that *all* northern waterfowlers prefer to hunt the early part of their season. In contrast, if a waterfowling survey was made in Mississippi or Louisiana, it might be discovered that poachers prefer the last weeks of the season—as do most southern hunters—which is when the majority of waterfowl finally arrive on their wintering grounds.

of those observed in Wisconsin rearranged their bags to circumvent the point system and then reported losing their high-point ducks as cripples when they had actually stomped them into the marsh or thrown them away. Although the typical violator expresses little regard for other hunters, he reports satisfaction with the "hunting experience." Finally, and paradoxically, violators use retrieving dogs more often than other hunters, possibly justifying the additional ducks they kill as part of the dogs' training or "getting their money's worth" from dog food or veterinary fees.

Because modern society frequently parodies the sportsman as a polite or overly privileged fool, and makes sentimental heroes out of outlaws, little wonder young hunters are more comfortable patterning themselves after vandals than gentlemen. According to a study commissioned by the National Shooting Sports Foundation, a research team from Batten, Barton, Durstine & Osborn discovered that antihunting feeling in America is focused on the crippling and nonrecovery of game and the belief that the typical hunter is untrained, incompetent, and ignorant of the law. The American nonhunting public has the impression the ordinary hunter does not know one species of game bird from another and does not even know what to do with a bird once it has been shot.

Unfortunately, the ordinary hunter is often as bad as society depicts him. However, aside from cussing sportsmen when hunting horror stories are printed in the local newspaper, the nonhunter is as indifferent to reforming the hunter as the ordinary hunter is interested in refining his personal knowledge and skills. When concerned sportsmen make defensive noises on behalf of our poorly trained colleagues, we are only accelerating the decline of public respect for hunting traditions in this country. There is only one way to reverse the downward trend, and that is with meaningful and mandatory hunter education. However, social inertia and the prevailing hostility to still more regulations prevent this step from being taken. One wonders how much longer the accumulated goodwill generated by sportsmen of earlier decades will mask many of the sordid realities of hunting today.

The National Shooting Sports Foundation study concludes: "The only way to improve the public image of the hunter is improve the training of those who hunt, and to utterly purge those who persist in their incompetence and irresponsibility. When we have done those things, or made significant strides in that direction, we can go to the public and tell our story with some hope of changing [the public's] negative attitudes. Not before."

All waterfowlers, whether they hunt in the Pacific Flyway where the Ross goose is protected, the Atlantic Flyway where special regulations govern the taking of canvasbacks and redheads, or the Central and Mississippi flyways where whooping cranes and trumpeter swans [2] are extending their ranges, should be required to take courses in natural history, wildlife management, and bird identification. Likewise, all waterfowlers, whose crippling loss rate is probably higher than the commonly cited one out of four, should have their firearms familiarity and marksmanship tested on a regular interval–perhaps, every other year. We don't allow people to drive automobiles without proving their competence. We should not allow people to hunt our nation's wetlands without passing similar examinations in fundamental skills and knowledge. The cost of administering this program could be taken directly from the taxes already levied on the sale of firearms, ammunition, and related equipment.

The point to be stressed is that the concept of hunter-education must provide definitive standards for determining who is to be licensed and who is not. It must not be assumed that just because a person is willing to be tested indicates he is qualified to pass. Hunter-education courses must be taught by well-paid, incorruptible personnel–not just volunteers–the best the wildlife management field can offer. The reputation of the courses should be such that nonhunters will want to take them to expand their own knowledge and understanding of nature. The testing should be independent of political influence and of state officials more concerned with boosting license sales than improving the character and quality of the hunting experience and wildlife management.

Management Versus Morality

If waterfowlers would support such genuine training for the would-be

[2] In December, 1978, a trio of trumpeter swans were shot by vandals at Thomas Hill Reservoir, Missouri. Although the last previous authenticated report of a trumpeter swan in Missouri was in 1907, these birds were not fully protected by federal law until 1913. Even as late as 1935, there were only 73 wild trumpeters south of Canada. Today the continental population may number as many as 5,000, and efforts are being made to re-establish the birds in former flyways, with as many as 190 trumpeters living as far east as La Creek National Wildlife Refuge in South Dakota.

sportsman, if we would be willing to submit to courses stressing the responsibilities, ethics, courtesy, and traditions of waterfowling, we would be able to do away with many of the moralistic and unenforceable laws that currently shroud our recreation. Probably the best example of a moralistic law that no longer serves the dubious purpose for which it was created is the federal regulation stipulating that no one can hunt ducks, geese, or swans with a shotgun holding more than three shells. If the daily limit is two black ducks, of what possible biological interest is it whether those two birds are killed with a right and a left from a Parker double or gunned down with five or six shots from an unplugged semiautomatic Browning? You may feel the man who uses the latter weapon is missing some of the esthetic pleasure of waterfowling, but the two ducks he killed are no more dead than the ones shot with your antique Parker.

In addition, many duck hunters can recall a time or two when a fourth or fifth round in their guns would have enabled them to kill a crippled duck that subsequently got away while they fumbled for more shells. However, these occasional losses of crippled birds must continue to be suffered to appease an abstract conscience, for we forget that this law was created over sixty years ago to bring additional pressure on the market gunner after his punt and battery guns were outlawed.

George Bird Grinnell and Ira Gabrielson both stressed that the daily bag limit—nothing more, nothing less—must be the foundation of scientific wildlife management. Neither of these gentlemen liked unplugged semiautomatic shotguns, but neither thought his feelings were a matter for law and order. They both knew that the ideal society is guided by customs and informal censorship, not laws, and that the contempt a man's peers express for something the majority finds disagreeable is a far better restraint on that man's behavior than half a hundred formal regulations on the matter. The fact that sportsmen in olden days looked down their noses at unplugged shotguns was enough—even without the law—to see them banned from most duck clubs.

In the British Isles, certain chapters of the Waterfowlers' Association of Great Britain and Ireland (WAGBI) hold that jump shooting is unethical because it disturbs resting ducks. However, no member of WAGBI has yet proposed (to my knowledge) that jump shooting should be made a legal offense. The British understand that fear of ostracism is a more potent tool for enforcing codes than passing laws. Furthermore, British hunting traditions stress that sport is found in *how* we do things and not in what we bring home. If Americans want to be so barbaric as to jump shoot ducks from streams and sloughs, then that fits in with everything else the British have heard about America, where daily limits are like shopping lists, and where people feel cheated unless they bring home all the "groceries" to which they are entitled.

It further amazes many British that Americans have outlawed the punt gun, which is actually a very proper sporting weapon for gentlemen-gunners. Sculling down on a flock of wary widgeon and positioning the boat so that the large-bore cannon cuts down a number of birds as the flock gets airborne ranks in many English and Scottish minds as the supreme experience of waterfowling.

The British know that in a week of hunting involving unpredictable winds, currents, and shy prey, the modern punt gunner will be lucky to fire one shot and kill half a dozen birds. Meanwhile, his jump-shooting colleague walking creek bottoms at low tide may down more birds in an afternoon than the punt gunner will all season. If punt gunning is dying out in Great Britain, it is more for a lack of opportunity (meaning time and access) than because of any keenly felt outrage regarding people who hunt with a gun capable of firing a pound or two of shot in one blast.

Other European hunting traditions that boggle the sensibilities of most American sportsmen include shooting at night, baiting, and the use of live decoys. In this country, it is illegal to discharge firearms at waterfowl after sunset and thirty minutes before sunrise. Indeed, there is a current attempt by wildlife protectionists to eliminate the 30-minute period before sunrise so that hunters will be better able to identify their quarry before pulling the trigger.

This controversy fascinates British waterfowlers who feel that if Americans can't tell from training, experience, and the context of their surroundings what they are shooting at in the clear, but colorless, light immediately before sunrise, whatever would we do lying out for geese on a dark night when shots are at shadows only slightly blacker than the sky? No wonder there are so many grotesque stories about untrained American hunters mistaking white pelicans for snow geese and grebes for diving ducks!

As for baiting, the capital sin of American waterfowling—the capital sin, that is, unless you own grainfields you can flood and, thereby, bait within the law—there is no better way to describe the English tradition than to quote A. Cadman's *Shouldergunning for Duck* (as distinguished from punt gunning for duck), first published in 1963:

[If you own or lease a shooting pond, and] if you use barley, you should feed every other day. Whole maize is better if there are large numbers of moorhen,[3] because they find it too large. Heaps of small, or bad, potatoes in the edge of the water are very good forms of feed, especially as this does not need renewing so often. A few whole sheaves of corn are useful. The quantity depends on how fast it is being eaten. On the one hand, you don't want surplus food lying around. But if it's all eaten in the first hour, then you are not getting the full effect. It's a very good idea to have bins with lids (dust bins will do) at each pond in which to store grain.

Don't forget it's most important to go on feeding after the season is over, through February and March. . . . Migrating duck will be held right up to the time of their departure. If that is done, they will return to the same place next autumn, together with their offspring. In this way, you help to build up the population using the pools.

In contrast to this British concern for sustaining the resource, season after season, many American farmers in goose concentration areas encourage birds to visit their fields during the hunting season when the farmers collect handsome guiding or blind leasing fees, and then as soon as the season ends, the farmers chase the birds out or file complaints about crop depredations in order to collect damages from the federal government. The way our baiting regulations are written makes inadvertent criminals of some of us, and hypocrites of us all.

Yet until all would-be waterfowlers submit to something approaching the European apprentice system for hunters, we must make do with our faulty antibaiting regulations. Without a proper grounding in the reasons why we have daily limits and restricted seasons, it is too much to expect that a majority of hunters will comprehend the responsibilities and restraints of baiting as well as its pleasures and privilege. American baiters may claim they feed more ducks than they shoot, but all evidence points to their shooting birds until they run out of shells or the ducks stop coming.

As for the tradition of live decoys, which the English condone and the U.S. federal government outlawed in 1935, this is what Ray Holland,

[3] The moor, mere, or lake-hen is *Gallinula chloropus,* the common gallinule. It is probably the United Kingdom's most common waterfowl and, like coots in this country, its abundance, mediocre flight, and reputedly poor flavor inspire the duck hunter's contempt. Too bad. Gallinule and coot are quite good eating, and their abundance may mark them as important game birds of the future. For more on this, see Appendix I.

Grover Cleveland saw nothing wrong with live decoys. Otherwise, he would not have used this drawing of a hunter setting off with his pet in the rain in *Fishing and Shooting Sketches*. So many moralistic laws have come to layer over the fundamental requirements of bag limits and seasons that waterfowl management is sometimes hard put to justify the modifier "scientific." *(Courtesy Elman Pictorial Collection)*

whose courage and persistence as a federal warden helped end the destructive practice of spring shooting, had to say about live decoys in 1945: "Many duck hunters thought of their decoys in the same light that the unpland gunner views his pointer or setter. They are pets as well as decoys. I have often seen decoys, allowed to swim free among the wooden stool, that come to the blind when they got cold or hop into the boat when called at taking-up time."

Live decoys—in almost every case, mallards or Canada geese—were outlawed ostensibly to protect canvasbacks and redheads. Yet such birds are divers and don't often associate with dabbling mallards and geese. As Holland pointed out, "All the canvas' and redheads killed in a given season through the use of live decoys could be carried in your hip pocket." He added, "I never could see the slightest excuse for this ruling, which took something very real out of the life of many duck and goose hunters."

The "slightest excuse"—besides the one about canvasbacks and redheads—was that only wealthy sportsmen could afford to feed live decoys during the Depression when so many people were going hungry. Moralists further argued that a man with live decoys had an "unfair advantage" over another hunter limited to wooden stool.[4] In other words, the prohibition of live decoys, like the later prohibition of electronic calls, were additional steps in the democratization of waterfowling.

Another American waterfowling taboo puzzling to residents of some European nations is the ban on rifles and shotguns with a bore larger than 10-gauge. Curiously, the prohibition against guns heavier than 10-gauge was created by moralistic sportsmen, not moralistic bureaucrats. Seventy-five years ago, most American sportsmen had given up rifles for waterfowling (except for swans),[5] and many of the fraternity's most distinguished members agreed that none of them would personally want to hold anything heavier than a 10-gauge gun to their shoulders for firing. It went without saying that unless a firearm is discharged from the shoulder, it cannot be considered a recreational weapon in America. Probably these worthies also associated the 8-gauge gun with the condemned market hunter who used the big-bore weapon to line up and kill several birds at the same time—often at longer ranges than were possible with the 12- or 16-gauge shotgun. In addition, since the 8-gauge shotgun tempts the casual nimrod to fire at birds at extreme range, converting many lightly struck birds into unrecovered cripples, a handful of influential sportsmen succeeded in their lobbying efforts to get the 8-gauge shotgun banned from waterfowling.

Ironically, modern 10 gauge and 3-inch, 12 gauge shotgun loads make

---

[4] This is the same reasoning used by opponents of depth recorders for fishing who had hoped to see such "unfair" electronic equipment "that only the rich can afford" banned in Minnesota and other states. Apparently such people have forgotten there are daily limits on walleye as well as ducks. Interestingly, the brouhaha may be dying down, less because a majority see the absurdity of the depth recorder issue than because low prices for many models now put depth recorders within the reach of most any angler.

[5] When Van Campen Heilner visited Danzig (Gdansk) to shoot geese in the thirties, he was asked where his rifle was. When he told his hosts Americans shoot geese with shotguns, the Poles were aghast. They pointed out you have to be a far better shot to kill a flying goose with a rifle than a shotgun; Heilner pointed out you have to be a far better hunter to get close enough to use a shotgun effectively. The debate was like the rivalry in this country between turkey hunters in the deep South who use shotguns, and those of the eastern mountain regions who prefer rifles. Members of both groups condemn the other group for their choice of weapon without understanding that for the bottomland hunter, the art of turkey calling is the point of the sport, while for the mountain hunter, imbued with the traditions symbolized by the Kentucky and Pennsylvania long-rifles, marksmanship is the point of his sport. The Mississippi hunter likes to outwit his bird, calling a proud gobbler through leafy cover to within ten yards of the hidden hunter. The West Virginia hunter likes to decapitate his bird at 175 yards. For both kinds of turkey hunting, the actual killing of the birds is a secondary, although necessary, objective.

These two pictures were made less than 30 miles apart in northern Minnesota. The real distance is not miles, but decades. In 1906 *(top)* a hunter measured his success by the size of his bag. In the 1970s we measure our success by whether the outing has provided us with *re-creation* in the most fundamental interpretation of that word. If it has, and we have shot a duck besides, we have had a successful day. *(Top photograph courtesy Library of Congress. Bottom by George Reiger)*

the old 8-gauge black-powder loads seem weak in comparison. In addition, novice nimrods today continue to shoot at birds at extreme range. Furthermore, there are no penalties as once existed at duck clubs where the sky-buster found his bags packed for him and a wagon ready to take him to the depot if he couldn't cure his long-range shooting habits. So how do we end modern sky-busting? Do we now outlaw the 10- and 12-gauge magnum shotguns along with the defunct 8-gauge? Or do we simply provide better training for hunters before they go afield?

It is further ironic that many of the same sportsmen who agreed to outlaw the 8-gauge shotgun thought it marvelous to hunt ducks with the .410 and 28-gauge shotguns. Outdoor writers a generation ago were impressed by the frequent use of such weapons at California and Louisiana duck clubs. The writers helped glamorize this ultralight artillery without bothering to explain that the ducks they saw centered by experts were killed at skeet-, not trap-equivalent, ranges. Ordinarily the .410 shotgun is a far mightier crippler of waterfowl than the outlawed 8-gauge ever was. Having banned the 8-gauge, should we now outlaw the .410? Or do we simply provide better training for hunters before they go afield?

In our shrunken and overcrowded world, we can no longer tolerate a laissez-faire attitude toward hunting. This does not mean, however, more piecemeal regulations. In fact, we can throw out most of our antiquated laws if we replace them with genuine training of hunters. We must stop making game wardens responsible for hunting ethics when, by definition of the word itself, *sportsmen* should be the people responsible.

It is wrong to create laws where cops are as confused by technicalities, ambiguities, and exceptions as the ordinary citizen. Waterfowling is plagued in this regard and, as a result, of all forms of hunting, it is the most vulnerable to attack by moralists who confuse the perpetuation of species and populations with the protection of individual creatures.

In order to work, conservation laws must be based on genuine need and common sense. People should be able to see the *reason* for such laws, and they should be enforced in such a way to make converts for the sport; not enemies of the resource. This requires rare judgment on the part of conservation law enforcers as when to be gentle and when to get tough. Overall, it means that wardens should presume innocence, not guilt, for the *majority* of people they find afield.

The Parable of Emile Dupont

Let me tell you about Emile Dupont. Emile immigrated to this country by way of Canada. He is no relation to the distinguished du Pont family of Delaware (for Dupont is a very common name in France). But as chance would have it, Emile bought a 40-acre farm in Delaware. His neighbors were thrilled to have a du Pont living near them, even if he spelled his name differently, and they were soon asking him to pay for a new church roof and a new ambulance for the rescue squad. Emile contributed $25, but since his neighbors had never heard of a du Pont who wasn't rich, they went away grumbling about the tightwad eccentric in the family who chose to live in an old farmhouse by himself.

Emile loved to hunt, and he loved especially to hunt the Canada geese that visited his farm in the fall. However, state and federal game wardens began to keep an eye on Emile, for anyone named du Pont who was too tight to pay for a church roof or an ambulance was a black sheep who bore watching.

One October afternoon, two wardens stopped by unexpectedly. Although Emile was in a hurry to get to town before the shops closed, he kindly set a kettle of water on the stove to make coffee.

"Been doing any hunting, Emile?" one of the wardens asked.

"Mais, oui! Three times I have sat in my field blind, and three times I have taken geese!"

"That's pretty good. Have you eaten all the birds?" asked the other warden.

"Ah, no. I'm saving them for the holidays for when my nephews come to visit from Quebec."

"How many geese are in the freezer?"

"Seven, but if you two would like to have one, I should be able to shoot another."

The two wardens looked at each other and nodded. "All right, Emile. That's what we want to know. You're under arrest for exceeding your federal possession limit, and for attempting to bribe an arresting officer. You may make one call to your lawyer, but we warn you that anything you say . . ."

"Zut alors!" said Emile. "I don't know any lawyer!"

"Ha! You du Ponts use lawyers just to carry your golf bags! Get your coat and come on."

Before establishing Emile's fine, the judge made an inquiry to discover whether this particular du Pont had any political connections that could cause the judge embarrassment. Reassured—and since it was only a first offense—Emile was fined $100 and the Christmas geese were confiscated.

Two weeks later Emile was walking with his nephews in the field behind his house when they flushed several mallards feeding in the corn stubble.

"Don't move!" yelled a voice from the woods. "I caught you rallying waterfowl!"

"Zut alors!" said Emile. "You are trespassing, but say I have done something wrong!"

"No wise stuff, du Pont," said the warden, emerging from the woods with his pistol drawn. "We're on to you. Show us your blind."

Emile walked ahead of the gunman to the pit he had dug in the field. As the warden began to check the area for corn, the nephews wandered off and began to throw corn cobs at one another the way restless young boys will do. A few of the cobs still had grain on them, and one missed its target and landed near the warden as he was inspecting the ground.

"Aha, baiting!"

"Zut alors! The children are but playing!" exclaimed Emile.

"Getting the kids to do your dirty work, eh?"

This time the fine was $1,500. Since the judge had not been hassled about the first fine, he figured he had nothing to fear from this du Pont. And since Emile was a du Pont, he could afford a hefty bite, and Delaware could always use the money.

And so it went. Throughout the rest of the season, Emile found himself harassed at every turn. He was unable to hunt, because incoming geese were constantly being flared by wardens skulking at the edge of his field. His neighbors condemned him for a scrooge and a convicted criminal. Emile took the only way out: He changed his name to Homer Jablonski and moved to Maryland.

This parable may be exaggerated, but it describes some of the pitfalls inherent in linking success in a conservation officer's career to the number of convictions he can get—particularly when some of the laws this officer literally and rigidly enforces were created for different purposes than the man perceives.

More than eighty years ago, George Bird Grinnell suggested a seasonal as well as daily bag limit. Canada adopted Grinnell's suggestion, and back in 1948 when the daily limit on ducks in New Brunswick, for example, was seven, the seasonal limit was 100; the daily goose limit was 5, and the seasonal limit was 25. Proportional seasonal limits based on daily limits still exist in Canada.

In the United States, however, seasonal limits are considered to be unenforceable, perhaps, because *wintering* waterfowl are available to many American hunters for a longer period than *migrating* waterfowl are to our Canadian counterparts. Yet we have equally unenforceable possession limits: that is, the equivalent of two days' bag limits. The restriction was created to permit the weekend and visiting non-resident sportsmen to convey a fair sample of his good luck home with him and to discourage meat hunters from crossing state lines to fill freezers. Thus the possession limit was intended to control the interstate flow of wildlife.

Nowadays, most wardens use the rule of thumb that enforcement of the possession limit stops at the hunter's door. Most wardens, that is but not all. In 1978 a resident of Delaware (who spells his name du Pont) was arrested by federal wardens for having several more geese than his possession limit (eight) in his home freezer.

The ambiguities and contradictions in waterfowling law are well-nigh endless. Virginia state law forbids a waterfowler from hunting on Sunday, but permits him to pursue crippled waterfowl in a motorized boat. Federal law permits a Virginian to hunt on Sunday, but forbids him to shoot cripples from a motorized boat. When law enforcement depends on which government entity or agency an officer works for, the law needs to be overhauled.

Some readers may think I lack a due regard for law and order. They know that of all law enforcers, wildlife protection agents are the most likely to suffer aggravated assault. My hat is off to the superb and generally thankless job being done by the overwhelming majority of conservation officers. At the same time, there is nothing subversive about suggesting that waterfowling laws can be made more coherent and less susceptible to personal interpretation or whim. I am sure most wardens would agree with me.

The Point System

Another controversy among modern waterfowlers concerns the point system for daily bag limits. According to Dennis Surrendi, former chief of the Migratory Bird Division of the Canadian Wildlife Service:

The point system encourages poor sportsmanship by not making a hunter more responsible before he pulls the trigger. We know how ignorant some waterfowlers are. At our waterfowl management areas, hunters will bring in gulls, loons, and herons to be recorded as part of their daily bags. This is an increasing problem. By allowing hunters to get away with shoddy identification of legal waterfowl, the point system appears to encourage hunters to shoot first and ask questions later.

Surrendi's appraisal of the ordinary waterfowler is as pessimistic as my own. However, the point system does not compound hunter ignorance so much as it tries to make allowances for it. Certainly, the point system does not kill the gulls, loons, and herons shot in Canadian waterfowl management areas, because the point system is not used in Canada. Furthermore, such cases of mistaken identity are just as illegal under the point system as under a body-count bag limit.

The only thing that will cure such ignorance is the kind of hunter training that I have been advocating throughout this chapter. Once a prospective hunter undergoes a rigorous apprenticeship, he will not likely kill loons or herons. And if he does, his license should be immediately revoked or suspended, depending on the circumstances of the error.

Dennis Surrendi has other reservations about the point system: "Canadians don't understand how Americans can value so many species of waterfowl at 10 points each, thereby permitting 10-birds-a-day limits. We *know* that in Alberta we have the best duck hunting in North America. Yet our daily limit is eight birds, period. It doesn't matter whether the duck is a mallard or a merganser. Each is equal in the eyes of Canadian law. We don't understand what omnipotent authority gives American biologists the right to declare one species or sex of waterfowl worth 100 or 70 points, and another 25 or 10."

No omnipotent authority is involved—only the fact that Alberta does offer some of the best duck hunting on earth, and there are few areas in the United States which can compare. Canadian hunters have to restrict themselves to eight birds a day in a province where sportsmen see little but pintail and mallards, canvasbacks and redheads. Under such circumstances, even the average hunter is not going to waste shots at stray scoters or mergansers, and the resulting pressure on such scarce species as canvasbacks and redheads may exceed what American gunners put on these same birds once they cross the border and become 70-, 100-point, or even completely protected, ducks.

In the Atlantic Flyway, our premier species is the black duck. Yet this bird is not as abundant as it once was, and American waterfowl managers would be hard put to justify even a 4-birds-a-day limit on black ducks— much less the 6-birds-a-day limit that exists in certain provinces at the Canadian end of the flyway. When U.S. biologists assign a point value of 70 to each black duck, and instruct hunters they must stop shooting when their combined total of points reaches or exceeds 100, this system permits American waterfowlers in several states of the flyway to shoot two black ducks (140 points total); one black duck (70) plus two goldeneyes or bufflehead (25 points each) for a combined total of 120 points; or three scaup or teal (10 points each) plus one black duck (70) for a combined total of 100 points.

Although "reordering" is a potential problem with certain combinations of species, there is no way the above, rather typical, flyway examples can be reordered so the hunter can kill still more ducks. Reordering, improper identification, and an inability to count are the weak elements of the point system. However, poaching and ignorance have been with us as problems long before the point system was conceived, and it would be a pity to deny sportsmen greater hunting opportunities in areas where prime species are in short supply merely to reduce temptation for the weakest members of the hunting fraternity.

Steel Shot

During the winter of 1893–1894, while George Bird Grinnell was on a shooting trip to Currituck Sound, North Carolina, he performed autopsies on a Canada goose and a whistling swan that had died of a disease which his guides called "croup." Since the birds suffered from labored and rattling breathing and discharged a yellowish fluid from their bills before they died,

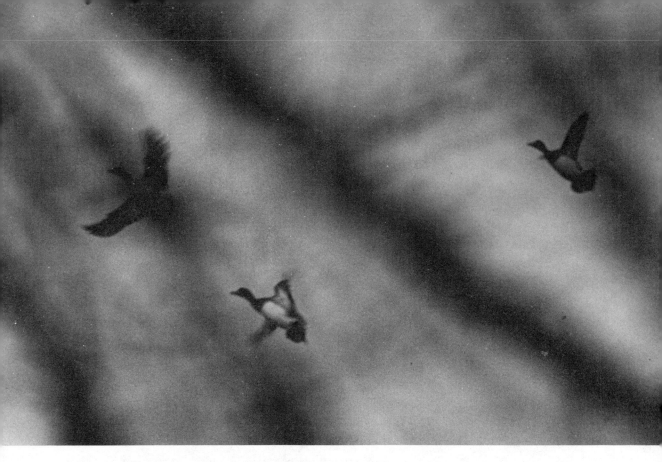

This view through the branches of a blind shows three ducks flaring over the decoys. Would the ordinary hunter be able to distinguish the mallard on the left from the widgeons on the right in the split seconds he has to make his shots before the birds are out of range? Probably not—which is why the point system evolved and has taken hold in so many states. *(Photograph by George Reiger)*

the guides thought the illness was centered in the respiratory system. They also told Grinnell they saw many such "croupy" birds each fall.

Grinnell's findings, which he later published in *Forest and Stream,* were quite different, and he concluded, "The birds dissected died from chronic lead poisoning, the cause of which was sufficiently obvious." He went on to describe the process:

Each season great quantities of shot are fired on the waters of this sound, and much of it falls on the feeding grounds of the wildfowl. In feeding, the geese, ducks and swans—whether by accident or design—take into the stomach with sand and gravel and food, more or less of this shot. When the shot has passed into the gizzard it is subjected to the same grinding process as the grass, grain or other food, and, being softer than the sand, it is ground into minute particles. These fine particles, acted on by the acids of the digestive organs, yield a soluble lead salt, which, being absorbed into the general system, causes death.

Over the next thirty-five years, hunters began finding increasing evidence that lead poisoning was a great and growing problem. If so many "croupy" birds were being discovered, thoughtful hunters asked, how many more must there be which die unnoticed or are quickly consumed by predators? And if lead poisoning from pellet ingestion can, also, affect pheasants and partridges, as reported in the London *Field* (1902), might not similar poisoning, also, affect the peregrine falcons and bald eagles which prey on crippled ducks? [6]

Despite this hand-wringing of a few, most sportsmen felt that since there was no substitute for lead, they had best do what they could to minimize the impact of lead poisoning (e.g., plowing upland areas and

[6] Technicians at the Patuxent (Maryland) laboratories of the U.S. Fish and Wildlife Service confirm that bald eagles can and have died from ingesting lead shot pellets, possibly consumed with the flesh of wounded ducks.

The best waterfowling art has always illustrated moments and perspectives unavailable to even the most skilled and luckiest of cameramen. Bob Kuhn's "Black Ducks on a River float" is just such a painting. *(Reproduction courtesy Remington Arms Collection of Game Art)*

raking the sands and muds in shallow lakes and bays) and then get on with the pleasures of hunting.

In August, 1931, More Game Birds in America, Inc., published *More Waterfowl By Assisting Nature,* which covered a spectrum of problems and proposals for improving duck hunting. One section concluded:

> Heavy concentrations of expended shot no doubt exist in numerous localities, especially on shooting grounds about blinds. A study should be made of the number of waterfowl killed by lead poisoning. If the losses of ducks from this cause are as large as many believe, an attempt should promptly be made to solve the problem.

Over the past half century, numerous studies have been made, and the search for a lead shot substitute began in earnest after the end of World War II. Today, estimtes of the number of waterfowl that die each year in North America from ingesting lead shot vary from hundreds of thousands to several million. Determining precise numbers has always been less important than realizing that hunters are inadvertently placing an enormous burden on waterfowl resources which, if an adequate lead shot substitute were adopted, could be alleviated to provide more recreational opportunities in the future—to say nothing of the unnecessary and lingering deaths that could be prevented.

In the search for a lead pellet substitute, even gold and silver were both tested and found to be superior to lead in every respect but cost! Copper- and nickel-plated shot were examined, and while their ballistic characteristics were superior to unplated lead, the copper and nickel plating wore off in the gizzards of tested birds, and the ducks succumbed to lead poisoning. Various metal alloys have been tested, but nothing has met the twin criteria of high duck mortality in the air, with little or no duck mortality on the ground or in the water from shot ingestion so well as soft iron—alias, steel—shot.

Although steel shot is lighter in weight than lead, it fires more perfect patterns with generally better penetration than lead over moderate ranges. It does not have the long-distance capabilities of hardened lead, and steel shot will scar the interior of inferior or antique shotgun barrels. Even Remington 1100s may wear out after a century of hard use, rather than the century and a half a shooter and his sons' sons might get from the gun by firing soft lead. On the other hand, there might not be as many waterfowl around in 150 years if the lead poisoning problem gets much worse.

While every waterfowler is enthusiastic in theory about saving ducks from lead poisoning, few like to imagine they have anything to do with the problem themselves. When the U.S. Fish and Wildlife Service first got around to promulgating regulations for the use of steel shot in selected areas of the Atlantic Flyway, the squawks of outraged hunters were heard from every state.

"We're clean as a whistle," insisted Long Islanders. "If our birds have ingested lead, they did so in New England."

"We're clean as a new knife," stressed Marylanders. "If our birds have ingested lead, they did so in New York."

So it went up and down the flyway, just as today we hear variations from western waterfowlers who insist their birds are as clean as a newborn calf; all the contaminated birds live east of the Mississippi.

"My grandfather shot thousands of ducks in this marsh, but you can't tell me there is still lead lying around from those days."

Or the corollary: "You can't tell me the little bit of shooting I do today is going to add a thimbleful of lead compared to what my grandfather fired."

Beginning back in the 1940s, Winchester-Western led the search for a lead shot substitute. More recently, however, this company has resisted the further introduction of steel shot, insisting the present iron alloy is an inadequate substitute for lead and will generate more waterfowl losses through crippling than we currently experience from lead poisoning. On the other hand, the Federal Cartridge Company has been a staunch proponent of steel shot partly because Federal helped develop one of the best early steel pellet and powder combinations. If the use of steel shot is made mandatory through all four flyways, Federal will be in an excellent position to capture a larger share of the waterfowling ammunition market currently dominated by the quality of Winchester's "Super X Double X" and Remington's "Nitro Mag" lead loads.

The trouble with allowing such subtle commercial overtones to play a role in the public debate surrounding the adoption of steel shot is that most sportsmen are unaware of these marketing nuances when they hear Winchester spokesmen say steel shot may bulge or blow apart the barrels of old shotguns (which is true of magnum lead loads as well) or read the courtroom testimony of federal officials who insist that steel shot performs as well as lead at all "reasonable ranges" (which is true, except that many waterfowlers think 70 yards is a reasonable range).

The most persistent argument against steel shot has nothing to do with either steel shot or the issue of lead poisoning of waterfowl. This is the theme that the introduction of steel shot is another example of Uncle Sam trying to regulate recreation to death. While waterfowling does have too many regulations, I can't view the introduction of steel shot either as a federal conspiracy or an example of moralistic manhandling. We must do something to alleviate the awful lead poisoning problem. The Toxic Substances Control Act would make that mandatory even if the federal courts had not. If there is a moralistic undercurrent in the lead shot/steel shot debate, it may involve ammunition dealers charging several dollars more for a box of 3-inch steel shot than a box of comparable lead shot, while ammunition manufacturers are insisting they know nothing about such scalping and that steel shot shells should be only about 10 percent more expensive than lead.

Although I have long supported the eventual adoption of a lead shot substitute, and I have been using steel shot (despite the cost and the fact I live in a zone where steel shot is not required) in much of my own waterfowling for the past six seasons, I have been concerned about the question of steel pellets fired at extreme range at our largest waterfowl targets. I found no significant difference in my ability to kill ducks with steel 4s and 2s when compared to lead 6s and 4s, but I had heard so many complaints, particularly from Marylanders, about the ineffectiveness of steel shot on Canada geese, I began to have doubts. When I expressed these doubts to Dick Dietz of Remington Arms, he asked me to visit Remington Farms in January 1978 in order to test fire the latest 2¾-inch steel load developed by his company.

"The problem is not with steel shot," Dick said, "but with how it is loaded. Of course, if people still insist on shooting at geese 80 yards out, and want to blame their failure on steel shot, we can't do anything about that."

Thus, one frozen morning I found myself standing in a clump of switchgrass overlooking the glazed surface of a tributary of Maryland's Chester River, waiting for geese sitting on the ice to fly into the fields behind me.

"How can 1⅛ ounces of steel in these new loads kill geese better than 1½ ounces of steel in the old?" I asked my Remington guide, Arthur Dierker.

"Improved velocity and retained energy are the answer. These new 2¾-inch shells are much superior to what Remington produced last year in the way of 3-inch shells. The proof of the pudding is we just don't have the crippling losses here at the Farms that we've been hearing about elsewhere."

Several small flocks of geese got up from the river and began moving to the fields, but far wide of our position. Then a flock of eight started our way, and, when they were still out in front and, perhaps, thirty yards up, Arthur, said, "Now!"

I swung on the nearest goose and fired as the bird disappeared behind my barrel. The goose folded. I watched it fall and hit the snow-covered ground with a thump. Almost too late I swung around to pick out another bird from the retreating flock and fired as my barrel dropped below its form, perhaps, 50 yards away. The bird jerked forward and began to tumble. It, too, was stone dead when it hit the ground.

A going-away shot at a goose is the toughest way to make a kill because of the bird's position and padding. Even 1⅞ ounces of lead fired from the rear will as often blow feathers as cut and kill the bird. But that is the glory of steel shot. It is not deformed by firing or contact and will penetrate better than lead.

"Get down!" warned Arthur.

Two more flocks of honkers were in the air and both were coming in our direction—but high. I was about to relax and watch the birds sail overhead when Arthur commanded,

"Take 'em!"

I jumped up, swung a long distance in front of the nearest bird, and pulled the trigger. The goose never missed a wingbeat. Putting my shotgun down, I cocked a suspicious eye at my companion.

"Arthur, those birds were too far away."

"I know it, but I wanted to see if you'd shoot at geese most hunters would think were in range—and then blame the shells for not killing the birds. Besides, you deserved to miss one after that double!"

The anger and bitterness expressed by dozens of *Field & Stream* readers whenever I have expressed support in one of my conservation columns for the adoption of steel shot makes me wonder at the motives of men who go waterfowling. We love the birds, but we often appear to love tradition more. At the root of much of the opposition to steel shot is the simple fact that steel shot is something new and different. After all, none of the grand gunners of yore ever hunted with steel!

Epilogue

Outsiders call us sadists or masochists; sometimes both. Others—mostly ourselves—describe our activities in romantic, even heroic, terms. We take ourselves very seriously and tend to forget that much of duck and goose hunting is fun and sometimes ridiculous.

For two days last season, I scouted a piece of salt marsh where several black ducks and mallards appeared to be in residence. I decided to go in the next day at dawn with my layout boat to try to decoy a limit. All night long, a northeast wind pushed the ocean through the inlets and over sod islands so that by first light, with my retriever tucked between my knees and myself tucked horizontally into the 9-foot punt, the tide began to float the boat off the point where I had hidden her.

I worried lest the boat's rocking would alarm ducks and wondered whether the brisk breeze wouldn't blow the punt completely clear of the reeds. I sat up, took one of the oars, shoved it hard down into the mud, and tied the painter to it. Now let her blow!

A half hour passed with no ducks to the decoys. Geese were flying high overhead, and ducks were trading in the distance. But the storm tide had lifted the boat well above the grass, and little white-capped waves slapped the hull and rocked my half-dozen decoys.

I was on the verge of packing it in when a pair of black ducks appeared low over the marsh obviously looking for company. I squiggled lower, hissed at my dog to stay down, and watched the birds approach from under the brim of my cap. My face was blackened, my pale hands were gloved, and only the stark bar of blued metal and wood resting across my camouflaged chest would spark the birds' suspicions.

Ordinarily they should have come straight in. But with all the marsh under water, they were wary of the curious "log" bumping near their rock-and-rolling buddies. Something wasn't right. They decided to swing by, look the situation over, and think about it.

"Just one," I pleaded. "Just one would make a perfect day. But, Lord, wouldn't a double be sweet!"

The ducks were gone half a minute. Then I noticed them to my right, flying wide of the decoys, but lower. When they turned upwind, no more than ten feet off the water, I knew they were coming—100 yards, 90, 80, 70 . . .

When the birds were less than 60 yards away, the oar suddenly pulled from the mud, surged into the air, slammed down on my head, startled the dog into jumping overboard, and the boat shipped a barrel of icy water that poured in like electricity around my crotch. I watched the black ducks blow away: 150 yards, 200, 300 . . . Then the sky broke loose and sleet obliterated the scene.

With the punt drifting away from the decoys, the dog paddling and whimpering in circles around me, and freezing water sloshing around my hips every time I made the slightest move, I did what any sane man would do: I laughed. I laughed and cussed and laughed again at all the follies of our magnificent recreation.

Halfway through the season, I left a dozen decoys out overnight in a pond. When I returned at dawn, I found two teal missing from the rig. Considerable searching turned up only one where an otter had pulled the bird—dragging the line and weight behind it—30 yards from the edge of the water. Somehow this otter, or a companion—the busy, back-and-forth tracks of otter never make such things clear—had contrived to carry off the other decoy to do with it what only an otter can tell.

I was fascinated; I was charmed. What a bizarre fate for a teal drake facsimile: that it becomes an otter's plaything. When I told one of my neighbors about the experience, he snorted and asked if I had shot enough ducks that day to make up the loss. But then, this man doesn't pretend to be a sportsman.

Two Washington, D.C., friends came down to share a seaside outing with me. An hour after dawn I was looking behind the blind and out to the ocean when I spotted a pair of puddle ducks coming down the coast. I provided the following, over-the-shoulder commentary for my companions:

"They're not too high—They should see the decoys—They have seen the decoys!—They're coming lower—They're going to circle—You should see them by now—They should be right over you—Why doesn't somebody shoot?!"

I turned and found both my companions peering around their end of the blind trying to see where I had been looking. No one was minding the store out front.

"Where are the ducks? " they whispered.

I looked up and saw a pair of gadwall hovering and staring down at me with something approaching bemusement.

"There! "

Guns began blazing and seven shots later we had one of the two birds.

"All right, guys, no more Gong Shows. Each person watches a different direction, and we'll use compass points to indicate where the birds are."

"Good idea," said Paul. "That's south."

"No, that's east."

"South."

"Paul, I live here; that's east."

"You're both wrong," announced Mel, uncapping a tiny compass he had tucked among his spare shells. "That's eastsoutheast."

Debating the fine points of the compass kept us busy until a goldeneye buzzed over the decoys without a shot being fired. We then decided to wrap up the compass conversation and concentrate on duck hunting. We compromised by calling "south" and "eastsoutheast," east and boxed the rest of the imaginary compass card accordingly. Going through the drill made us feel better. It was as though we had actually learned something—as though this time we were prepared for any and all contingencies, even though experience indicates that each fiasco in waterfowling is somehow unique and unforeseeable.

Suddenly we heard the distant murmer of geese.

"North," said Mel, "and coming this way! "

"More like northwest," said Paul, "and the wind will carry them wide."

"Start calling," I ordered. "And stay back in the blind. We don't want to spook them while trying to get a look."

The sound of Canada geese carries a long distance under most any atmospheric condition. Biologists suspect the birds may use their calling to echolocate their way through fog. When Canadas are flying downwind toward a trio of expectant hunters, the honking seems to come from a public address system mounted on the roof of the blind—even when the birds are still half a mile away.

But this time there was no rubber-necking. This time we were ready. My companions and I scrunched into the corners of the blind and matched yelp for yelp the calling of the geese behind us. We didn't go into action until we saw a wingtip flash about 30 yards above the edge of the plywood roof.

"NOW!"

Mel and Paul leaped up and did an audition for a movie called "Abbott and Costello Go Hunting." Paul stepped on Mel's foot, and Mel recovered his balance by knocking Paul back into the corner. Then swinging on the nearest bird, which looked as large as a bomber, Mel squeezed the trigger of his empty gun. He had forgotten to reload after the gadwall farce.

Meanwhile I had somehow contrived to insert the thumb tang on the bolt of my semi-automatic shotgun through a hole in my right glove and couldn't get my hand free. My frantic gyrations and furious oaths brought the dog around to the entrance of the blind where he peered in to see what was going on.

A dozen geese flew by unscathed, but our imprecations quickly turned into such uproarious laughter it took still another missed opportunity to sober us up. No, we hadn't been drinking. And we did quite well when we finally got organized. Funny though: I don't remember those details half as well as the foolish way we began.

How do you explain waterfowling to anyone who does not share your faith? How can you even describe events to those who care but were not there?

With my final shot last season, I killed a black duck. That is a simple statement of fact. But those few words mask a range of sensations which could not be duplicated with a sound-and-light replica of the outing.

This is because you'd have to know my dog is old and that day lame, and I wanted to get his mind off his hurt by doing something he loves and does well: jump shooting. You'd also have to know that I had watched half a hundred black ducks angle down in the afternoon mist toward a series of meanders in two drains of the high marsh, and despite a following wind which blew every crunch of spartina grass underfoot ahead of us to spook the wary birds, I was confident that eventually Rocky and I would find an elbow of water to which we could turn upwind and find an unsuspecting duck.

You'd have to hear the whispering wings of birds in the air, and see how I'd periodically squat, less with the hope of having a shot, than to pause and watch the panorama of waterfowl returning to the evening marsh. You'd have to see the pair of mallards pitch to a pond several hundred yards away, and know that because I'd rather kill one of these interlopers of the salt lands than a native black duck, I made a special effort to reach the alert drake and his oblivious hen. You'd see the mallards sitting close by the opposite shore and then noisily flushing out of range. You'd watch Rocky and me turn back to our original course, and when we were 75 yards away, you'd glance back in time to see a solitary black duck take to the air a few feet from where we'd stood while contemplating the fleeing mallards. You'd hear me chuckle and tell my dog that I hoped the crafty bird lived another decade, and you'd see Rocky look up as if he understood every word.

Other ducks were getting up in the mist, but only a few were at extreme range, and you'd know that once the gun was fired, every bird in the marsh would be up and gone. So you wait with me for the shot that can't be missed.

You'd watch me come to a deep, unwadable creek, and while I look for a possible ford, two black ducks leap up from the other side. Despite the fact you are hunting them, the sudden rise of a pair of ducks is always a strangely unexpected event.

You are behind my eyes as I fire at the furthest bird in an attempt to score a double, miss, swing on the nearest, and kill it with a charge of steel 2s. While Rocky swims the channel to retrieve the fallen bird, you let the sight and sound of dozens of ducks rising from all parts of the darkening marsh and the cold mist on your cheek saturate your senses.

My watch tells me there are still seven minutes left in the season. But my day, my year, is done. I turn back toward the distant blind and calculate that in a narrow, ten-square-mile band of salt marsh, I am the only human being, and the proud, head-high sashaying dog striding before me with a black duck in his mouth is all the human companionship a waterfowler needs.

An oar, an otter, a tangled glove, and a last-chance duck. These are the memories of waterfowling. These are the words and experiences we seek to recover or revise each time we return to the marsh. If we weren't dedicated, we would not suffer the small tribulations surrounding our recreation. And it is this dedication—call it "obsession" if you like—that provides hope for the future.

Thousands of years ago, men crouched at the edge of ponds to fling their stones and arrows at ducks and geese lured by crude facsimiles of themselves. So long as waterfowl and men exist, we will hunt the wings of dawn.

Appendix:

SEA DUCKS AND HOW TO COOK THEM, MAYBE

I N THE DECEMBER 1924 issue of *Field & Stream,* Richard Warren Hatch provided the readers with two famous "sea coot" recipes, said to make any bird "delicious for the most epicurean hunter":

The easiest way is to place the coot in a pot to boil with a good flat-iron or an anvil. Let it boil long and merrily, and when you can stick a fork in the flat-iron or the anvil, as the case may be, then that coot will be ready to eat.

If that takes too much patience, take the goodly coot and nail it firmly to a hardwood board. Put that board in the sun for about a week. At the end of that time, carefully remove the coot from the board, throw away the coot, and cook the board.

The "poor coot" has been suffering parodies of its table qualities for as long as the bird has been hunted for sport. Yet freshwater coots in the South, and scoters, eiders, and oldsquaw in New England have had fans of their flavor longer than they have had sophisticates making cooking jokes at their expense.

Nelson Bryant, *New York Times* outdoor editor and a native of Martha's Vineyard, Massachusetts, writes:

There are various recipes for coot (scoter) stew—and the breasts do make a good stew—but I prefer my own [way of preparing the birds.] Remove the skin from the breast of a scoter by making a small slit with a knife and then tearing the rest away by hand. You will immediately discover that the scoter's skin is tough and thick, a suitable undergarment for the weather it must endure. Slice the meat away from the breastbone, one chunk on each side; remove any fat that might cling to the edges, and marinate the breasts in a mild mixture of vinegar and water—about four parts water and one part vinegar—for a half-hour. Pat dry on paper toweling and cook in butter in a hot frying pan for a short time. Don't overcook. Make sure the center of the meat is at least pink. I prefer it red. Slice in thin pieces across the grain and serve on buttered toast with a suitable orange marmalade or currant jelly.

Long Island outdoor writer, Nick Karas, is partial to sea duck dinners, but he believes in the power of positive seasoning. With his recipe, he "defies anyone to tell me that it is scoter and not mallard they are eating" :

First, remove only the breasts from young birds,[1] discarding all skin and fat. Marinate the breasts overnight in a dry, cheap red wine. The cheaper the better. Then cut small pouches into the outside of the breasts and stick small plugs of garlic into them. Season well with salt and pepper until you can no longer see the meat. Place the breasts in a broiler and cover with fresh, thinly sliced onions. Broil for 15 minutes.

Well, Nick, that's not exactly how I'd prepare a mallard–or a sea duck–but, *chacun à son goût*. For a little less spicy "sea coot" recipe, here is Oliver Hazard Perry Rodman's suggestion. Incidentally, Ollie is one of the grand old men of the sport and was Van Campen Heilner's hunting host on Cape Cod in the 1930s when Heilner was gathering experiences for *A Book on Duck Shooting*. In personal correspondence dated July 9, 1973, Ollie writes:

First skin the bird, then cut out the entire breast, bone and all, snipping off the rough short ends of rib which may break away when the breast is taken out of the body.

From here you can go two ways: first, cook the entire breast, or, better yet, cut off the breast meat on both sides of the breast bone, which leaves you wih two fillets from a single bird. Use a heavy old-fashioned iron skillet. Fry up several pieces of bacon. Then, while the bacon fat is really hot, put in the fillets and cover the frying pan. It takes only about three or four minutes cooking on each side–and you should have two medium rare, very tender, "steaks" that will melt in your mouth. One important thing which I almost forgot: after you skin the bird and take out the breasts, be sure to take a sharp knife and skim off absolutely all of an yellow fat. This takes away the possibility of any "fishy" taste.

For generations, New Englanders have made a "coot stew." The ingredients vary from place to place along the Maine and Massachusetts coasts, but all use sea ducks as their principal meat. Decades ago, there was even a restaurant on Federal Street in Boston that featured this popular dish.

---

[1] As indicated in chapter six, distinguishing immature scoters of either sex from mature females is not always an easy job.

However, since this gourmet spa was known as the Shoe and Leather Club, one wonders whether the name didn't inspire Richard Warren Hatch's parody of coot cookery.

I've sampled several varieties of coot stew and found the concoctions range in taste from savory to sordid. A lot depends on whether you've been brought up on a particular recipe. And, for some variations, a lot seems to depend on how hungry you are. Here is one of the better coot stew recipes, supplied by the late John G. Mackenty, of Edgartown, Massachusetts:

Skin the scoter and cut him up in sizeable pieces. Don't use the carcass. Employ only the wings, leg, and each breast cut into four or five pieces. Sauté the pieces in butter and onion until the meat is well browned. Then place potatoes, carrots, and more onions in a casserole; add the meat and the gravy from the sautéing. A little poultry seasoning will help to dull the strong scoter taste. You will probably need to add a little water, too, and, is you like the gravy thickened, a little flour can be stirred gradually in before it is added to the mixture. Put the covered casserole in a low oven for about two hours. Check your water content from time to time. Finally, if the scoter flavor still comes through too strong, add two or three ounces of Bordeau or red Burgundy to the stew about half an hour before serving, and stir it well.

Outdoor and western writer, Zane Grey, was taught much of his early woodcraft by a hermit who lived in a cabin near Dillon's Falls, not far from Zanesville, Ohio. Old Muddy Miser, as people called him, had several ways for preparing muskrat and coot, which Zane Grey later adapted for sea ducks when he lived along the coasts of New York and California. For several ways to prepare sea ducks over an open fire—in Dutch ovens or on a grill—we immodestly recommend *The Zane Grey Cookbook* by Barbara and George Reiger (Prentice-Hall, 1976).

If what happens to wildlife resources and recreation in the East eventually happens in the West as well, the currently preferred dabbling ducks may be increasingly scarce in the years ahead, and optimum shooting will be provided by true coots and the various species of sea ducks. Long after prohibitions against hunting within one mile of a building, road, telephone pole, or discarded beer can will have eliminated much of our recreation near small towns and waterways throughout the continent, scoter shooters will still be allowed to hunt well off the crowded coasts of Oregon, Michigan, New Hampshire, and Maryland. Furthermore, what with escalating food prices, as well as the moral inhibition against throwing away something you've killed, I suspect more hunters will not only be sea duck shooting in the years ahead, but sea duck eating as well.

Limits are generous—in most states, you may shoot between 7 and 10 a day; in Alaska, the daily limit is 15—and considering the abundance of most eiders, scoters, and oldsquaw, limits will not likely be reduced before the end of this century. The birds nest far enough north so it will still be a few decades before the drainers, channelizers, and industrial developers take over all the spring latitudes of our oceanic divers.

There is another positive, although oblique, rebate to sea duck shooting. Every year, tens of thousands—and some years, millions—of sea ducks and other marine birds die in oil slicks caused by the illegal discharge of oily ballast water or the grounding of oil barges and tankers. At present, because eiders, scoters, and oldsquaw are ranked as "trash ducks," even by some wildlife biologists, there are few people to protest this preventable waste of waterfowl resources. However, if a majority of the wildfowling fraternity took up and enjoyed sea duck shooting, oh, my, how the politicians would hop to make the shipping lanes a safer place for sea birds! Then, perhaps, Van Campen Heilner's ironical words would reverberate with a new, more literal meaning:

Let others have their canvasback and mallard. Let others have their honkers and their wavies.[2] Give me the long lines of dories anchored off Barnstable or Gurnet Point, the ever-wheeling gannets and the flash of the light at North Truro. And when I'm too old to gun any more, take me down on Monomoy the day of a big northwester and sit me in a chair to watch the skunk-heads run the gantlet.

And when you take me home that night I want a big red-hot steaming plate-full of good old coot stew!

[2] Snow geese.

Bibliography

BIBLIOGRAPHIES are of primary interest to bibliophiles. Writers generally include a long list of reference materials to indicate how much they know about their subject. The longer the list, the more they know—supposedly.

My list is long for this reason, I'm sure, but I have an additional excuse. Originally I was going to include only those American authors and titles bearing directly on the subject of waterfowl and waterfowling. Yet that would have meant rejecting many excellent British titles, beginning with Lieutenant Colonel Peter Hawker's *Instructions to Young Sportsmen in all That Relates to Guns and Shooting,* first published in London in 1824 and with enormous influence on our own hunting customs and traditions. In addition, since no modern writer on waterfowling can call his book "complete" without at least passing reference to dogs, decoys, and shooting skills, I can't very well have a bibliography that neglects these subjects.

Thus, in gathering my reference materials, the pendulum swung so far the other way that the present bibliography includes some titles of only the most marginal interest to the pure waterfowler. For example, Colonel H. P. Sheldon's *Tranquility* series and several of Archibald Rutledge's books are included because these gentlemen personified the finest traditions in outdoor writing and sportsmanship found in their respective parts of the country—Sheldon in New England; Rutledge in the Carolinas.

The books of Charles G. D. Roberts and Ernest Thompson Seton have long been favorites with American outdoorsmen, and much of the awe we feel for wildlife stems from our youthful readings of these two Canadian naturalists. Although I have not included any of his works in this bibliography, still another important Canadian naturalist/writer was Archibald Stanfield Belaney, who wrote under the pseudonym "Grey Owl." Someday,

I hope, a bright young graduate student will do a thesis on the effect such turn-of-the-century writers and illustrators had in developing the conservation ethic of today.

As I put this bibliography together, it occurred to me that while not all the best books on waterfowling have been written, most of them have. Certainly the halcyon days are gone, days to be measured not only by the quantity of game available, but by the scarcity of other shooters. Both factors are critical to quality hunting. As described in chapter six, we once knew fabulous shooting along the shores of Lake Okeechobee because the U.S. Army Corps of Engineers had not yet ruined the lake for waterfowl, because tourists had not yet discovered interior Florida, and because locals thought duck hunters were mad. Some mornings, with great strings of lesser scaup, ringbills, and mallards trading in all directions and at different altitudes, we were in a kind of hunter's ecstasy. Such rapturous feelings are sometimes hard to recollect on today's overcrowded public marshes.

More people taking up duck hunting has created demands for more how-to books on the subject. In the last century, waterfowling books were written by amateurs who, in the best sense of that word, composed their tomes based on a love of the birds and the sport of hunting them. Sometimes these books were written for a handful of friends or as diaries for no eyes but the author's.

Gradually, and then rapidly following the widespread introduction of television, books were created to appeal more to the eye than to the inner ear, and writers on waterfowling were asked to prepare attractive "packages" telling a mass audience where to find birds, what kind of decoys to use to lure the birds, and what kinds of guns and loads to use to kill the birds. The traditions and ethics of waterfowling are sometimes lost in the rush to the army-navy surplus stores and the discount catalogues.

If contemporary British hunting books still emphasize the esthetic pleasures of hunting over the tangible rewards, this may be because the British still have other ways to measure a man's contribution to society than his annual income. The British also have other ways to honor such contributions. Charles Roberts and Peter Scott, for example, were knighted for their translations of natural history into art. George Bird Grinnell and John C. Phillips, on the other hand, were merely given long obituaries in *The New York Times*.

Although I tend to share Oscar Wilde's impression that "journalism is unreadable, and literature is not read," two important outdoor writers of the previous generation were Corey Ford and Ernest Hemingway, who did their best work while still under the influence of their newspaper training. Furthermore, most of the best outdoor writers of this generation—Bob Boyle, Bil Gilbert, Bob Jones, Frank Graham, Jr., John McPhee, and John G. Mitchell, just to name half-a-dozen—are graduates of the Manhattan pulp mills. I only wish more good writers wrote about duck hunting.

The initials "p.p." mean the cited book was privately printed. The abbreviation "n. pub." means there is no listing for this title in the Library of Congress. In certain instances, I have included all of an author's names or given his real name alongside his pseudonym, because as time passes, such details are often lost to literary historians, and some trivia expert may need these facts a century hence.

Unfortunately, there is no way to cite the many thousands of duck hunting stories and articles in the numerous perodicals that have catered to such sporting activities over the last 100 years, beginning with the original *American Sportsman, Rod and Gun,* and *Forest and Stream;* continuing with *Outing, Outdoor Life, Sports Afield,* and *Field & Stream,* and including the modern and mostly defunct *The American Sportsman, The American Gun, Rod & Gun,* and *Gray's Sporting Journal.* Hopefully, one or more university libraries will take it upon themselves to develop a complete collection of such periodical sporting literature as well as waterfowling books. As far as I can determine, there are only about a dozen libraries in the world that have all the issues of *Forest and Stream,* either in original form or on microfilm. Equally disappointing, only a few more libraries keep microfilm records of *Field & Stream, Outdoor Life,* and *Sports Afield,* before about 1960. The problem is storage and cost. Yet microfilm takes less space than magazines and is more critically needed with today's publications than those in the nineteenth century, for the paper used by modern mass magazine publishers will not last much more than 30 years.

While I doubt I'll ever have a chance to amend this bibliography, I'm at that stage in life when I find greater pleasure in rereading good, old titles than risking disappointment on unproven, new books. If you know of a good waterfowling title I've overlooked, please write me. Such a surprise will be almost as welcome as a northeast wind with a taste of snow.

G. W. R.

Ackley, Parker O. *Home Gun Care & Repair*, Stackpole Books, Harrisburg, Pa., 1969.

Arnold, Richard. *Automatic and Repeating Shotguns*, A. S. Barnes and Co., New York, 1958

———*The Shooter's Handbook*, N. Kaye, London, 1965.

———*The Shoreshooter*, Seeley Service, London, 1953.

Askins, Charles. *Game Bird Shooting*, Macmillan, New York, 1931.

———*Modern Shotguns and Loads*, Small-Arms Technical Publishing Co., Marshallton, Del., 1929.

———*The American Shotgun*, Outing Publishing Co., New York, 1910.

———*The Shotgunner's Book: A Modern Encyclopedia*, The Stackpole Co., Harrisburg, Pa., 1958.

———*Wing and Trap Shooting*, Outing Publishing Co., New York, 1911.

———*Wing Shooting*, The Outers' Book Co., Chicago, 1923.

Askins, Charles, JR. *Wing and Trap Shooting*, Macmillan, New York, 1948.

Babcock, Havilah. *My Health Is Better in November*, University of South Carolina Press, Columbia, S.C., 1948.

Babcock, Philip H. *Falling Leaves*, The Derrydale Press, New York, 1937.

Bailey, Robeson, ed. *The Feld and Stream Gamebag*, Doubleday, Garden City, N.Y., 1948.

Baird, Spencer Fullerton; Brewer, Thomas M.; and Ridgeway, Robert. *The Water Birds of North America* (1884), Arno Press, New York, 1973.

Barber, Joel D. *'Long Shore*, The Derrydale Press, New York, 1939.

———*Wild Fowl Decoys* (1934), Dover Publications, New eyork, 1954.

Barton, Frank Townend. *The Retriever: Its Points, Management, Training and Diseases*, Everett & Co., London, n.d.

Bashline, L. James, and Saults, Dan, eds.

America's Great Outdoors, J. B. Ferguson Publishing Co., Chicago, 1976.

Bates, Frank Amasa. *The Game Birds of North America*, B. Whidden, Boston, 1896.

Bauer, Erwin A. *Outdoor Potography*, Outdoor Life Publishing Co., New York, 1965.

Bauer, Erwin, Jr. *The Duck Hunter's Bible*, Doubleday, Garden City, N.Y., 1965.

Beach, Rex Ellingwood. *Oh, Shoot! Confessions of an Agitated Sportsman*, Harper & Bros., New York, 1921.

Becher, A. C., Jr. *Decoying Waterfowl*, A. S. Barnes and Co., South Brunswick, N.J., 1973 .

———*Waterfowl in the Marshes*, A. S. Brnes and Co., Cranbury, N.J., 1969.

Bellrose, Frank C. *Ducks, Geese & Swans of North America*, Stackpole Books, Harrisburg, Pa., 1976.

Bennett, Logan Johnson. *The Blue-winged Teal, Its Ecology and Management*, Collegiate Press, Inc., Ames, Ia., 1938.

Bent, Arthur Cleveland. *Life Histories of North American Wild Fowl*, Part 1 (1923) and Part II (1925), Dover Publications, New York, 1962.

Berkey, Barry R. *Pioneer Decoy Carvers*, Illustrated by Henry Andrew Fleckenstein, Jr., Tidewater Publishers, Cambridge, Md., 1977.

Bernsen, Paul S. *The North American Waterfowler*, Ballantine Books, New York, 1972.

Bewick, Thomas. *Ducks*, Gentry Magazine, New York, 1951.

Bigelow, Horatio. *Flying Feathers*, Garrett & Massie Publishers, Richmond, VA., 1937.

———*Gunnerman*, The Derrydale Press, New York, 1939.

———*Gunnerman's Gold*, p.p., Stanaford, W. Va, 1943.

Bishop, Richard Evett. *Wildfowl: A Collection*

of Etching and Oil Painting Reproductions, Brown & Bigelow, St. Paul, Minn., 1948.

Bliss, Anthony A., ed. *The Chesapeake Bay Retriever,* The American Chesapeake Club, New York, 1936.

Blogg, Percy Thayer. *There Are No Dull Dark Days,* H. G. Roebuck & Son, Baltimore, Md., 1944.

Bonner, Paul Hyde. "A Bitter Dawn," *The Glorious Mornings,* Charles Scribner's Sons, New York, 1954.

Bonvouloir, Comte J. de. *Les Retrievers et Leur Dressage,* Librarie des Champs-Elysées, Paris, 1948.

Book of the Shotgun, Sports Illustrated, New York, 1967.

Bourjaily, Vance. *The Unnatural Enemy,* The Dial Press, New York, 1963.

Bovey, Martin Koon. *The Saga of the Waterfowl,* illustrated by Francis Lee Jaques, The Wildlife Management Institute, Washington, D.C., 1949.

———*Whistling Wings,* Doubleday, Garden City, N.Y., 1947.

Bradford, Charles Barker. *The Wild-Fowlers, or, Sporting Scenes and Characters of the Great Lagoon,* G. P. Putnam's Sons, New York, 1901.

Brewer, Frances G. *Labrador Retriever,* All-Pets Books, Fond du Lac, Wis., 1958.

Bright, Ira. "The Stork and the Pintail," *Great Hunting and Fishing Stories,* edited by J. Hammond Brown, Grosset & Dunlap, New York, 1947.

Brister, Bob. *Moss, Mallards and Mules,* Winchester Press, New York, 1973.

———*Shotgunning: The Art and The Science,* Winchester Press, New York, 1976.

Broadley, Gwen. *The Retriever Owner's Encyclopedia,* Pelham, London, 1968.

Brown, William Francis. *Retriever Gun Dogs,* A. S. Barnes and Co., New York, 1945.

Bruette, Dr. William Arthur. *American Duck, Goose, and Brant Shooting,* G. Howard Watt, New York, 1929.

———*The Complete Dog Book,* Steward Kidd Co., Cincinnati, Ohio, 1921.

———*Guncraft,* p.p., Chicago, 1912.

———*Sportsmen's Encyclopedia* (2 volumes), Forest and Stream Publishing Co., New York, 1923.

Brusewitz, Gunnar. *Hunting,* Stein and Day, New York, 1969.

Bryant, Nelson. "The Hunt," *Hunting Moments of Truth,* edited by Eric Peper and Jim Rikhoff, Winchester Press, New York, 1973.

———*The Wildfowler's World,* Winchester Press, New York, 1973.

Burch, Monte. *Waterfowling,* Harper & Row, New York, 1978.

Burk, Bruce. *Game Bird Carving,* Winchester Press, New York, 1972.

———*Waterfowl Studies,* Winchester Press, New York, 1976.

Bush, Walter L. *A Saga of Duck and Goose Shooting,* illustrated by Leslie C. Kouba, American Wildlife Pub., Minneapolis, 1978.

Butler, Alfred Joshua. *Sport in Classic Times* (1930), William Kaufmann, Inc., Los Altos, Ca, 1975.

Butler, David F. *The American Shotgun,* Winchester Press, New York, 1973.

Buxton, Aubrey. *The King in His Country,* Longmans, London, 1955.

Cadman, W. Arthur. *Goose Shooting,* Percival Marshall & Co., London, 1963.

———*Shouldergunning for Duck,* Percival Marshall & Co., London, 1963.

Cameron, Jenks. *The Bureau of Biological Survey: Its History, Activities, and Organization* (1929), Arno Press, New York, 1973.

Camp, Raymond Russell. "Waterfowl: Ducks–Geese–Shore Birds," *All Seasons Afield with Rod and Gun,* McGraw-Hill Book Co., New York, 1939.

——*Duck Boats, Blinds, Decoys, and Eastern Seaboard Wildfowling,* Knopf, New York, 1952.

——*The Hunter's Encyclopedia,* The Stackpole Co., Harrisburg, Pa., 1948.

Cartier, John O. *Getting the Most Out of Modern Waterfowling,* St. Martin's Press, New York, 1974.

Cartwright, B. W. *Sports Afield Treasury of Waterfowl,* Prentice-Hall, Inc., Englewoods Cliffs, N.J., 1957.

Casson, Paul W. *Decoys Simplified,* Freshet Press, Rockville Centre, N.Y., 1972.

Cay, John E. *Ward Allen: Savannah River Market Hunter,* p.p., Savannah, Ga., 1958.

Cellini, Benvenuto. *Autobiography,* translated by John Addington Symonds, Modern Library edition, New York, n.d.

Chapman, Frank Michler. *Bird-Life, A Guide to the Study of Our Common Birds,* illustrated by Ernest Thompson Seton, D. Appleton and Co., New York, 1897.

——*Handbook of Birds of Eastern North America,* D. Appleton and Co., New York, 1907.

Charlesworth, W. M. *The Book of the Golden Retriever,* Fletcher & Son, Norwich, Eng., 1947.

Cheever, Byron, ed. *L. T. Ward & Bro. Wildlife Counterfeiters,* North American Decoys Pub., Heber City, Utah, 1971.

——, ed. *Mason Decoys,* A Hillcrest Publication, Heber City, Utah, 1974.

Claflin, Bert. *American Waterfowl: Hunting Ducks and Geese,* Knopf, New York, 1952.

Clark, Roland. *Gunner's Dawn,* The Derrydale Press, New York, 1937.

——*Pot Luck,* Countryman Press, A. S. Barnes and Co., New York, 1945.

——*Roland Clark's Etchings,* The Derrydale Press, New York, 1938.

——*Stray Shots,* The Derrydale Press, New York, 1931.

Clarke, Eileen. *How to Raise and Train a Curly-coated Retriever,* T. F. H. Publishers, Jersey City, N. J., 1966.

Cleveland, Grover. *Fishing and Shooting Sketches,* The Outing Publishing Co., New York, 1906.

Cochrane, Robert L. "Crippling Effects of Lead, Steel and Copper Shot on Experimental Mallards," *Wildlife Monographs No. 51,* The Wildlife Society, Washington, D.C., November, 1976.

Cofield, Thomas R. *Training the Hunting Retriever,* D. Van Nostrand Co., Princeton, N.J., 1959.

Connett, Eugene Virginius, III. *A Decade of American Sporting Books & Prints by The Derrydale Press, 1927–1937,* The Derrydale Press, New York, 1937.

——*Duck Decoys: How to Make Them, How to Paint Them, How to Rig Them,* D. Van Nostrand Co., New York, 1953.

——*Duck Shooting Along the Atlantic Tidewater,* William Morrow & Co., New York, 1947.

——, ed. *Wildfowling in the Mississippi Flyway,* D. Van Nostrand Co., New York, 1949.

Cook, Earnshaw. *Hollica Snooze,* illustrated by Bob Hines, Smith Pub., Rindge, N.H., 1957.

Cory, Charles Barney. *How to Know the Ducks, Geese and Swans of North America, All the Species Being Grouped According to Size and Color,* Little, Brown & Co., Boston, 1897.

Cottam, Clarence. *Food Habits of North American Diving Ducks,* U.S. Department of Agriculture, Bulletin #643, Washington, D.C., April, 1939.

Cox, Nicholas. *The Fowler; Containing Rules for Taking Every Species of Land & Water Fowl; Whether By Fowling Piece,*

Net, Engine or Otherwise, J. Dixwell, London, circa 1800.

Coykendall, Ralf. *Duck Decoys and How to Rig Them,* Henry Holt, New York, 1955.

Crowe, Philip K. *Sport Is Where You Find It,* Van Nostrand, New York, 1953.

Curtis, Paul Allan, Capt. *American Game Shooting,* E. P. Dutton & Co., New York, 1927.

———*Guns and Gunning,* The Penn Publishing Co., Philadelphia, Pa., 1934.

———*Sportsmen All,* The Derrydale Press, New York, 1938.

———*Sporting Firearms of Today in Use,* E. P. Dutton & Co., New York, 1922.

Dalgety, C. T. *Wildfowling,* Charles Scribner's Sons, New York, 1937.

Daumier, Honoré. *Hunting and Fishing,* Leon Amiel Publisher, New York, 1975.

Davis, Richard Harding. *With the French in France and Salonika,* Charles Scribner's Sons, New York, 1916.

Dawson, Major Kenneth. *Marsh and Mudflat,* Country Life, London, 1931.

———*Son of A Gun,* Country Life, London, 1929.

Day, Albert M. *North American Waterfowl,* The Stackpole Co., Harrisburg, Pa., 1949.

Day, James Wentworth. *Coastal Adventure,* G. G. Harrap and Co., London, 1949.

———*Harvest Adventure on Farms and Sea Marshes,* G. G. Harrap and Co., London, 1946.

———*A History of the Fens,* George G. Harrap and Co., London, 1954.

———*The Modern Fowler,* Longmans, Green and Co., London, 1934.

———*The Modern Shooter,* Jenkins, London, 1952.

———*Sport in Egypt,* Country Life, London, 1938.

———*Sporting Adventure,* G. G. Harrap and Co., London, 1937.

———*Rum Owd Boys: On Poachers, Wild-fowlers, Longshore Pirates, Cut-Throat Islanders, Smugglers and Fen-Tigers,* East Anglian Magazine, Ipswich, England, 1974.

———*Wild Wings and Some Footsteps,* Blandford Press, London, 1948.

Delacour, Jean. *The Waterfowl of the World,* (4 volumes), Country Life, London, 1954.

Duncan, Stanley, and Guy Thorne. *The Complete Wildfowler,* Outing Pub., New York, 1912.

Dunlap, Roy. *Gun Owner's Book of Care, Repair and Improvement,* Harper & Row, New York, 1974.

Earnest, Adele. *The Art of the Decoy: American Bird Carvings,* Clarkson N. Potter, New York, 1965.

Einarsen, Arthur Skogman. *Black Brant: Sea Goose of the Pacific Coast,* University of Washington Press, Seattle, Wa., 1965.

Eley, Charles C. *The History of Retrievers,* The Field Press, London, 1920.

Eley, W. G. *Retrievers and Retrieving,* Longman's, Green and Co., London, 1905.

Elliott, William. *Carolina Sports by Land & Water* (1846), Arno Press, New York, 1967.

Ellis, Melvin Richard. *Wild Goose, Brother Goose,* Holt, Rinehart and Winston, New York, 1969.

Elman, Robert. *The Atlantic Flyway,* Winchester Press, New York, 1972.

———*The Great American Shooting Prints,* Knopf, New York, 1972.

Erskine, Anthony J. *Buffleheads,* Canadian Wildlife Service Monograph Series, Number 4, Ottawa, 1971.

Errington, Paul L. *The Red Gods Call,* Iowa State University Press, Ames, Ia., 1973.

———*Of Men and Marshes,* Macmillan, New York, 1957.

Etchen, Fred. *Commonsense Shotgun Shooting*

with *Fred Etchen,* Standard Publications, Huntington, W. Va., 1946.

Evans, George Bird, ed. *The Best of Nash Buckingham,* Winchester Press, New York, 1973.

Falk, John R. *The Practical Hunter's Dog Book,* Winchester Press, New York, 1971.

Farrington, Selwyn Kip, Jr. *The Ducks Came Back,* Coward-McCann, New York, 1945.

——— *Labrador Retriever, Friend and Worker,* Hastings House, New York, 1976.

The Field and Stream Reader, Doubleday & Co., Garden City, N.Y., 1946.

Fiennes, Richard and Alice. *The Natural History of Dogs,* Bonanza Books, New York, 1968.

Finn, Frank. *Wildfowl of the World,* Hutchinson & Co., London, 1923.

Fischer, Gertrude. *The Complete Golden Retriever,* Howell Book House, New York, 1974.

Fleckenstein, Henry A., Jr. *Decoys of the Mid-Atlantic Region,* Schiffer Publishing, Philadelphia, 1979.

Folkard, Henry Coleman. *The Wild-Fowler: A Treatise on Ancient and Modern Wild-Fowling, Historical and Practical,* Longman, Green, Longman, and Roberts, London, 1864.

Forbush, Edward Howe. *Birds of Massachusetts and Other New England States,* Berwick and Smith Co., Norwood, Mass., 1925–1929.

——— *A History of the Game Birds, Wild-Fowl and Shore Birds of Massachusetts and Adjacent States,* Massachusetts State Board of Agriculture, Boston, 1912.

——— *Important American Game Birds,* E. I. Du Pont de Nemours & Co., Wilmington, Del., 1917.

Forbush, Edward Howe and May, John Richard. *Natural History of the Birds of Eastern and Central North America,* Houghton Mifflin Co., Boston, 1939.

Fosdick, Charles Austin [Harry Castlemon, pseud.]. *The Rod and Gun Club,* Porter & Coates, Philadelphia, Pa., 1883.

——— *The Young Game-Warden,* H. T. Coates & Co., Philadelphia, Pa. 1896.

——— *The Young Wild-Fowlers,* Porter & Coates, Philadelphia, Pa. 1885.

Fowler, Ann and Walters, D. L., ed. *Charles Morgan on Retrievers,* October House, New York, 1971.

Free, James Lamb. *Training Your Retriever,* Coward-McCann, New York, 1949.

Gabrielson, Ira Noel. *Concepts in Conservation of Land, Water, and Wildlife,* U.S. Government Printing Office, Washington, D.C., 1949.

——— *Wildlife Conservation,* Macmillan, New York, 1941.

——— *Wildlife Refuges,* Macmillan, New York, 1943.

——— *Wildlife Management,* Macmillan, New York, 1951.

Gallico, Paul. *The Snow Goose,* Knopf, New York, 1941.

Gardner, Herbert. *Come Duck Shooting With Me,* The Knickerbocker Press, New York, 1917.

Garwood, G. T. *Gough Thomas's Gun Book,* Winchester Press, New York, 1970.

——— *Gough Thomas's Second Gun Book,* Winchester Press, New York, 1972.

Gill, Joan. *Golden Retrievers,* W. & G. Fyle, London, 1962.

Gilley, Wendell. *Bird Carving: A Guide to a Fascinating Hobby,* Van Nostrand, Princeton, N.J., 1961.

Gilmore, Jene C. *Art for Conservation,* The Federal Duck Stamps, Barre Publishers, Barre, Mass., 1971.

Graham, Edward Harrison. *The Land and Wildlife,* Oxford University Press, New York, 1947.

——— *Natural Principles of Land Use,* Oxford University Press, New York, 1944.

Graham, Edward Harrison and Van Dersal,

William R. *Water for America: The Story of Water Conservation,* Oxford University Press, New York, 1956.

——*Wildlife for America, The Story of Wildlife Conservation,* Oxford University Press, New York, 1949.

Gresham, Grits. *The Complete Wildfowler,* Winchester Press, New York, 1973.

Grey, Hugh and McCluskey, Ross, eds. *Field & Stream Treasury,* Holt, New York, 1955.

Grinnell, George Bird. *American Duck Shooting,* Forest and Stream Publishing Co., New York, 1901.

Hallin, Emily Watson and Robert Kingery Buell. *Wild White Wings,* illustrated by Larry Toschik, David McKay Company, New York, 1965.

Hallock, Charles. *The Sportsman's Gazetteer and General Guide,* Forest and Stream Publishing Co., New York, 1878.

Hamilton, Charles William. *Shooting Over Decoys and Other Hunting Tales,* D. D. Nickerson & Co., Boston, 1923.

Hanson, Harold Carsten and Jones, Robert L. *Canada Geese of the Mississippi Flyway, with Special Reference to an Illinois Flock,* Natural History Survey, Urbana, Ill., 1950.

——*Characters of Age, Sex and Sexual Maturity in Canada Geese,* Natural History Survey, Urbana, Ill., 1967.

——*The Biogeochemistry of Blue, Snow, and Ross' Geese,* Southern Illinois University Press, Carbondale, Ill., 1976.

Hanson, Harold Carsten. *The Giant Canada Goose,* Southern Illinois University Press, Carbondale, Ill., 1965.

Harrison, Jeffrey G. *A Wealth of Waterfowl,* André Deutsch, London, 1967.

——*Estuary Saga, A Wildfowler Naturalist on the Elbe,* H. F. & G. Witherby, London, 1952.

——*Pastures New: A Wildfowler Naturalist Explores North-West Germany,* H. F. & G. Witherby, London, 1954.

Hawes, Harry Bartow. *Fish and Game, Now or Never,* D. Appleton-Century Co., New York, 1935.

Hawker, Peter, Lt. Col. *Instructions to Young Sportsmen in All that Relates to Guns and Shooting,* Lea and Blanchard, Philadelphia, Pa., 1846.

Haynes, William Barber. *Goose and Duck Shooting,* The Naylor Co., San Antonio, Texas, 1961.

Hazelton, William Chester. *Ducking Day,* n. pub., Chicago, 1918.

——*Duck Shooting and Hunting Sketches,* n. pub., Chicago, 1916.

——*Supreme Duck Shooting Stories,* n. pub., 1934.

——*Tales of Duck and Goose Shooting,* Phillips Bros., Springfield, Ill., 1922.

——*Wildfowling Tales from the Great Ducking Resorts of the Continent,* n. pub., Chicago, 1921.

Heilner, Van Campen. *A Book on Duck Shooting,* The Penn Publishing Co., Philadelphia, Pa., 1939.

——*Our American Game Birds,* Doubleday, Doran & Co., Garden City, N.Y., 1941.

——"Brant: Harvest on the Marsh," *The American Gun,* Vol. 1, No. 3, Madison Books, New York, 1961.

Heintzelman, Donald S. *North American Ducks, Geese & Swans,* Winchester Press, New York, 1978.

Harris, Albert W. *The Chesapeake Bay Retriever,* Harris, n.p., 1946.

Held, John. *Danny Decoy,* A. S. Barnes and Co., New York, 1942.

Heller, Eliose, ed. *A History of the Chesapeake Bay Retrievers,* American Chesapeake Club, Sonoma, Calif., 1967.

Henschel, Stan. *How to Raise and Train a Chesapeake Bay Retriever,* T. F. H. Publishers, Jersey City, N.J., 1965.

——*How to Raise and Train a Labrador Retriever,* T. F. H. Publishers, Jersey City, N.J., 1964.

Herbert, Henry William [Frank Forester]. *American Game in Its Season,* Charles Scribner, New York, 1853.

——*Frank Forester's Field Sports of the United States and British Provinces of North America,* 2 Vols., Stringer & Townsend, New York, 1848.

——*The Complete Manual for Young Sportsmen,* Stringer & Townsend, New York, 1856.

——*The Hitchcock Edition of Frank Forester,* 4 vols., The Derrydale Press, New York, 1930.

Hester, F. Eugene and Dermid, Jack. *World of the Wood Duck,* Lippincott, Philadelphia, Pa., 1973.

Hill, F. Warner. *Labradors,* Arco Publishing Co., New York, 1976.

Hill, Gene. *A Gallery of Waterfowl and Upland Birds,* illustrated by David Maass, Peterson Publishing, New York, 1978.

——*A Hunter's Fireside Book,* Winchester Press, New York, 1972.

——*Hill Country,* E. P. Dutton, New York, 1978.

——*Mostly Tailfeathers,* Winchester Press, New York, 1975.

Hines, Bob. *Ducks at a Distance,* U.S. Department of the Interior, Washington, D.C., 1963.

Hinnan, Bob. *The Duck Hunter's Handbook,* Winchester Press, New York, 1974.

——*The Golden Age of Shotgunning,* Winchester Press, New York, 1971.

Hochbaum, Hans Albert. *The Canvasback on a Prairie Marsh,* Stackpole Books, Harrisburg, Pa., 1944.

——*To Ride the Wind,* Harlequin Enterprises, Ltd., Toronto, 1973.

——*Travels and Traditions of Waterfowl,* University of Minnesota Press, Minneapolis, 1955.

Hochbaum, Peter Weller. *The Delta Marsh,* Dept. of Mines, Resources and Environmental Management, Ottawa, 1971.

Holder, Charles Frederick. *Life in the Open: Sport with Rod, Gun, Horse, and Hound in Southern California,* C. P. Putnam's Sons, New York, 1906.

Holland, Raymond Pruty. *Now Listen, Warden,* A. S. Barnes and Co., New York, 1946.

——*Shotgunning in the Lowlands,* A. S. Barnes and Co., New York, 1944.

——*Scattergunning,* Knopf, New York, 1951.

Howe, Dorothy. *This is the Labrador Retriever,* T. F. H. Publishers, Hong Kong, 1972.

Hunt, Lynn Bogue. *An Artist's Game Bag.* The Derrydale Press, New York, 1936.

Hunter, Alexander. *The Huntsman in the South: Virginia and North Carolina,* The Neale Publishing Co., New York and Washington, D.C., 1908.

Hyde, Dayton O., ed. *Raising Wild Ducks in Captivity,* E. P. Dutton & Co., New York, 1974.

Innis, Pauline. *The Wild Swans Fly,* McKay, New York, 1964.

Janes, Edward C. *Hunting Ducks and Geese,* The Stackpole Co., Harrisburg, Pa., 1954.

Jaques, Florenc Page. *Francis Lee Jaques: Artist of the Wilderness World,* Doubleday & Co., Garden City, N.Y. 1973.

——*The Geese Fly High,* illustrated by Francis Lee Jaques, University of Minnesota Press, Minneapolis, 1939.

Job, Herbert Keightley. *Among the Water-Fowl, Observation, Adventure, Photography,* Doubleday, Page & Co., New York, 1902.

——*How to Study Birds,* Outing Publishing Co., New York, 1910.

——*The Blue Goose Chase: A Camera-Hunting Adventure in Louisiana,* The Baker & Taylor Co., New York, 1911.

——*The Sport of Bird-Study,* Outing Publishing Co., New York, 1908.

——— *Wild Wings,* Houghton, Mifflin & Co., Boston, 1905.

Johns, Rowland, ed. *Our Friend the Retriever: Curly-Coated, Flat-Coated and Golden,* Methuen & Co., London, 1935.

———, ed. *Our Friend the Labrador,* Methuen & Co., London, 1933.

Johnsgard, Paul A. *Handbook of Waterfowl Behavior,* Comstock Publishing Associates, Ithaca, N.Y., 1965.

——— "Flight of the Sea Ducks," *Natural History,* August/September, 1976.

——— "The Triumphant Trumpeter," *Natural History,* November, 1978.

———*North American Game Birds of Upland and Shoreline,* University of Nebraska Press, Lincoln, Neb., 1975.

———*Song of the North Wind: A Story of the Snow Goose,* Anchor Press/Doubleday, Garden City, N.Y., 1974.

———*The Bird Decoy: An American Art Form,* University of Nebraska Press, Lincoln, Neb., 1976.

———*Waterfowl of North America,* Indiana University Press, Bloomington, Ind., 1975.

———*Waterfowl: Their Biology and Natural History,* University of Nebraska Press, Lincoln, Neb., 1968.

Keith, Elmer. *Shotguns by Keith,* Stackpole & Heck, New York, 1950.

Kersley, J. A. *Training the Retriever: A Manual,* Howell Book House, New York, 1971.

Kesting, Ted, ed. *Lowland Game Birds,* Thomas Nelson & Sons, New York, 1962.

Kimball, David and Jim. *The Market Hunter,* Dillon Press, Minneapolis, 1969.

Kimball, Kendrick. "Pintail Point," *The Field and Stream Reader,* Doubleday & Co., Garden City, N.Y., 1946.

Klapp, H. Milnor, ed. *Krider's Sporting Anecdotes* (1853), Arno Press, New York, 1966.

Knap, Jerome J., ed. *All About Wildfowling in America,* Winchester Press, New York, 1976.

Kortright, Francis H. *The Ducks, Geese and Swans of North America,* The American Wildlife Institute, Washington, D.C., 1942.

Labisky, Wallace R. *Waterfowl Shooting,* Greenberg, New York, 1954.

Lanier, Henry Wysham. *A. B. Frost: The American Sportsman's Artist,* The Derrydale Press, New York, 1933.

Lanman, Charles. *Adventures in the Wilds of North America,* Longman, Brown, Green and Longmans, London, 1854.

Latham, Sid. *Great Sporting Posters of the Golden Age,* Stackpole Books, Harrisburgh, Pa., 1978.

Laycock, George. *The Sign of the Flying Goose,* Natural History Press, Garden City, N.Y., 1965.

———*Wild Refuge,* The Natural History Press, Garden City, N. Y., 1969.

LeClerc, Maurice J., *The Retriever Trainer's Manual,* Ronald Press, New York, 1962.

Leffingwell, William Bruce, ed. *Shooting on Upland, Marsh and Stream,* Rand, McNally & Co., Chicago, 1890.

———, ed. *The Art of Wing Shooting* (1894), Arno Press, New York, 1967.

———, ed. *Wild Fowl Shooting,* Rand, McNally & Co., Chicago, 1888.

Leitch, W. G. *Ducks and Men, Forty Years of Co-operation in Conservation,* D. W. Friesen and Sons Ltd., Altona, Manitoba, 1978.

Leopold, Aldo. *A Sand County Almanac,* Oxford University Press, New York, 1949.

———*Game Management,* Charles Scribner's Sons, New York, 1933.

Lewis, Elisha J. *The American Sportsman* (1863), Arno Press, New York, 1967.

Lincoln, Frederick. *Migration of Birds,* U.S. Department of the Interior, Circular 16, Washington, D.C., 1950.

Linduska, Joseph P., ed. *Waterfowl Tomorrow,* U.S. Department of the Interior, Washington, D.C., 1964.

Liu, Allan J., ed. *The American Sporting Collector's Handbook,* Winchester Press, New York, 1976.

Long, Joseph W. *American Wild-Fowl Shooting,* J.B. Ford and Co., New York, 1874.

Long, William J. *Fowls of the Air,* Ginn & Co., Boston, 1901.

Lorna, Countess Howe (Katherine Curzon) and Waring, Geoffrey. *The Labrador Retriever,* Popular Dogs Publishing Co., London, 1975.

Lyell, Sir Charles. *Travels in North America in the Years 1841–42,* Wiley and Putnam, New York, 1845.

McAtee, Waldo Lee. *Wildfowl Food Plants,* Collegiate Press, Inc., Ames, Ia., 1939.

McCawley, Edmund S.Jr. *Shotguns and Shooting,* D. Van Nostrand Co., Princton, N.J., 1965.

McGuire, Harry, ed. *Tales of Rod and Gun,* Macmillan, New York, 1931.

Mackay, John W. *Mark!,* Coward-McCann, New York, 1956.

MacKenty, John G. *Duck Hunting,* A. S. Barnes and Co., New York, 1953.

Mackey, William J., Jr. *American Bird Decoys,* E. P. Dutton & Co., New York, 1965.

McLean, Colin. *At Dawn and Dusk: Being My Record of Nearly Sixty Years of Wildfowling,* Batchwood Press, London, 1954.

MacQuarrie, Gordon. "Pothole Guys, Friz Out," *Great Hunting and Fishing Stories,* edited by J. Hammond Brown, Grosset & Dunlap, New York, 1947.

——*Stories of the Old Duck Hunters & Other Drivel,* edited by Zack Taylor, Stackpole Books, Harrisburg, Pa., 1967.

——"Geese! Get Down!" *The Field and Stream Reader,* Doubleday & Co., Garden City, N.Y. 1946.

Marcham, Frederick George, ed. *Louis Agassiz Fuertes & The Singular Beauty of Birds,* Harper & Row, New York, 1971.

Martin, A. C. and Uhler, F. M. *Food of Game Ducks in the United States and Canada,* n.pub., Washington, D.C., 1939.

Martin, John Stuart. *Learning to Gun,* Doubleday & Co., Garden City, N.Y. 1963.

Martin, Richard Mark. *Wildfowl in Captivity,* Gifford, London, 1972.

Matthiessen, Peter. *Wildlife in America,* The Viking Press, New York, 1959.

Mayer, Alfred M., ed. *Sport With Gun and Rod in American Woods and Waters,* The Century Co., New York, 1883.

Mayo, Clayton [Clay Emery]. "A Remarkable Shot," *Cap'n Titus, Sketches of New England Country Folk,* Doubleday, Page & Co., N.Y. 1902.

Mendall, Howard. *The Ring-Necked Duck in the Northeast,* University of Maine Press, Orono, Me., 1958.

Merne, Oscar J. *Ducks, Geese and Swans,* St. Martin's Press, New York, 1974.

Migliorini, Mario. *Labrador Retrievers,* Arco Publishing Co., New York, 1971.

Millais, John Guille. *The Wildfowler in Scotland,* Longmans, Green and Co., London, 1901.

Miller, Evelyn. *How to Raise and Train Golden Retrievers,* Sterling Publishing Co., N.Y., 1960.

Miner, Jack. *Jack Miner and the Birds,* The Ryerson Press, Toronto, 1923.

——*Wild Goose Jack,* Simon and Schuster of Canada, Richmond Hill, Ont., 1971.

More Waterfowl by Assisting Nature, More Game Birds in America, Inc., New York, August, 1931.

Musgrove, Jack W. and Mary R. *Waterfowl in Iowa,* Conservation Commission, Des Moines, Ia., 1953.

Nichols, Bob. *The Shotgunner,* n. pub., New York, 1949.

Nichols, Margaret. *Bird Sculpture: A Native American Art Form, Refined,* Birmingham, Museum of Art, Birmingham, Al., 1976.

Nicklaus, Ronald H. "Effects of Lead and Steel Shot on Shooting of Flighted Mallards," *Wildlife Monographs No. 51,* The Wildlife Society, Washington, D.C., November, 1976.

Nye, Russell Scudder. *Scientific Duck Shooting in Eastern Waters,* Independent Press (Spencer & West, proprietors), Falmouth, Mass., 1895.

Oates, W. C. *Wild Ducks: How to Rear and Shoot Them,* n. pub., London, 1905.

O'Connor, Jack. *Complete Book of Shooting,* Harper & Row, New York, 1965.

———*The Shotgun Book,* Knopf, New York, 1965.

Olson, Sigurd. "A Shift in the Wind," *Great Hunting and Fishing Stories,* edited by J. Hammond Brown, Grosset & Dunlap, New York, 1947.

Ortega y Gasset, José. *Meditations on Hunting,* translated by Howard B. Wescott, Charles Scribner's Sons, New York, 1972.

Osborn, Robert Chesley. *How to Shoot Ducks,* Coward-McCann, New York, 1941.

Outdoor Life's Gallery of North American Game, illustrated by Francis Lee Jaques, Outdoor Life Publishing Co., New York, 1946.

Ovenden, Lou. *Ducks & Spaghetti,* Vantage Press, New York, 1972.

Parmalee, Paul W. and Loomis, Forrest D. *Decoys and Decoy Carvers of Illinois,* Northern Illinois University Press, Dekalb, Ill., 1969.

Parker, Eric. *Colonel Hawker's Shooting Diaries,* P. Allan, London, 1931.

Parker, John and Phyllis. *Ornamental Waterfowl,* A. S. Barnes and Co., South Brunswick, N.J., 1970.

Parker, Willie J. with Robinson, Conway. *Halt! I'm a Federal Game Warden,* David McKay Co., New York, 1977.

Payne, H. T. *Game Birds and Game Fishes of the Pacific Coast,* News Publishing Co., Los Angeles, 1913.

Peterson, Roger Tory. *A Field Guide to the Birds* (1934), Houghton Mifflin Co., Boston, 1947.

Petzal, David E., ed. *The Experts' Book of Upland Bird & Waterfowl Hunting,* Simon and Schuster, New York, 1975.

Phillips, John Charles. *A Bibliography of American Sporting Books: Sport, Natural History, Hunting, Dogs, Trapping, Shooting, Early American Travel, Fishing, Sporting Periodicals, Guide Books, Forestry, Conservation, etc. 1582–1925,* E. Morrill, Boston, 1930.

———*A Natural History of the Ducks,* Houghton Mifflin Co., Cambridge, Mass., 1930.

———*A Sportsman's Scrapbook,* Houghton Mifflin Co., Cambridge, Mass., 1928.

———*A Sportsman's Second Scrapbook,* Houghton Mifflin Co., Cambridge, Mass., 1933.

———"Fluctuations in Numbers of the Eastern Brant Goose," *Auk,* 49: 445–453, 1932.

———*Experimental Studies of Hybridization Among Ducks and Pheasants,* n. pub., Cambridge, Mass., 1915.

———*Migratory Bird Protection in North America,* n. pub., Cambridge, Mass., 1934.

———, ed. *Shooting Journal of George Henry Mackay, 1865–1922,* Cosmos Press, Cambridge, Mass., 1929.

———*Shooting Records Wenham Lake, 1897–1925,* n. pub., Cambridge, Mass., 1926.

———*Shooting Records Wenham Lake and The "Farm Bag," 1926–1935,* n. pub., Cambridge, Mass., 1936.

———*Shooting-Stands of Eastern Massachusetts,* The Riverside Press, Cambridge, Mass., 1929.

——*The Sands of Muskeget,* n. pub., Cambridge, Mass., 1931.

——*Wenham Great Pond,* n. pub., Salem, Mass., 1938.

Phillips, John Charles and Lincoln, Frederick C., *American Waterfowl, Their Present Situation and the Outlook for Their Future,* Houghton Mifflin Co., Cambridge, Mass., 1930.

Phillips, John Charles and Hill, Lewis Webb, M.D., eds. *Classics of the American Shooting Field,* Houghton Mifflin Co., Cambridge, Mass., 1930.

Pickering, Harold Gregg William. *Neighbors Have My Ducks,* The Derrydale Press, New York, 1937.

Pirnie, M. D. *Michigan Waterfowl Management,* Michigan State Univ. Press, East Lansing, Mich., 1935.

Pitman, Ian Robert. *And Clouds Flying: A Book of Wild Fowl,* illustrated by Peter Scott, Faber and Faber, London, 1947.

Pollard, Hugh Bertie Campbell. *Wildfowl & Waders, Nature & Sport in the Coastlands,* Country Life Press, London, 1928.

Pough, Richard H. *Audubon Water Bird Guide,* Doubleday & Co., Garden City, N.Y., 1951.

Purdey, T. D. S. and Capt. J. A. *The Shotgun,* Charles Scribner's Sons, New York, 1937.

Queeny, Edgar Monsanto. *Prairie Wings,* Ducks Unlimited, Chicago, 1946.

Rae, William E., ed. *A Treasury of Outdoor Life,* Outdoor Life, New York, 1975.

Rand, Austin Loomer. *American Water & Game Birds,* Dutton, New York, 1956.

Reiger, Barbara and George. *The Zane Grey [Outdoor] Cookbook,* Prentice-Hall, Inc., Englewood Cliffs, N.J., 1976.

Reiger, John F. *American Sportsmen and the Origins of Conservation,* Winchester Press, New York, 1975.

Richardson, R. H., ed. *Chesapeake Bay Decoys,* Crow Haven Publishers, Cambridge, Md., 1973.

Ripley, Aiden Lasell. *Sporting Etchings,* Barre Publishers, Barre, Mass., 1970.

Ripley, Dillon. *A Paddling of Ducks,* Harcourt, Brace and Co., New York, 1957.

Robbins, Chandler S.; Brunn, Bertel; and Zim, Herbert S. *A Guide to Field Identification: Birds of North America,* Golden Press, New York, 1966.

Roberts, Sir Charles George Douglas. "The Terror of the Air," *The Haunters of The Silences,* The Page Co., Boston, 1907.

——"The Homesickness of Kehonka," *The Kindred of the Wild,* Duckworth & Co., London, 1908.

——"The Decoy," *The Watchers of the Trails,* L. C. Page & Co., Boston, 1904.

——"A Gentleman in Feathers," *They Who Walk in the Wilds,* Macmillan, New York, 1924.

Robinson, Ben Carl. *Woodland, Field and Waterfowl Hunting,* David McKay Co., Philadelphia, Pa., 1946.

Robinson, James (Jimmy) Merlen. *Forty Years of Hunting,* n. pub., Minneapolis, 1947.

——*Hunting Adventures With Jimmy Robinson,* T. S. Denison, Minneapolis, 1958.

——*Wing Shooting,* Trap & Skeet, n. pub., Minneapolis, 1955.

Roosevelt, Robert Barnwell. *Florida and the Game Water-Birds of the Atlantic Coast and the Lakes of the United States,* Orange Judd Co., New York, 1884.

——*The Game-Birds of the Coasts and Lakes of the Northern States of America,* Carleton, New York, 1866.

Roslin-Williams, Mary. *The Dual Purpose Labrador,* Pelham, London, 1969.

Ross, Robert Erskine. *Wings Over the Marsh,* Batchworth Press, London, 1948.

Ruthven, John A. and Zimmerman, William H. *Top Flight Speed Index to Waterfowl of North America,* Crown Publishers, New York, 1965.

Rutledge, Archibald Hamilton. *Children of Swamp and Wood,* Doubleday, Page & Co., Garden City, N.Y., 1927.

——*Days Off in Dixie,* Doubleday, Page & Co., Garden City, N.Y., 1924.

——*Home By the River,* Bobbs-Merrill Co., Indianapolis, Ind., 1941.

——*Hunter's Choice,* A. S. Barnes and Co., New York, 1946.

——*Plantation Game Trails,* Houghton Mifflin Co., Boston, 1921.

——*Santee Paradise,* Bobbs-Merrill Co., Indianapolis, Ind., 1956.

——*Those Were the Days,* Dietz Press, Richmond, Va., 1955.

——*Wild Life of the South,* Frederick A. Stokes Co., New York, 1935.

Salisbury, Howard M. *Duck Guns, Shooting and Decoying,* Crown Publishers, New York, 1947.

Samson, Jack. *The Sportsman's World,* Holt, Rinehart and Winston, New York, 1976.

Samson, John (Jack) G., ed. *The Worlds of Ernest Thompson Seton,* Knopf, New York, 1976.

Sanford, L. C.; Bishop, L. B.; and Van Dyke, T. S. *The Water-Fowl Family,* Macmillan, New York, 1903.

Scales, Susan. *Retriever Training, the Modern Way,* Newton Abbot, North Pomfret, Vt., 1976.

Scharff, Robert. *Complete Duck Shooter's Handbook,* G. P. Putnam's Sons, New York, 1957.

Schoonmaker, W. J. "Leader of the Flock," *Great Hunting and Fishing Stories* edited by J. Hammond Brown, Grosset & Dunlap, New York, 1947.

Scott, Sir Peter Markham. *A Coloured Key to the Wildfowl of the World,* W. R. Royle for the Wildfowl Trust, London, 1968.

——*Morning Flight.* Country Life Ltd., London, 1936.

——*Our Vanishing Wildlife,* N. Doubleday, Garden City, N.Y., 1966.

——*The Eye of the Wind,* Houghton Mifflin, Boston, 1961.

——*Wild Chorus,* Country Life Ltd., London, 1938.

——*Wild Geese and Eskimos,* Charles Scribner's Sons, New York, 1951.

Scott, Sir Peter Markham and Bratby, Michael. *Through the Air,* Country Life Ltd., London, 1941.

Scott, Sir Peter Markham and Boyd, Hugh. *Wildfowl of the British Isles,* Country Life Ltd., London, 1957.

Scott, Sir Peter Markham and Fisher, James. *A Thousand Geese,* Collins, London, 1953.

Scott, Sir Peter Markham and The Wildfowl Trust. *The Swans,* Houghton Mifflin, Boston, 1972.

Sedgwick, Noel Mostyn; Whitaker, Peter; and Harrison, Jeffrey G., eds. *The New Wildfowler in the 1970's,* Barrie & Jenkins, London, 1970.

Seton, Ernest Thompson. *Bird Portraits,* Ginn & Co., Boston, 1901.

——"The Mother Teal and the Overland Route," *Lives of the Hunted,* Charles Scribner's Sons, New York, 1906.

——*The Best of Ernest Thompson Seton,* Hodder & Stoughton, London, 1949.

Sharp, Henry. *Practical Wild Fowling,* n. pub., London, 1895.

Shaul, H. Edwin. *The Golden Retriever,* Indian Springs Press, Boston, 1954.

Sheldon, Colonel Harold Pearl. "Trash Ducks," *The Field and Stream Reader,* Doubleday & Co., Garden City, N.Y., 1946.

——*Tranquility Regained,* The Countryman Press, West Hartford, Vt., 1945.

——*Tranquility Revisited,* The Derrydale Press, New York, 1940.

————Tranquility: Tales of Sport With the Gun, The Derrydale Press, New York, 1936.

Sheldon, Colonel Harold Pearl and Lincoln, Frederick C. Sportsman's Guide to Wild Ducks, Outdoor Life and The Wildlife Management Institute, Washington, D.C., 1946.

Shoemaker, Paul E. Training Retrievers for Field Trials and Hunting, Superior Publishing Co., Seattle, Wa., 1970.

Shortt, Angus Henry and Cartwright, B. W. Know Your Ducks and Geese, Sports Afield Publishing Co., Minneapolis, 1948.

————Sports Afield Treasury of Waterfowl, Prentice-Hall, Inc., Englewood Cliffs, N.J., 1957.

Simmons, Albert Dixon. Photography for Sportsmen, D. Van Nostrand Co., New York, 1951.

————Wing Shots, The Derrydale Press, New York, 1936.

Skinner, T. S., The Dog and the Sportsman, n. pub., Philadelphia, Pa. 1845.

Smith, Lawrence (Lon) Breese. American Game Preserve Shooting, Windward House, New York, 1933.

————Fur or Feather; Days with Dog and Gun, Charles Scribner's Sons, New York, 1946.

————Modern Gun Dogs, Their Uses and Care, Charles Scribner's Sons, New York, 1935.

————Modern Shotgun Shooting, Charles Scribner's Sons, New York, 1935.

————Shotgun Psychology, Charles Scribner's Sons, New York, 1938.

Sorenson, Harold D. "Decoy Collector's Guide" p.p., Burlington, Ia., 1963–68.

Soper, J. Dewey. The Blue Goose, F. A. Acland, Ottawa, 1930.

Sowles, Lyle K. Prairie Ducks, The Stackpole Co., Harrisburg, Pa., 1955.

Sprake, Leslie Cecil. The Labrador Retriever, H. F. & G. Witherby, London, 1933.

————The Popular Retrievers, Popular Dogs Co., London, n.d.

Sprunt, Alexander. Wildlife Refuges, N. Doubleday, Garden City, N.Y., 1957.

Sprunt, Alexander, IV and Zim, Herbert S. Gamebirds: A Guide to North American Species and Their Habits, Golden Press, New York, 1961.

Squire, Lorene. Wildfowling With A Camera, J. B. Lippincott Co., Philadelphia, Pa., 1938.

Stanford, J. K. The Complex Gun, Pelham, London, 1968.

Starr, George Ross, Jr. Decoys of the Atlantic Flyway, Winchester Press, New York, 1974.

Stearns, Jean P. A Catalog of the Duck Stamp Prints with Biographies of the Artists, p.p., Stevensville, Md., 1972.

Stetson, Joe. Hunting with Retrievers, T. F. H. Publishers, Jersey City, N.J. 1965.

Stockton, M. L., Jr. Duck Hunters' Determinant, The Stackpole Co., Harrisburg, Pa., 1940.

Strung, Norman. Misty Mornings and Moonless Nights, Macmillan, New York, 1974.

Stuart, Frank S. Wild Wings, McGraw-Hill, New York, 1952.

Sutton, George Miksch. High Arctic, Paul S. Ericksson, New York, 1971.

Taverner, P. A. Birds of Eastern Canada, Department of Mines, Memoir 104, no. 3, Biological Series, Ottawa, 1922.

Taylor, Zack. Successful Waterfowling, Crown Publishers, New York, 1974.

Tennyson, Jon R. A Singleness of Purpose, Ducks Unlimited, Chicago, 1977.

Trefethen, James B. Crusade for Wildlife, Boone & Crockett Club, Harrisburg, Pa., 1961.

Tryon, Aylmer. The Wildfowler's Year, Collins, London, 1952.

Tudor, Joan. The Golden Retriever, Popular Dogs Publishing Co., London, 1966.

Unkelbach, Kurt. Knowing, Training and En-

joying Those Lovable Retrievers, McGraw-Hill, New York, 1973.

Vale, Robert B. *Wings, Fur & Shot,* Stackpole Sons, New York, 1936.

Van Wormer, Joe. *The World of the Canada Goose,* J. P. Lippincott, Philadelphia, Pa., 1968.

——*The World of the Swan,* J. P. Lippincott, Philadelphia, Pa., 1972.

Vincent, John, Rev. *Fowling, A Poem in Five Books,* A. Constable and Co., Edinburgh, 1812.

Wade, Margaret. *The Wild Goose: An Appreciation of Jack Miner, Naturalist,* n. pub., Detroit, Mich., 1923.

Walsh, Harry M. *The Outlaw Gunner,* Tidewater Publishers, Cambridge, Md., 1971.

Walsh, Roy E. *Gunning the Chesapeake, Duck and Goose Shooting on the Eastern Shore,* Tidewater Publishers, Cambridge, Md., 1960.

——*Sanctuary Pond,* Barre Publishers, Barre, Mass., 1967.

Warwick, Helen. *The Complete Labrador Retriever,* Howell Book House, New York, 1964.

Waterman, Charles F. *The Hunter's World,* Random House, New York, 1970.

Waters, Bernard. *Fetch and Carry—A Treatise on Retrieving,* p.p., New York, 1895.

——*Modern Training, Handling and Kennel Management,* The Blakely Printing Co., Chicago, 1889.

Webster, David S. and Kehoe, William. *Decoys at Shelburne Museum,* Museum Pamphlet Series, No. 6, Shelburne, Vt., 1961.

Where to Hunt American Game, United States Cartridge Co., Lowell, Mass., 1898.

Whitehead, Charles Edward. *Wild Sports in the South; or, The Camp-Fires of the Everglades,* Derby & Jackson, New York, 1860.

Whitney, Leon F. *The Complete Book of Dog Care,* Doubleday, Garden City, N.Y., 1953.

"Wildfowler," [pseud.] *Shooting Adventures, Canine Lore, and Sea-Fishing Trips,* Chapman and Hall, London, 1879.

——*Shooting and Fishing Trips in England, France, Alsace, Belgium, Holland and Bavaria,* n. pub., London, 1878.

Williams, Eugene Russell. *The Ways of Wildfowl,* J. G. Ferguson Publishing Co., Chicago, 1971.

Willock, Colin D. *The ABC of Shooting,* André Deutsch, London, 1975.

——*The Bedside Wildfowler,* André Deutsch, London, 1966.

——*Town Gun,* André Deutsch, London, 1973.

Wilmore, Sylvia Bruce. *Swans of the World,* Taplinger Publishing Co., New York, 1974.

Wilson, Eugene E. *A North Woods Rendezvous,* Connecticut Printers, Inc., Hartford, Conn., 1953.

Wolf, Bill. *Reveries of an Outdoor Man,* G. P. Putnam's Sons, New York, 1946.

Wolters, Richard A. *Water Dog: Revolutionary Rapid Training Method,* Dutton, New York, 1964.

Woods, Shirley E., Jr. *Gunning for Upland Birds and Wildfowl,* Winchester Press, New York, 1976.

Wright, Bruce S. *Black Duck Spring,* E. P. Dutton & Co., New York, 1966.

——*High Tide and An East Wind,* Stackpole Books, Harrisburg, Pa., 1954.

Zern, Edward Geary. *The Classic Decoy Series,* illustrated by Milton C. Weiler, Winchester Press, New York, 1969.

——*To Hell with Hunting,* D. Appleton-Century Co., New York, 1946.

Zimmerman, William H. *Waterfowl of North America,* Frame House Gallery, Louisville, Ky., 1974.

INDEX

Numbers in italics refer to illustration captions. N indicates footnote.